SACRED TRUSTS

SACRED

TRUSTS

Essays on Stewardship and Responsibility

Edited by Michael Katakis

With Illustrations by Russell Chatham

Mercury House
San Francisco

Published in the United States by
Mercury House
San Francisco, California

United States Constitution, First Amendment: Congress shall make no law respecting an establishment of religion, or prohibiting the free exercise thereof; or
abridging the freedom of speech, or of the press; or the right of the people peace-
ably to assemble, and to petition the Government for a redress of grievances.

Cover illustration, *August in Paradise Valley,* © 1991 by Russell Chatham (oil on
board 12 x 16).

Mercury House and colophon are registered trademarks of
Mercury House, Incorporated
Printed on acid-free paper
Manufactured in the United States of America

Library of Congress Cataloging-in-Publication Data
Sacred trusts : essays on stewardship and responsibility / edited by
    Michael Katakis.
        p.   cm.
    Includes bibliographical references
    ISBN 1-56279-056-0 (pbk.) :
        1. Environmental responsibility. 2. Human ecology—Moral and ethical
    aspects. I. Katakis, Michael.
    GF80.S23   1993
    179'.1 — dc20   93-872
                                                                 CIP

5   4   3   2   1

Really it is rather strange, for
   the angels
Have all the power on their side,
All the importance: —men turn away from them,
   preferring their own
Vulgar inventions, the little
Trivial Sirens. Here is another sign that the age needs
   renewal.

—Robinson Jeffers, 1941, from his poem "The Sirens"

CONTENTS

This volume would be incomplete without this editor's thanks to the many writers who have contributed their time, insights, and good humor to this project. I would also like to thank my friend, George Anderson, who, from the beginning, encouraged me to follow through with this book and who made many calls on this volume's behalf. I thank Henry Chapman for his listening and thoughtful comments in regard to some essays and the introduction. To Tim Gable and the Clark City Press staff I wish to extend my great appreciation for their support and graciousness. To Russell Chatham, who believed in and supported this book from the beginning and who used his own resources and artwork to keep this coalition together in good times and when times got tough, I extend my sincere appreciation, thanks, and best wishes. A thank you to Mercury House for keeping *Sacred Trusts* alive after Clark City discontinued publishing operations and for making the transition a pleasure. And to Mr. Burt England my thanks for his friendship and the many stories of his life, a life spent afield. Finally I want to thank my wife, Kris, for her endless patience, good counsel, and unwavering support.

Michael Katakis

SACRED TRUSTS

Introduction
Michael Katakis

AS A BOY GROWING UP IN ILLINOIS I LEARNED MANY LESSONS FROM my father, the most vivid of which took place around the kitchen table on November 23, 1963. The day before, President John Kennedy had been assassinated, and within a few hours my mother would die. I was young, scared, and felt sick to my stomach. I recall my father's pale face and moist eyes as he sat with his hands neatly folded. We moved, barely, as if in a bad dream. After a long silence my father said "Honor, duty and courage are just words until we breathe life into them." I stared at my father trying to take it in, trying unsuccessfully to understand. "Papa, how do you make a word alive?" I asked. "By our deeds, Michael," he replied.

I remember that morning for many reasons, the President and my mother, of course, but mostly because of that exchange with my father.

I've often wondered why he said those words at that time. Perhaps he was reminding himself of those simple truths that he lived by as he looked at the small son he would now raise alone. Because of that experience, among others, I have learned three important things. First, that our deeds have significant consequences that are often unforeseen. Second, that duty is seldom easy or without sacrifice and, finally, that from time to time people must remind themselves and each other of their duties and responsibilities.

This volume is about stewardship and its underpinnings, which I believe to be honor, duty, and courage. Stewardship is never as easy as signing a check to your favorite cause but is rather a way of seeing, thinking, and acting on this planet. It is not a static view; its definitions and actions are continually redefined by wider experiences and more knowledge. Stewardship is not confined to any regional border. Its value is as relevant to the inner cities of America as it is to the mountains of Montana. Stewardship's limitations or applications are dependent on our choices. With this understanding comes the responsibility to become the teacher while remaining the student. We live in cynical times, however, and often these words and ideas become nothing more than fodder in election year speeches, word symbols used to elicit certain reactions from the electorate. As my father said, these are just words, valueless really, until our deeds give them life. It is ultimately, and finally, our choice. David Hume believed that reason alone was insufficient to move the will, and I believe that when the heart is touched substantive action can follow.

The authors gathered here are from different walks of life with different experiences. They have written personal essays for this book, something from their lives. It is my hope that this volume will help people reflect on the remarkable and delicate natural world around them and their responsibilities to that world. The authors offer their insights so that readers may refer to this volume not as an answer, but rather as one step in a long journey in which we must all participate.

In our youth we are bathed in that wonderful perceived light of immortality. We cannot see the end of our time. But as we age we learn the truth that we and our surroundings are finite. We may abrogate our responsibilities at any time, but collectively and individually we are always responsible—always. No excuses will suffice or be accepted by those who inherit our legacy.

In his 1950 introduction to *Measure of the Year*, Roderick Haig-Brown wrote, "When all is said and done, a writer can have no more serious purpose than this. His duty is to stir echoes in his readers, to touch thought and ideas that might otherwise have remained idle and forgotten in the back of the mind. It is a rare book that changes a life, a poor one that adds nothing to it."[1] We all have a sacred trust to the future to stir those echoes in ourselves and others and perhaps, most importantly, to inspire.

1. Salem, NH: Ayer Company Publishers Inc., 1950.

Into the Trees
Mary Catherine Bateson

DEATH TOO IS A TRUST, ONE THAT REQUIRES US TO GO BEYOND individual consciousness and to be aware of natural process.

Walking through the woods, I am reminded that there is as much death here as there is life. It is a mistake to think the word *forest* refers only to the living, for equally it refers to the incessant dying. It is a mistake to speak of preserving forests as preventing the death of trees. Forests live out of the deaths of toppled giants across the decades, as well as the incessant dying of microscopic beings. Without death, the forest would die. Ultimately, it is only the removal of trees that can deplete the forest. Both fallen giants and fallen leaves collaborate with the bacteria of decay to produce the fertile soil from which new growth comes. By itself, no single organism can long survive. The forest is its own memorial, the conclusion of its own conversation. You can lift a log, the corpse of a fallen tree, and find a whole community at the rotting face where it touches the moist ground.

Within organisms, living means the continual death of cells. Some are replaced; some linger, no longer living but still providing protection or support; some wither and are reabsorbed, part of an organ no longer needed, like the tadpole's tail. Within the human body, death is, from moment to moment and day to day, an essential part of life. Within the ongoing process of healthy functioning of an organism, there is a steady rhythm of cell death and replacement, and this, we now know, is not only a matter of replacing casualties but also, in many cases, a programmed process in which cells themselves switch into an active mode of self-destruction, synthesizing the enzymes that will shut them down. The cells that live on memorialize the others, but these will also die. Only cancerous tissue can be kept alive indefinitely. Death is apparently not a failure of life but a mode of functioning as intrinsic to life as reproduction. To see life without seeing death is like believing that the earth is flat and matter solid—a convenient blindness.

◆

HUMAN COMMUNITIES are unlike the forest, for dying and decay are often concealed, the story distorted. In our society, we treat dying as if it were separable from living, and we surround the process of dying and its aftermath in secrecy and expertise, much as we treated birth until recently. Decay, the same process that in the forest undergirds all new life, is denied. The all-too-perishable bodies of the beloved dead are both beautiful and horrible. They could continue their journey, back into the unity of natural cycles, but instead we struggle to deny this return and bodies are segregated from the cycle of living things, preserved with chemicals and sealed in metal-lined caskets. In many societies the preparation of the dead—washing them, closing the eyes—is a final act of loving intimacy. They are laid out in the home, where both caring and grieving nourish ongoing love and those who live on become familiar with death.

Respect could be expressed in other ways. For years I have had the fantasy of buying a hillside suitable for terracing, where the dead might be buried without coffins and chemicals, and fruit or olive trees be planted above each one. No waste of fertile land, no whispering between rows of statuary; rather, an annual harvest and families coming for laughing picnics. And for the dead, the slow intimacies of groping roots and a merging with organic process rather than protected separation from the earth or the quick, furtive transition to sterile ash and gases in cremation. After a time, especially for the children, it would be easy to believe that the lives ended had passed into the trees.

That is what I believed after my father's death. Every tall tree is my father now, I thought.

✦

HEALTH HAS A DIFFERENT face in a society where death and aging are denied. We have come a long way in the unwinnable warfare against death. More and more, human beings are products of technological interference with natural process. Whenever I enter a room filled with people, as thickly gathered as underbrush, I am reminded that I am in the presence of an artifact. Not the hall, with its air-conditioning or heating, its loudspeaker system and lighting, but the assembly of human beings. I share the room with others who except for technology would be dead or would never have been born, the creations of public health and immunization programs, of surgery and medication of all sorts, of treatments both heroic and routine. As infants, some were kept alive in incubators; others have had open-heart surgery. More and more of us are started on our way by parenthood consciously chosen, rather than by nature taking its course, and increasing numbers now are brought into life by in vitro fertilization. Any gathering today is likely to include vital "senior citizens" actively enriching their retirement with lectures and seminars into their eighties and beyond. Most of them would not have been alive under the circumstances of human life only half a century ago. It is curious that so many religions that define the prevention of conception as an interference with divine will do not question the prevention of death.

Not only life but also health, youth, and beauty are artificially sustained. Looking around I see skin, hair, and teeth kept healthy and shining; sight and hearing corrected; age camouflaged. Physical pain is anesthetized. Each of our bodies is a declaration that technology can overcome nature, not perfectly, not indefinitely, but to a significant degree. Yet there is a shadow side to this achievement. Almost everyone in the room is dissatisfied with the reality of his or her body, trying to pummel it or squeeze it into a new shape, to mask its natural odors. The consequences include eating disorders, addictive exercising and dieting, and steroid abuse. Huge sums of money are spent on cosmetic surgery, which can itself be addictive, and on the less drastic cover-ups of makeup and clothing. Rejecting death, we reject ourselves. In a society that rejects the beauty of mature bodies, forcing people to strive to be endlessly adolescent, it is also predictable that there will be some who follow this obsession with youthfulness into the sexual exploitation of children.

Finally, after looking around me at others, I look at my own hands. The joints ache sometimes now and will probably get worse. The skin hangs rather loosely, showing the beginning of age spots, and there are new ridges in my fingernails. My culture tells me I too should want to resist these gradual changes. After years of arguing that the desire to dominate nature is leading to its destruction, I am at that moment of transition when for almost everyone, the battle against nature begins to be fought within the boundaries of the body. The rhetoric of longevity is full of references to natural foods, the outdoors, and exercise but not to the natural necessity of return to the earth. Do I then want to defeat old age, to control death? It is the transient body that we hold in trust.

None of us have known our parents as they were as children, so we must invent childhood for ourselves. Usually we have known our parents in maturity and old age, so we might have learned from them something about dying. Yet as a society, we have failed in the duty of teaching to new generations the process of dying, knowledge traditionally passed on through contact with the peaceful courage of the old and the passionate expression of grief that is then allowed to heal. Death, so often taken for granted like the air and often so difficult to accept, will someday again be treasured for the meaning it gives to life. Dying, a natural process too often masked by medical heroics, will someday be embraced as a final stage of maturation.

I knew people in my childhood who died, and I saw their bodies laid out for mourners. I learned something of death from reading the poems of a friend who committed suicide and from the death soon after birth of a premature son. But I did not begin to learn about dying until the death of my father. He had been impatient for years of medical and dental care, so his body was a clear testimony to aging. At the end, his death was expected and accepted, awaited without tubes and monitors, shared as an extraordinary gift. If my own aging brings me closer to him, does it bring me closer to the trees and to the forest?

Every tall tree is my father now.

✦

SOME NATURAL PROCESSES have been taken for granted, while others have been matters of artifice and effort, concern and prayer. I doubt that any human group has prayed that gravity continue—on the contrary, mythology and technology are full of efforts to outwit it. Even a tepee, after all, is a negotiation with gravity. Gravity is a fact of the natural order so reliable and so pervasive that the entire body is constructed to come to terms with it. We remain, as a species, handicapped by lower back pain— the result of a recent and imperfect defiance of gravity. Only when it became possible to send human beings into space did lack of gravity become recognizable as a problem, complicating the simplest activities, like eating and elimination. Without gravity to work against, bodies deteriorate rapidly. Walk through the forest and notice that "up" and "down" are reflected in the structure and behavior of every visible being. Sunlight above and the downward pull of gravity are mast and unseen keel for every motion. Gravity is a servitude that gives shape to our lives.

Death is like gravity, shaping and balancing our lives. Legends offer immortality as they offer flight, sometimes combining both in the image of an afterlife above the clouds. There are cautionary tales that suggest that immortality would be a burden without eternal youth, innocence, or the companionship of contemporaries—that death might be longed for in the absence of these. But, in general, death has been reliable, and so it is survival that has been longed for and pursued through ritual and technology.

In nature, effort often seems one-sided when you look at a single organism, for the characteristics of the organism are balanced by the characteristics of the environment, with the two together forming the unit of survival. Eating, breeding, even moving, the behavior of every creature takes much for granted and is organized around what is scarce. In the rain forest, species may be sorted by their adaptations to the filtered light; in the desert they can be classified by their strategies for storing moisture. The effort to survive is intrinsic in life, but when we humans gain the capacity to make our desires effective, our one-sided struggles can be disastrous. We are like people who have been walking against a high wind, leaning into it; when the wind drops, we risk falling over.

Where food is plentiful, human beings are slow in learning not to overeat; where almost all infants survive, we have difficulty learning not to overbreed; where death can be staved off by ever more elaborate technologies, we have trouble learning when to let go. We go on struggling against death because this has been a battle impossible to win. Death has been a safe enemy, since we have never had to face the disaster of victory. We have not in the past needed to ensure our own dying, for death has been the one thing we could count on.

All pathologies of immoderation must be one side of the coin of survival, emerging as problems when the coin no longer spins true. Human greed and human hoarding have been adaptive responses to scarcity and tenuous survival, but, backed by the power of technology, these can come to threaten survival. For humankind, aware of struggling for millennia against predictable natural processes, the extent of reliance upon our opponents has been obscured.

The mythology of wish fulfillment underlines the fact that what human beings strive for is not desirable when it disrupts the environment in which they survive. Of all the many stories, the most poignant perhaps is that of King Midas, who wished for and was granted the golden touch and found that he could no longer eat or drink, that his touch caused the death of those he loved. Midas suffered the fate of being cut off from those exchanges necessary for life and happiness; his error was the assumption that he could prosper in separation from the environment. What you want as a single organism is not what you want as a system consisting of an organism in an environment.

Years ago, at a conference on conscious purpose and human adaptation, Tolly Holt said, "It's the idea of the conceivable existence of anything which is independent of process. It's the confusion that what I strive for is what I strive for, which is nonsense. . . . The illusion that if strawberry shortcake is a good thing, then more strawberry shortcake is a better thing."[1] Good and evil are contextual, and even orchids and roses are weeds in the wrong setting. We have believed that prolonging life is always good and always an obligation for family members and medical personnel. This is not true. The individual who wishes too efficiently may disrupt the larger system. The mechanism of wishing may have evolved to push against environmental constraints, but not to succeed in overcoming them. Now, with so much power, we must learn to override our own wishes. Kierkegaard once said, "Purity is to will one thing," but it seems possible that a divided will is the beginning of wisdom.

Struggles and anxieties change and new solutions give birth to new concerns. Infants seem at first to take the mother's breast for granted, as if it were a part of themselves. Fear of loss comes into being when they discover their fundamental separateness. Then, as adults, they learn that the possibility of separation is an essential and poignant element in the understanding of love. At times, human beings have worried about the sun, about whether it would rise the next morning or whether after the winter solstice the days would once again lengthen and warm, and green leaves appear. In other places, the perennial focus of anxiety was the rain or the salmon run or the arrival of migratory flocks of birds. Ceremonies

MERCURY HOUSE

In a world of exploding information, fine writing still communicates to readers in a unique and lasting manner. At Mercury House, we are devoted to writing that will endure because of its distinction, and we publish books that reflect that distinction with innovative design, fine typography, and lasting acid-free paper.

If you would like to see a catalog of Mercury House titles, please fill out this card and return it to us.

Which book did you find this card in?

_____

How did you hear of this book?

_____

Which types of books are you particularly interested in?

❏ FICTION & LITERATURE
❏ LITERATURE IN TRANSLATION
❏ POLITICS & CURRENT AFFAIRS
❏ ENVIRONMENTAL CONCERNS
❏ BIOGRAPHY & MEMOIRS

❏ ARTS & FILM
❏ LITERARY TRAVEL
❏ PHILOSOPHY & PERSONAL GROWTH

Name _____

Address _____

City _____

State _____ Zip _____

MERCURY HOUSE

201 Filbert Street
Suite 400
San Francisco, CA 94133-9841

were held that were believed to sustain and regulate the natural order; humans were participants, with a part to play and limitations they were required to accept.

One of the modern nightmares is the loss of those goods that have always been trustworthy in the past. Yet the notions of air as a free good and of the ocean as an unfillable garbage dump have not been universal, even among peoples who lack our modern experience. For these groups, it is often an essential courtesy to avoid certain kinds of pollution. Now we face the awareness that the destruction of the ozone layer will make the very sunshine dangerous, the recognition that rain can be poisoned by airborne wastes. We are preoccupied with failures in parental care, the discovery that the desire and wisdom to bear and nurture children are not reliable universals of human behavior, that parental caring is not a free good that can be drawn on, but rather must be cherished and rewarded, and only flourishes in an appropriate context. The battles about incest and child abuse, about abortion, about family leave and day care all reflect the horrifying discovery that the care needed by the next generation of human beings cannot be taken for granted, any more than it can be taken for granted that running water will always purify itself.

Forest peoples may revere the forest and treat it with respect, but rarely do they imagine that the forest might simply cease to exist. Yet today the great trees are at risk, the forests are at risk, the seas are at risk. Some argue that forests that were protected should be opened up to loggers to preserve jobs, jobs that will disappear soon enough when the trees are cut. Lumber companies claim they restore the forests—sometimes— but what they do is plant young trees for harvesting later. In this system no trees will be allowed to mature like the ancients, and the elders of the forest will not be permitted to die and melt into the ground.

Whenever I hear of ancient forests being cut down in the American Northwest, the tropical rain forests, the Siberian taiga, I know that living graves and cradles are being destroyed. During the memorial service for my father at Big Sur, held on a wide lawn, I looked up at a great tree and thought, there is my father. Every tall tree is my father now.

✦

WAITING BY THE DEATHBED of someone we love, we want to salvage every day or hour of life; but looked at from the perspective of the future, unless there are key tasks to be completed, important farewells to say, those extra hours are trivial. Later we learn to ask about the completeness of the life ended, the dignity and surcease granted, the grace afforded to the entire composition by its closure. My father had a book he had begun and wanted to finish, a book I eventually completed for him. When his final illness began, we took him to the hospital and prepared to fight for more time. It's natural when you love someone to want to keep that person alive. Soon, however, my father realized that the medical efforts being made did not correspond to his idea of life and that it was time to die.

One of the ways of affirming death today is the living will. Sometime in the fifties, early in my adolescence, my mother wrote such a document. I doubt that she was the first to do so, but the idea was a new one at that time, with no clear legal standing. Now we are beginning to believe that it is not obligatory to sustain human beings in permanent coma if they have clearly expressed a different preference, and a few believe that human beings have the right to be helped to end their lives if they are confronted with painful terminal illness. The creation of hospices frees patients and staff from the obligation of deferring death when it is no longer preventable. But we still resist any social affirmation that ending life might also be an obligation: Death has been left to take care of itself.

Death is not regarded as natural but as an intrusion on primordial harmony, instituted as a punishment for sin. The act of ending a life is not yet accepted as an act of caring but only as an act of hatred, a crime, a maximum punishment, or a necessity of warfare. Suicide is regarded in many places as a criminal act. People may be medicated to destroy the desire for death, and patients who ask to be allowed to die are often treated against their will, since the desire for death is seen as pathological.

Perhaps we will only progress to the affirmation of death if we no longer use death as a punishment and no longer withhold the prolongation of life on a class basis. At present, in American society, death rates are an index of inequality: African Americans can expect to die some eight years sooner than Caucasians. Death rates of black infants show the same inequality: less education, worse nutrition, more toxic environments, less disease prevention, less conviction that a black individual's life is valuable. To learn to value each person's death, we will need to conserve and value life equally.

Whenever humans gain greater power to affect the course of events, they become responsible for new choices. Ethics follow efficacy. Eventually, just as it will be necessary to bring birthrates into balance with death rates around the world, we will need a new affirmation of the positive value of death. Indeed, we will need to learn to choose and cherish death. We cannot continue to believe that death is always an enemy and extended life always good, a right of the individual to demand and an obligation of the community to provide. Soon we will want, instead, to own our deaths.

The living will that my mother prepared was troubling to me, not because it affirmed the necessity of death but because it contained a criterion of life that I rebelled against. She listed the circumstances under which she wanted medical intervention withheld, and together these added up to a definition of what she valued in her life: intellectual functioning and ability to communicate about ideas. She drew sharp distinctions, asserting that she could learn to function effectively with the loss of one sense or of mobility but not if both these conditions occurred. She also asserted that preserving her life would be inappropriate given any intellectual diminution.

At fifteen this seemed wrong to me. Even though I could reject the evidence of a heartbeat or wavy lines drawn by an electroencephalograph as a meaningful criterion of life, I would not accept as criteria the gifts that made one individual extraordinary—intellect or beauty or athletic skill. I was threatened by the fact that my mother did not define the give-and-take of love as central, but rather the working of intellect. Yet it is not surprising that an individual might say, on the loss of a skill or the death of a loved one, "My life is over." Today, I believe my mother's choice was her right. If we assert the right to make choices in life, we surely must uphold the right to express those values in death. Decisions about dying offer the opportunity to explore basic values: human dignity, recognition and response to others, moral autonomy. Dying has always been a measure of dedication and courage.

✦

TODAY I BELIEVE WE must work toward a pattern in which human beings deliberately reverse the struggles that were necessary at one stage of human evolution: to reproduce as many young as possible and to stay alive as long as possible. We have been engaged in a tug-of-war that required that every muscle be strained in one direction. Now, when resistance is overcome, we may collapse through our own unbalanced effort. We have spent millennia struggling against death; now we must find a way to reclaim it. Judging by the conflict surrounding responsibility for reproduction, this new effort will not be easy. The ancient words of poets and religious teachers that preceded modern technology will help, but we need more than resignation as a model for choice.

Each time I am closely involved with a death, I find myself rethinking these issues: the death of a premature firstborn, the death of my parents and my parents-in-law, the death of elderly friends and of friends in mid-life. I have three times been closely involved in caring for someone during the process of dying when they have rejected medical intervention. With each encounter, my understanding spirals back over the same issues and I gain a new level of intimacy.

Several years ago, a friend was dying of metastatic melanoma in an Israeli hospital. He had read things I had written about my parents' deaths and knew I was one of the few people in his circle, perhaps the only one, with whom he could discuss not only the struggle to survive but also the decision to let death take its course. Others pressed on him the obligation to hope for miracles and cling tenaciously to every moment and every treatment. Even after he had decided to discontinue medical intervention, that decision had to be worked through with every family member and every staff member.

All of us were learning. It was clear that friends and family and even hospital personnel were ignorant of death except as a threat to be resisted and were strangers to the capacity to choose to die. I could see how uncomfortable the decision made them, how sharply it undercut their very reason for being. Whatever new patterns emerge, they must be developed without squandering the resources of medical compassion. When the medical team ceased trying to control the course of the illness and were confronted with an unknown process, it was striking that they had little ability to predict its course. In the same way, generations of doctors had no idea how to manage childbirth without anesthesia. Medical personnel overemphasize the suffering created by lack of treatment and lose the awareness of how burdensome medical treatment can be. Without this burden, my friend survived longer and with greater clarity than the doctors expected.

We know something now about the process of coming to terms with terminal illness, of maturation in dying, but we know little about how individuals might come to terms with death gradually, throughout the course of a life. Dying may be a choice that needs to be made in health, for pain and medication and impaired awareness throw us back on instinctual responses that are no longer appropriate. We will no doubt continue to use technology to protect and lengthen life, but perhaps someday we will develop the convention of writing and revising living wills at multiple stages in the life cycle and accept these testaments as ways of exploring and constructing meaning, of savoring the treasure of life. It will take time to develop new attitudes toward death, to recognize that we will only learn to hold this living earth in trust when we acknowledge our own dying. No one can know the form this new outlook will take, the debates about legislation and medical ethics and funding that lie ahead.

✦

IT IS HARD TO IMAGINE how those who live by the rejection of mortality and fallibility can care for and protect our natural landscapes. Surely they may be tempted to turn them into manicured parklands, to remove the signs of decay—memento mori, the reminder of death. Surely the temptation to cut and clear and destroy, the assertion of power, is a rejection of the inevitability of death. For me, it works the other way: I can accept the fact of death as long as the trees remain, as long as natural cycles continue and lives are reabsorbed into the larger life of the planet.

In the life of the forest, nothing is lost. One day, I too want to be a tree.

1. M. C. Bateson, *Our Own Metaphor: A Conference on Conscious Purpose and Human Adaptation,* 2nd ed. (Washington, D. C.: Smithsonian Institution Press, 1991), 90.

Life on the Myopian Frontier
Dan O'Brien

WHEN I SIT ON THE STEPS OF OUR RANCH HOUSE AT NIGHT, I CAN see a single electric light somewhere near the top of the Black Hills. The light first appeared a couple months ago, and it annoys me because it creates the sensation that humans have finally elbowed their way to the top of the mountains that are, in many ways, the central feature on my life. I can't help imagining that the Black Hills are filled with people to the point of overflowing.

For thirteen years after I started making payments on this little ranch, there was no sign of civilization from the porch at night. I liked it that way, enjoyed the feeling that I was folded harmonically into the landscape of the Great Plains, that I belonged and that neither I nor any of my kind was disturbing the beauty and precision of the Hills in any significant way. I was profoundly thankful not to be living in the congestion I have seen in this country and around the world. I felt safe, remote from the deprivations of crowded cities and countryside.

Of course I knew the ranch was not a truly remote place. There are no such places anymore. It was mostly a quirk of geography that made the view from the porch seem pristine. Sitting in the exact right place on the top step, I didn't notice the light from the bedroom window above, and I could feel totally alone. The yard lights of the neighbors and the small town ten miles south are mercifully hidden by ridges and buttes. But because this new light shines from somewhere high in the Black Hills, it is conspicuous. It draws my eyes every time I step from the house and reminds me that human population pressures have pushed people to even the marginal land of the Earth, resulting in tragic destruction of ecosystems and other species. The light is a symbol of that pressure, and it drives me wild.

When I moved to the little ranch from an even smaller one in the southern Black Hills, I fell in love with the solitude that came with the night. As is the case with most people, the quiet and seclusion were restorative for me, and I have come to think of them as unprotected rights, like the right to free speech or to worship is in lesser countries. Some of us out here have learned to savor those qualities and feel they are part of what makes our lives special. But special as it may be, life in the shadow of the Black Hills has a severe economic reality, and we've also learned that you can't eat solitude. These ranches are often not able to sustain us through the hard times that seem to keep on coming out here. Four years ago I married a woman with a good job in the nearby town of Rapid City. Her job is economically more important to us than our little ranch could ever be, and since she needs to be near her work, we moved to town. So even though I drive to the ranch every day, I don't get to spend many nights out there anymore. Now most of my nights are spent in the nice little midwestern-type town of Rapid City. It's a pleasant place and still part of the Black Hills, which we love and need. But I greatly miss sitting on that porch and seeing nothing but bright dancing stars above the dark reptilian spine of the Hills.

The new electric light in the Hills could be ten miles off, or it could be forty. It's hard to say, because from our front porch you can see a very long way. All of western South Dakota and the northern plains is a land where vision is still very important. The animals, and some of the people, depend on their eyes much more than any other sensory organ. There is a feeling that you need to see things coming from a long way off, so vision is primary out here. In the daytime the antelope and mule deer watch me from a mile away as I go about my daily routine. The hawks, falcons, and eagles watch from somewhere too high for me to see. Even at night the distances one can see are amazing. On the moonlit nights I can see silvery ridge lines thousands of yards away and the silhouette of Bear Butte six miles to the southeast.

Even though the electric light in the Hills is probably much farther away than Bear Butte, I can see it clearly. But it does not aid my vision; it detracts from it. That light does not have the soft edges of the moon and stars. It takes the silver from the night and forces me to focus on a pin-point. It's impossible to regard it as anything other than a foreign object in this landscape. It appears ostentatious and intrusive.

Unfortunately, ostentatious and intrusive objects are not that rare out here. In fact, the recent human history of the Black Hills might well be summarized as a string of reactions to things foreign, ostentatious, and intrusive. I say recent because the only written history we have is barely a hundred years old. To be sure, there were important events that took place in the Hills before 1874 when General George Custer directed the first significant white penetration. For centuries, small groups of indige-nous North Americans evicted each other from the Hills, but the first real changes to the land or people since the last Ice Age have come in the last two generations. Changes to the Black Hills came late in the saga of North American settlement. But when they finally came, they came fast and brutally, with a lack of foresight that has been common throughout the world but is particularly acute in the conquest of North America. The pace of change, the coarseness of its application, and the indifference to what is lost has slackened only slightly in the Black Hills of South Dakota.

White people had been on this continent for nearly four hundred years before there was a European dwelling in the Black Hills. American inde-pendence had been fought for and won a century earlier. The United States had divided in a great civil war and was on the mend by the time the first white army laid eyes on the land that is believed by some to be the birthplace of humanity. It was only curious twists of fate that allowed the Hills to remain unsullied long after most of the continent had been overrun by European Christians. Lewis and Clark's path tracked several hundred miles north of the Black Hills when they inspected the newly purchased land in 1804. The Bozeman trail led settlers south and west. Colorado, Oregon, California, and Nevada had earned their statehood years before Europeans cast their consumptive gaze toward the Black Hills. In addition to the discouraging label of "The Great American

Desert," the Black Hills and a large portion of the present state of South Dakota were protected from encroachment by being designated as a reservation for the indigenous pantheists of the Great Plains in the famous Treaty of 1868. Of course when Custer found gold in the Black Hills in 1874, all bets were off. The government reneged on the treaty, and the drive to civilize and Christianize the native Lakota people was intensified. The push to populate the "empty" land was begun in earnest, and the nearsighted belief that there would always be room in the American West established itself firmly in national dogma.

From that time the Black Hills raced to find their place in the jigsaw puzzle of manifest destiny. In eighteen months the brand-new town of Custer swelled to a population of eleven thousand. By 1876 the Black Hills boasted over fifteen thousand white souls, each with the dream of finding his or her fortune in the clear streams or black earth of America's latest promised land. Of course only a few found a fortune—to this day South Dakota remains one of the poorest states—but many found work in the mines and supporting businesses that sprang up around the boom towns. By 1910 the population of the Black Hills was over fifty-seven thousand, and the night view from my front porch, had there been a house there then, was still uninterrupted, gray above when the moon was new and always solid black below where the Hills were known to be.

Stories of the richness of the Black Hills fueled the fires of greed through an ongoing gold rush and an extended period of homesteading. Most of the stories were lies, but they brought thousands of people from Europe and the eastern states, where the natural vitality of the land was already being sapped by the crush of human population. A huge percentage of those people were bitterly disappointed by their Dakota experiences. They blamed the weather, the government, and just plain bad luck for the fact that they did not prosper. No one, until recently, seemed to realize that this land actually could be a paradise if humans were spread thinly among the other species instead of displacing them.

It's true that the majority of immigrants were poor, uneducated people who were only trying for a better life. They were simple people who had not read Malthus and did not have the time to consider that each ecosystem, according to its fertility, has a fairly rigid carrying capacity. There was no way for them to understand that each piece of land can only supply a given number of individuals with all they need for a happy existence. There was certainly no great plan to overtax the ecosystem. The reality, as in most places, is that things simply got out of hand. It would have taken individuals of great vision indeed to see that too many people was a possibility. Even Thomas Jefferson, perhaps our premier visionary, made a profound and uncharacteristic miscalculation by arguing effectively that Kentucky would never become a state because it would never reach the required population of twenty-five thousand voters. Given such a blind spot in a vision as farsighted as Jefferson's, it is hard to condemn the early emigrants to the Black Hills. It's hard, in fact, to condemn the present inhabitants of the cluttered little housing developments jammed into the once fertile and pristine valleys. Our politicians and civic leaders may be a different story, but probably one should not harbor evil thoughts about the person who turns on that electric light I see from my porch.

Greed is still a factor in the continuing population growth of our area, but more and more, people are moving to the Black Hills for different reasons. Now many people choose the Hills as a place to live for the quality of life that it has always offered. Of course the twentieth-century irony of the Black Hills is the irony of many places. People come because it is beautiful, sane, and abundant in life. There is relatively clean air, clean water, and still an adequate supply of topsoil. They begin to build an ethic and a heritage around these things, and as the population grows, the very things that brought the people begin to be destroyed, leaving whole communities to discover they are built on eroding and irretrievable foundations.

Rapid City is the second largest town in the state. Depending on who's counting, the estimates of the city's population run from fifty to seventy-five thousand, perhaps half the total population of the Black Hills. There are few large hardwood trees in western South Dakota, and a large portion of them must be in Rapid City. That means there is probably more deep shade in Rapid City than in most northern plains communities. Our neighborhood is the kind of place where Americans live in the movies. Fred MacMurray and his boys could live down the block; Jimmy Stewart could run the local mortgage company. Our end of town is a good place to raise kids. But it is still an American city, and so there is another end of town. That's where the Indians live.

North Rapid, as it is called, is not Harlem. It's not L.A.'s Watts or Cleveland's Hough, but it is still a ghetto. And in some ways it is a particularly tragic ghetto. Perhaps the greatest tragedy lies in the fact that the grandparents or great-grandparents of many of these people frequented the Black Hills in pre-European days. Their recent forebears moved in and out of the Hills as freely as the buffalo. Their more distant ancestors, or people like them, existed for thousands of years without altering the environment in any significant way. Whether this was the result of cultural beliefs or the simple fact that they lacked the technology and human numbers to impact the environment is debatable—there were probably fewer than thirty thousand Lakota scattered over all the western Dakotas, eastern Wyoming, and parts of Nebraska and Montana in the early nineteenth century.

But for whatever reason, it must be difficult for some of those folks living in North Rapid to watch what is happening to the Hills. It must be difficult to watch the gold strip mines of the Northern Hills tearing out untold tons of ore each day, must be hard to abide the circus atmosphere of tourist traps and the newly relegalized gambling in Deadwood. It must be hard to see the attempts to turn parts of the Hills into huge garbage dumps for waste from all over the country. It must be difficult to watch the elk herd going the way of the buffalo, the water in the trout streams being funneled off for irrigation, industry, and green golf courses. It must add greatly to their minority sense of powerlessness to see the destruction of the Hills continuing pretty much unabated.

The Lakota Sioux have never given up the dream of regaining the Hills. They fought first in the draws and valleys of the Great Plains with bows and arrows, then in the courts of white cities with legal briefs to accomplish this goal. The Sioux claim on the Black Hills finally was upheld by the Supreme Court in 1980. The court ruled that the U.S. government illegally took the Black Hills from the Sioux Nation when the government broke the Treaty of 1868. They awarded the tribe the largest cash settlement ever levied against the U.S. government in an Indian land claim: over $106 million. But the Sioux have refused the money, which with interest is now closer to $250 million. The official line is that the Black Hills are not for sale. Never mind that in a bigger sense the Hills were sold years ago and continue to be sold every day. Still the Sioux insist that land must be part of any settlement and that sounds right. Notwithstanding their poor stewardship of the huge reservations to the south and east, it is hard to imagine that they could manage the Black Hills with much less respect and foresight than the U.S. Forest Service and private owners.

It is true that the Sioux have been deeply wronged, but the greater wrong has been to the Hills themselves, and turning over ownership, while it might act to salve our national consciousness, probably would not bring an end to the assault of the Black Hills. It might well turn out to be a failed attempt to step back in time, when what is needed are imaginative steps toward the future. Some people, white and Indian, are more concerned with the welfare of the Hills for posterity's sake than in righting one of many wrongs of the past. When you consider the shaky record of tribal government's ability to look ahead, the age-old jealousies and divisions within the Sioux community, and the fact that many whites who also revere the Black Hills as a special place would be disenfranchised by such a settlement, one begins to wonder if a change in ownership would serve any real purpose other than substituting red exploiters for white ones.

You don't have to be Sioux or live in North Rapid to feel impotent in the face of the anthropocentricity that is maiming the Black Hills. Many Black Hills residents feel a need to protect the Hills, but almost none have had the courage to focus on the problem. It is not a question of going back in time in search of old solutions, because in Black Hills time, the problem is quite new and more sinister than anything that has happened before. Rather, it is a matter of going beyond and coming up with fresh, farsighted solutions.

For years, a lot of people have felt helpless over what is happening in the Hills and all over the West. I'm afraid I am one of them. Some nights I lie in our bed thinking about what will become of the land to which I belong. I sometimes get a suffocating feeling that keeps me awake. But at least one night last month, I was fast asleep by ten o'clock. My wife and I go to bed early in our little house in the shady end of Rapid City. It's old-fashioned, I realize, but I like to be up before the sun, like to see the morning colors spread across the countryside on my drive to the ranch. Though there has been a Colt .357 in the drawer of the bed stand for years, we have never locked the doors of our Rapid City house. That kind of faith in our security is one of the reasons we live in the Black Hills, and we have always taken a certain amount of pride in the fact that we have never felt a need for dead bolts and safety chains.

That night last month, I was dreaming a pleasant dream of the time when I spent all my nights at the ranch. In the dream there was a cold evening breeze and the smell of stacked prairie hay that I would feed the cattle the next morning. I suppose I was staring at the Black Hills and marveling that there was no light in sight. But there was sound. It was footsteps, and then there was my wife's voice, "Hey, Hey!"

About then I came fully awake. "Get out of here. Get out!" she was yelling. And when I turned, already fumbling in the bedside drawer, I saw a head stuck through the door of our bedroom.

"Hey!" I was shouting this time. Then, footfalls ahead of me on the stairs, and suddenly I was standing naked and alone in our kitchen. The .357 was in my hand, and I was staring at the back door that was now flung open. The cool evening breeze that chilled me was exactly like that of my dream but there was no smell of prairie hay. When I turned, my wife was standing at the dining room door, clutching her housecoat at the throat. Our eyes caught and held for several seconds before our shoulders slumped. What on Earth was happening?

The policeman had an accent that I mistook for Chicago. "No," he said. "New Jersey. I'm a little mixed up. I've been out here a couple years." He was young and big and exuded confidence. He walked through the house ahead of me, poking his nightstick under all the beds, into the back of the closets. He had done this before, was very professional, and made us feel a little more secure. "It's your business," he said as he readied to leave, "but if it was me, I'd start doing things differently. I'd lock the doors."

Sometimes it seems that the state government's top priority is to make South Dakota as much like Illinois or Ohio as they can. To watch the local news, you would think that every farmer, rancher, teacher, merchant, white man, or Indian longs for more factories, more highways, more jobs. But when I move among the people of the Black Hills, this is not what I hear. What I hear is that there is only a fraction of the sharp-tailed grouse and pheasants there used to be, that it's nearly impossible to find a place to cross-country ski or hunt deer where you can be alone. Many conversations end with a dazed shaking of heads and talk about traffic, lines at restaurants, beer cans thrown into trout streams, the morning smog over the Hills.

When I visit places I've read were once beautiful and uncorrupted, it strikes me that the human characteristic that is perhaps most unfortunate is our ability to get used to almost any insult to our senses if it comes gradually enough. It's probably the fact that changes have come, and continue to come, so fast out here that makes the sense of loss so profound. I used to feel cheated for never having seen the buffalo. Now I suspect that it's a blessing that they were gone before my time. Maybe if I had waited in traffic as a child, I would be adjusting better to Rapid City's rush hour. Maybe I wouldn't notice the cluttered subdivisions along the highway if I had never seen mule deer standing in the meadows that were sacrificed for those housing starts. Maybe I wouldn't notice the topsoil blowing away if I couldn't remember when those wheat fields were prairie, if I didn't remember what switch grass, blue stem, and grama grass look like. And maybe that damned light at the top of the Hills wouldn't bother me if I had never sat on the porch steps and enjoyed the sensation of a few moments of solitude.

I've tried to find that light. I've gotten in my pickup and driven toward it, but it always disappears. A ridge of pine trees or a hill blocks it from sight, and when I come to where I think it should be visible again, there's nothing but the blackness of the Hills. I want to think the light is fastened to a pole above some senseless materialistic venture. I want its existence to be ridiculous. I want it to be simply wrong. But most likely it's not simply anything. Most likely it is someone's home. I may well be seeing a light shining from someone's bedroom window.

So perhaps it is best that I can't find the source of that light. As long as it is just a glow in the distant night, I can imagine that it is a huge mercury vapor light illuminating the night shift's work at a new strip mine, the beacon at the top of another ski hill, the yard light for a sawmill or a factory of some kind. As long as I don't know for sure, I can keep myself out of the equation. I'm not sure what I would do if one night I located that light at the end of someone's driveway. It would sicken me to find a person sitting quietly on his own front porch, staring downcountry at a light glimmering from the direction I had just come.

Symbols
Kris L. Hardin

THIS IS NOT AN EASY ESSAY. IT WILL NOT CONJURE UP IMAGES of alpine meadows alive with the sounds of clear running streams or describe the clarity and beauty of standing in a trout stream as the setting sun bathes a summer landscape in layers of amber. As many of us spend more and more of our lives in landscapes and mindscapes shaped by concrete, steel, and asphalt, only a very lucky few have access in daily life to such idyllic scenes. While descriptions of the natural world are an important way of reminding ourselves of the necessity of protecting the possibilities and alternatives that unpopulated, wild, even dangerous places offer, I will instead focus on a less glamorous aspect of stewardship: the ease with which we have chosen to take symbolic and relatively ineffective action rather than tackle the more difficult choices that stewardship implies. Symbols are tricky things: they stand for something, but they are *not* that something in themselves. Grape juice in a Baptist communion cup stands for the blood of Christ, but it is not blood. Driving a BMW may be a symbol of being successful, but it may also hide the lack of success.

While most people still take pleasure in a beautiful landscape, many have difficulty facing the fact that their lives must change dramatically if their children and grandchildren are to experience such pleasures too. Unless we begin to address the side of stewardship that requires us to take a hard look at the effectiveness of our mostly symbolic efforts over the last twenty-five years, our options within the natural world will continue to dwindle. While fighting to save a particular piece of land or species is a noble cause, we continue to fight these battles in the same ways and on the same terms. The real battle, the one that changes the nature of the way we think about ourselves and our place in the natural world, has yet to be fought and, in fact, is probably hidden from us by the symbols we have chosen to use. My fear is that putting energy into smaller battles keeps us from taking part in the larger battle that must take place if we are to survive.

My journey to this position has been long and circuitous. It begins with growing up in central California and memories of seeing the Sierra Nevada range out of our dining room window. Blue and gray in the summer, white with snow in the winter, the massive distant presence provided me with a sense of permanence and solidity. In what was a predominantly flat suburban landscape, the sight of these mountains fueled my imagination and filled me with the possibility of other places and other stories to be explored.

By the time I was eleven or twelve, in the mid sixties, I could only see the mountains occasionally. Looking back, it seems that as air quality in the San Joaquin Valley deteriorated and the mountains faded, my attachment to local things increased. Thoughts about other times and places, a habit instilled by my early imaginings of the distant people and places of the Sierras, got in the way of my pursuit of activities typical of most adolescents and teens.

It wasn't until high school (by then I could only see the Sierras after a rainstorm) that I found my own cause in an ecology club started by a biology teacher. Here were issues that seemed more pressing than prom dresses or football games, and I pursued them wholeheartedly. I read Rachel Carson, Paul Ehrlich, Thoreau, and more; I knew the statistics on America's overexploitation of natural resources; I was at the local college campus for the first celebration of Earth Day; I helped organize one of the first recycling centers in my hometown; I was one of the first students to begin riding a bicycle to school at a time, not so long ago, when cycling was a sure sign of social backwardness.

But, more important, I began making forays into the Sierra Nevada range. Backpacking trips with my brother and his friends replaced an earlier decade's imaginings with experience. The vanillalike smell of a Jeffrey pine, the bone-chilling cold of a sudden snowfall, encountering bear on their own terms, standing on a high mountain peak watching a bird of prey as it circled below—these were new experiences for me, and they opened up new avenues for thinking about the world around me as well as my place in it. The summer of my senior year, as a cook and general hand at a small riding camp, I made even longer trips into the Sierras and hardened my resolve about the possibilities such wild places provided. Preservation of these areas became important to me because of their natural beauty and the importance of biodiversity, but also because of the alternatives that wild places offered. They were places where the answers were less obvious, less readily available. Wild places offered me another kind of diversity: the space to think about life and myself in alternative ways.

Throughout this period, during the late sixties and seventies, I was convinced that education and small steps taken by individuals in their daily lives could make a difference. My experiences and resolve likely were not very different from many of the middle-class youth of my generation. We entered college toward the end of the Vietnam era, wore old faded clothing and long hair, used drugs as an escape, and saw environmentalism as another way of working against the establishment.

Over time, however, I noticed that the fervor of my environmentalist friends began to wear off as they left school, got jobs, and became car and home owners and parents. I remember being disappointed and puzzled. I moved away from the San Joaquin Valley and the shadow of the mountains when I went to graduate school in the Midwest, but continued the activities I associated with being an environmentalist: bicycling, recycling, shopping at a food co-op, buying products in bulk. Looking back now I see this bent in my thinking was as much economic necessity as real choice or sacrifice.

Then, in the early eighties, as a doctoral student in anthropology, I spent several years doing research in a rural community of subsistence farmers in Sierra Leone. There was no electricity, no running water, little motorized transport, no supermarkets, few consumer goods, and very little garbage. Plastic bags were reused again and again, empty plastic containers, like those used for antifreeze, were cleaned and then used to store palm oil or other goods; even run-down radio batteries were set to dry in the sun as a way of eking out the last bit of electricity from them. Farmers who practice shifting cultivation, as these people did, must rely on the natural world in ways that most Americans can hardly imagine. The yearly appearance of certain species of termites and caterpillars signaled the time for farmers to begin clearing land for the year's farm. Trees were felled and brush was cleared, dried, and burned to provide a layer of ash fertilizer for the year's rice crop. Planting was closely tied to the rains. If the rice seed was sown too early in the season, it would not sprout for lack of moisture; if it was sown too late, it would rot before it could germinate. At the end of the yearly harvest, farm families moved their farms to a new area, leaving the depleted farm fallow for a number of years.

I was constantly impressed both by the knowledge these people had of their natural world and the degree to which they lived their lives in its shadow. As I learned more about the history and values of the area, however, it became clear that the close attention paid to the natural world was driven by necessity rather than ideals about appreciation or stewardship, and that the small size of this community, rather than a conscious choice, was all that kept the level of environmental destruction somewhat in check. I found, for example, that primary forests in the area had been destroyed and that in one or two generations the length of time allowed for fallowing had dropped from fifteen years to between four and seven years. When I was there in the early eighties, there were only stories about elephants and other large game. Even monkeys had been hunted out, and the duiker (a small deer), boa constricters, forest lizards, and other medium-sized game were becoming harder and harder to find and would most likely disappear within the coming twenty years. Population pressures and more efficient technologies fostered these changes. It was all too clear that as more efficient alternatives became available, the overwhelming attitude was one of exploitation rather than stewardship or preservation. These people were hungry for consumer goods, for roads and transportation systems that would make education and better medical care a reality, for water systems and electricity—in short, for all the things they knew others in the world had. Here, it seemed, was one answer to my puzzlement about my fellow environmentalists a decade earlier. The reason, I saw now, that I had been frustrated by how quickly people's values had changed was that I had confused necessity and a kind of youthful resistance with real change. I had not known that once other possibilities became available, either through the introduction of new choices (as in Sierra Leone) or increased income (as among my U.S. friends), values would change accordingly. Perhaps there is something in human nature that leads people in almost every culture to the attitude that the individual's wants take precedence over everything else and this blinds us to the costs of such single-mindedness.

It happened to me too. When I returned to the United States from Africa, I remember being initially overwhelmed by the waste. It was months before I could bring myself to throw away a plastic bag, and clothes dryers and washing machines seemed an ultimate luxury. Having lived without so much for several years I reveled in the choices and possibilities of American life in a way I would not have imagined before I left. As I finished my degree and moved out of the marginal world of the student, the seeming imperatives of adult life descended on me almost without my awareness. I bought a car and began to rationalize my choices. The costs of taking the time to bicycle to work or otherwise live a smaller-scale existence were weighed against the extra time that driving or other conveniences and shortcuts offered. For a number of years, donations to Green Peace, the Chesapeake Bay Foundation, the Sierra Club, and other organizations assuaged my guilt about living a life-style I knew was destructive, but in time even those donations stopped.

The point of this narrative is to show how I continued to fool myself, as, I believe, most of us do. The actions many of us have taken in the name of environmentalism or conservation have made little difference other than to make us feel somewhat better about ourselves in the short run. We, as a species, are still on a downward spiral. We are unwilling to assume any responsibility for this decline, and few have taken significant action against it.

What I mean by this very simple, yet very pessimistic conclusion can best be illustrated by relating a conversation that took place among a group of my friends in a restaurant in a small town in Montana. One of those in the group had grown up in the town, left Montana to go to school, but returned after graduation. The conversation began with development and the fact that he barely recognized the small town he had returned to six or seven years before. In fact, he was thinking about moving to a smaller town about thirty miles away to escape the onslaught of people who had invaded from the west and east coasts and had brought all of their bad habits with them—people who had been drawn to this small western town because of its friendliness and slow pace of life, but whose tastes and excesses were changing the very fabric

of the community. At the same time, we all agreed that the ranchers who
had worked hard all their lives could not be blamed for selling large tracts
of land to subdividers if it meant their families would be comfortable for
the rest of their lives. In the same way, the Main Street storeowners could
not be blamed for catering to the desires and tastes of the newcomers,
particularly when one realized that much of Montana had missed the economic boom of the eighties.

I am sure similar conversations have taken place in numerous small
communities across the country as Americans search for ways of preserving the communities they grew up in and city dwellers try to escape
the confines of urban life. Somewhere deep into this discussion the topic
shifted to the meaning of conservation. My friend admitted that newcomers were the main exponents of conservation policies in the last
twenty years. In Montana, recent newcomers have been a major force in
fights to limit the timber industry, reintroduce the wolf to Yellowstone
National Park, and keep the Army Corps of Engineers away from the Yellowstone River (the longest as yet undammed river in the United States).
But he went on to say that conservation hadn't really been necessary
before these newcomers flooded in. As with my Sierra Leonean friends,
the local townspeople tended not to see changes as degradation, but
rather as the necessities of economic life. There was also anger that the
newcomers were beginning to dictate what Montanans could do with the
state's resources. Someone recounted two current jokes in Montana: that
outsiders would not be so anxious to come to Montana if they hadn't
already spoiled the places they were from, and that life in the big cities is
so terrible it's no wonder Montanans don't trust people from the city to
make decisions for them.

Our laughter helped us escape the complexity of the real issues. We all
knew change was inevitable, and yet we all longed for the return of a
more pristine time and feared the impersonality that seems to characterize communities that grow too large or change too quickly. Then my
friend noticed a bumper sticker on a passing car. It was on one of those
four-wheel-drive Isuzu Troopers or Toyota Land Cruisers that are fast
becoming *de rigueur* for the set that cannot quite afford a Range Rover. It
had out-of-state plates.

"'Think habitat,'" he read. "But, what does that *mean?* I see it everywhere, but how does that translate into action?"

"It demonstrates a kind of concern," someone said.

"I suppose it means that this guy does what he can to preserve the habitat of endangered species, but more generally it means things like recycling, contributing to environmental organizations—things like that," I added.

Then my friend asked two very simple questions: "But how many people who have that bumper sticker really do those kinds of things, and what good do those things do anyway?"

At that point a kind of clarity came to me about the environmental movement as I had known it. It was a realization that had been lurking in half-consciousness for some time and that had probably fueled my inactivity for the last decade. Despite Earth Days, bumper stickers, monetary contributions, and recycling, I saw that we are no closer to seeing ourselves as part of the natural world, rather than its dominators, than we had been twenty years before. Like my environmentalist friends of twenty years ago and my Sierra Leonean friends, most of our actions are fostered by necessity and the image of doing the right thing. The newest revival of America's flirtation with environmental concerns is also fundamentally rooted in the contingencies and needs of the moment. What has often passed as concern and activity is merely symbolic action, action that does not fundamentally aid us in rethinking our relationship with the natural world but merely allows us to feel good about our participation in issues of preservation or to be recognized as an environmentally concerned person. We do not explore what kinds of participation would take us where we hope to go, what an ideal world might look like, what we would have to give up if we want to get there, or, more important, what we would gain if we did.

There may be something even more insidious about our reliance on symbolic action. In this age of easy answers, readily visible symbols pit timberman against ecologist, city dweller against rancher, and businesspeople against intellectuals by making it immediately apparent which camp one belongs to. You have the wrong bumper sticker? You're a reactionary. You own shotguns? Not at my dinner table. Our symbolic polemics become more numerous and distancing day by day. Such labels have the capacity to freeze battle lines before we even know what the real issues are, what commonalities we share, and what solutions we might propose. The conspiracy theorist in me longs to see this as a plot by those who want us to ignore the long-term costs of environmental degradations for short-term gains. But, of course, that means someone else would be pulling the strings, thereby absolving us from any responsibility. The anthropologist in me sees these divisions as an outgrowth of discourses that have become more and more limited and thus less flexible and open to explore alternatives: we cannot or will not engage in conversations with those who think in other ways.

The conclusion remains: symbolic action has not worked. If it had worked, we wouldn't have mountains of glass, tin, aluminum, newsprint, and plastic waiting to be recycled. We wouldn't have produced so much to begin with.

If it had worked, people would consider environmental records along with the profit margins of the corporations they invest in.

If it had worked, Americans' response to the Gulf War would have been to begin car pooling and otherwise reduce the consumption of petroleum products instead of waving yellow ribbons that tacitly supported American policies and our continuing overexploitation of the world's resources.

If it had worked, we would be seriously discussing population control.

If it had worked, mass transit would be more than a dream in all but our largest cities.

If it had worked, there would be no question about the importance of saving the smallest and "lowliest" tree frog, just as there is little question about the importance of preserving a species as majestic as the California condor or as symbolic as the bald eagle.

If it had worked, we would be seriously thinking about ways of curtailing our life-styles and developing healthy economies that are not premised on continual growth.

There are countless examples of environmentally conscious actions that have been adopted in the flurry of a cause only to be abandoned when the next cause appears. We live in an era in which social issues are consumed and cast off much as last year's shoe makes way for this year's style or a new and improved detergent replaces last month's miracle cleaner. I was in Los Angeles during the 1984 Olympics long enough to see that the carpooling and no-drive days that were organized to help the athletes breathe more easily can reduce air pollutants substantially. Yet people have chosen not to pursue these efforts. Have you noticed in grocery stores lately how we have so easily gone back to using plastic bags instead of requesting paper, or better yet bringing our own reusable carriers? The hype of the twentieth anniversary of the first Earth Day must be wearing off.

These and many more instances show that we have chosen the easy way out. Anyone interested in stewardship must begin to ask why this is so. The answer can only be that we really don't want to make changes or even adjustments to the life-style and consumption patterns that are embedded in the American or, perhaps, human psyche. It is much easier to decide to put a bumper sticker on the family car than to decide not to use that car three days a week. Our life-styles reflect both domination over other countries, as we continue to utilize a disproportionate percentage of the world's resources at alarming rates, as well as domination over the natural world. Our approach is shaped by an ethos that says we have the right to take what we have the ability to exploit. Recognizing this is a first step toward, if not changing, at least working against this ethos. Another step is to begin to ask questions about our place in the world and the consequences of our actions for that world.

At face value these are simple questions. The next step is the hardest. Will we take those answers seriously and translate them into actions that are more than symbolic, actions that do more than make us feel good about ourselves in the short term?

The Only Last Best Place
Todd Wester

EMMETT WESTER ENTERED THE WORLD AMID THE REVERBERATION of a scream, a dissonant expression of unimaginable hurt and fear mixed with joy and relief. Yet as quickly and unexpectedly as the note crescendoed, it tapered off into a tearful, hushed incantation of the unique sentiment of my wife's pain-purged mind: "Oh, he's beautiful. He's our baby. *He's our baby.*"

Even as Lynn spoke, the attending nurses removed our newborn child from atop her stomach, wrapped him in blankets, handed him to me, and more or less shuffled the two of us off to the side. The long labor and slow, difficult delivery had taken their toll on Lynn's body, and her obstetrician wanted to work quickly to avoid any postpartum complications. Between anxious glances toward the flurry of activity going on around my wife, I looked into the remarkably clear, blue eyes of our first child. He stared back quizzically, as if to ask what the world might have in store for him over the next few years. I had given much thought to the question, but as yet I had no answer.

Emmett represents the fifth generation of my family to call Montana home, but he is certain to experience a much-abbreviated version of the wild, expansive land of his ancestors. The popular modern appellation of Montana as "the last best place" signifies the fervor with which people have rushed to take advantage of what the state has to offer before it is all gone. Humans have undeniably exploited the resources of this area since they first arrived here, and many Montanans (myself included) have relied on outside interest to make a living. But the current rapid increase in the rate of growth and change has generated concerns that with the promotion of our state we have opened a Pandora's box. The problem is a complex one that seems to have no simple solution or any single cause. The effects of an influx of people and money on matters of economy, tourism, property values, fish and game populations, nonrenewable resources, access, Native American rights and heritage, farm and ranch foreclosures, subdivision, and crowding, among others, form the diverse components of a confusing issue, one that is most often dealt with not by application of logic or philosophy, but rather by emotion, resulting in a sort of "I was here first" selfishness. "What can be done about it" becomes at once the question and also the resigned answer. Nevertheless, my query remained simple and focused: What could I do to ensure that my son could enjoy this place as I had?

The answer came in a rather inconspicuous form. I was preparing to take Lynn and Emmett home from the Livingston hospital when my parents arrived with a few gifts. Some of them were things I had used as a small child, among them a tiny pair of black rubber hip boots. When my dad handed them to me, he reminded me that he had worn them as a child, as had I and my younger brother, and that as a result they showed considerable wear. But, he said, half in jest, perhaps they could be patched up so that Emmett could use them. We both knew that since even brand-new hippers often fail to perform their intended purpose of keeping more water out than in, the only chance that these little boots, now nearly half a century old, will keep my son dry is the possibility that the cracks and tears will vent off perspiration. Nor will the smooth soles provide much purchase on the slick, moss-covered rocks of a trout stream. And I'm sure that at only fourteen inches high, they were never really meant to give little three-foot boys who can barely cast, let alone wade, access to the fish of waters distant from shore. But they reminded me of the story of my grandfather—his life and death, his all-consuming passion with fishing, and his character. Therein lay their usefulness—and the answer to my question.

✦

My grandfather, Leo Wester, was definitely, though not exclusively, a fly-fisherman. He was born in 1910 in Hayworden, Saskatchewan, and five years later moved with his family to the tiny eastern Montana community of Forsyth. The town grew up on either side of the Northern Pacific railroad tracks, over which coal-fired steam engines pulled cattle to distant markets and sugar beets to the Billings refinery. Protected by the breaks and rims of the lower Yellowstone River, Forsyth is a peaceful oasis in the dry, wind-blown prairie. But a fly-fisher's paradise it is not: the Yellowstone is warm and slow moving there; hence, the trout population tapers off almost completely in the river well upstream of Forsyth. Except for the occasional shad or carp, Leo would have found the warm-water species of the lower river almost impossible to catch on flies. Furthermore, fly-fishing was next to unheard of in Montana in the 1920s, so I am sure my grandfather found it no less noble a venture to pursue with bait the denizens of the Yellowstone near Forsyth: the nocturnal catfish, the prehistoric sturgeon, the eel-like burbot (ling), and toothy predators such as sauger and northern pike.

In 1936 he met and married Mary Wills, my grandmother, who, when I inquired, replied only that she was born "out in the prairie" north of Forsyth somewhere near Mildred, Montana. She had moved to town to work as a waitress when she met my grandfather. Shortly after they were married, Leo found work with the Sawyer chain of grocery stores, and they relocated two hundred miles west of Forsyth in Livingston. There Leo found two new fascinations: the fly rod, and his daughter, Persis, born in the spring of 1937.

Though busy with work and a baby, Leo still spent most of his evenings and weekends learning to fly-fish the trout streams of Park, Sweet Grass, and Gallatin counties. Dan Bailey and Walter "Red" Monical had not yet opened their fly shop in Livingston, and no one seems to know where Leo purchased his fishing equipment, but he owned at least one split-cane bamboo fly rod and a couple of reels. My grandmother recounts how they would frequent a now-popular spot on the Yellowstone River near where Depuy's Spring Creek empties in through a culvert. She would pack a picnic and would play with their daughter while

Leo fished, the entire place to himself. A novice at the fledgling sport, his object was not so much to catch fish as it was to learn a new method and to spend his days out on the stream.

But my grandfather's fly-fishing was abruptly interrupted when in the fall of 1938, after rapid and inexplicable loss of motor function, he was diagnosed with multiple sclerosis. Short-circuited by the degeneration of its insulative layer, his nervous system sent crossed signals to his muscles, and he lost coordination of movement, became weak and bedridden. I am told that he once dragged himself outside the house and there lay and sobbed, devastated by the condition of his body. Yet he never ceased to maintain that he could get better, nor did his wife ever give up hope in her constant care of him. My grandfather was fortunate—MS is little understood and has claimed the lives of many equally strong-willed individuals determined to stop its progression—nevertheless, he was one of the rare few to see the disease through to complete remission. After nearly eight months fraught with frustration, he was finally able to move about on crutches, and later with a cane. Eventually, with the help of friends, Leo would walk to the Yellowstone, sit in a chair, and fish a few hours every other day. A year and a half after his diagnosis, he was well on his way to a total recovery.

It was really during the years that followed his bout with MS that my grandfather became enraptured with fly-fishing. Turned away from volunteer service during World War II because of his previous illness, he found work with the U.S. Employment Office in Livingston and resumed his pursuits with the fly rod. He learned quickly, and soon became as efficient at catching fish as he was adept in knowing their habitudes. At a time in Montana when catch-and-release meant "letting the little ones go," Leo found it necessary to put back most of the fish he caught, lest his family eat trout morning, noon, and night. Those who knew him speak of Leo as a man who was not so wild about eating fish as he was about fishing, who savored every moment out on the stream regardless of the numbers of fish he caught or brought home.

Many of his friends hit upon Leo's infatuation with fishing as a novelty and teased him about his practice of returning the fish he caught to their waters, none so acutely as one Donald McCausland, publisher of the Forsyth *Independent*. McCausland found great pleasure in counting weekly coup on my grandfather in Newsy Notes, a regular feature of his newspaper, and my grandfather derived no less satisfaction from his counterattacks. Once McCausland wrote that the reason his friend "Leo 'Isaak Walton' Wester" had returned home with an ice box empty of fish

was simply because he had no knowledge of how to prepare the same, to
which my grandfather sent him the following reply dated September 8,
1944:

> For your information, McCausland, my ice box is now, as it has always
> been since coming here, full of fish, and contrary to your editing I can
> boil, fry, or do anything with a fish that can be done. But, I ask you, if
> after having been on a continuous fish diet for the last two months, if
> it is too much to expect something diversified in the way of subsis-
> tence?
>
> P.S.—That moniker of "Isaak Walton" attached to my name is, I
> can assure you, of no credit to me. What has he or did he have that
> I haven't?

What, indeed? My grandfather learned to fly-fish at a time before Montana was referred to as "the last best place," when abundant, eager trout
saw few fishermen and fewer decent imitations of their foodstuffs. It was
certainly a time of great opportunity, but he had even more to be thankful
for: against all odds he had returned to perfect health and was able to
spend time with his family, had work, and could fish just about as often as
he pleased. Each healthful day a gift in itself, he reveled in the joy of the
hours spent hiking with his wife and daughter to small high-mountain
streams in search of native cutthroat trout.

Fishing in high-mountain streams is tantamount to gambling. I suspect it is because each involves some degree of random reward that both
are so addictive. Rarely is it a matter of casting to sighted fish; more often
it is a wager that a cast to a particular spot will elicit a rise. Each time a
fish takes the fly, something is learned about its behavior and preference
for particular structures, depths, and currents. And while the largest and
easiest-to-catch fish may lie in deep, open pools, the greatest prizes are
tucked in behind some log or overhanging branch or lie in the tiny step-
like pools formed by a series of deadfalls. Most often the technique
required to catch such fish is a unique one never tried before, and successful or not, the attempt evokes the anticipation of discovery. For my
grandfather, fishing *was* the anticipation of discovery. The promise of
new insight, the chance that some novel and creative method would be
necessary, and maybe even effective, made high-mountain streams his
favorite haunts.

His endeavors rendered him a wellspring of information and a much-
desired fishing companion. Still, he endured the sporting jabs of news-
paperman and raconteur McCausland. Transferred to the U.S. Employment

office in Helena in April of 1945, Leo received a copy of the *Independent* in which McCausland had printed the following:

> Leo "Isaak Walton" Wester has changed addresses again. Must be he doesn't live at Livingston anymore. Well, the fine people of that mountain metropolis certainly tolerated his boasting longer than I thot they would. Just how a man (?) can go to a place like that and create more wind than a small tornado singing of his piscatorial abilities, I can't conceive. There are real fishermen in that town.
>
> A friend of Wester's told me some time ago that the only trout of legal size he brought home were some that had become stranded in shallow water and Leo waded in and knocked them out with a stick. Some fisherman!

In another such article, McCausland suggested that Leo's infant son— my father, Milton, born in April of 1946—was already a better fisherman than his father. At the end of a long letter of rebuttal dated May 18, 1946, Leo refutes,

> Now I have wasted enough of my valuable time in trying to put you "hept" to yourself and should I continue writing and relate in detail what I have stored up as endurance against you, McCausland, you would have to bury your head like the ostrich. As I said, "Time's a wastin'"—for on the morrow fishing season opens and since I have fished this part of the country out, I must seek more lucrative fields. I shall, therefore, arise early in the morning and take a jaunt up on the Madison. (Trust I am making you feel good) and there, my landlocked friend, I will be catching fish and you can dream about them sitting under your cactus bush. When I return and relate my experiences to you, your spirits will be lower than the alcoholic content of Forsyth's water supply.
>
> P.S.—That son of mine may get to be about as good a fisherman as I, but never a better one!!!

Leo and Mary had a third child, another daughter, Marylin Jo, in 1948. Back in Livingston as director of the new Montana State Employment Office, Leo's passion for fishing remained insatiable, so his wife and their three red-headed children found themselves tagging along on many an evening or weekend trip. But he expected his son to participate, and so it was that in the spring of 1949 he purchased the little black hip boots.

My grandfather took a photograph of my father in the hip boots at age four, the back of which is stamped "July 1950." They had spent the day on the Boulder River, a stream not far from Livingston, and were preparing to head home. The scene is of a little boy side-saddle behind the wheel of a brand-new Plymouth two-door sedan. The high bench seat just barely permits his feet to reach the running board, and visible behind the seat is the grip of a bamboo fly rod with an automatic reel. He holds his own wool baseball cap in his hand and peers out from under the too-large brim of his father's fedora that has several flies stuck in around the band. He looks slightly propped up, and his father's hat does little to conceal an expression unencumbered by any notion of his identity beyond the moment, wherein he is what his father wants him to be: a fisherman. It's a good-times-last-forever photograph that belies the tragedy that lay ahead, for Leo died just two months later at age 39.

A bizarre consequence of his triumph over sickness, it was my grandfather's preoccupation with a life he knew he was fortunate to lead that caused his death. For it was not in the throes of illness, but rather as a result of the excitement over a caught fish that Leo lost his life. I found the following account of the incident on the front page of the September 14 issue of the *Park County News,* then Livingston's weekly newspaper. At noon on Sunday, September 10, 1950, Leo and friends Bill Anderson and Harry Thomas were adrift in a metal boat on the southwest side of Lewis Lake, Yellowstone Park (Wyoming), fishing for spawning mackinaw trout.

> Wester . . . had caught a large mackinaw trout, and in the excitement among the group in landing the fish, the boat was capsized. . . . An airlock in one end kept a part of the boat above water. The men clung to the boat for some time before Wester, who was unable to swim, lost his hold. Thomas and Anderson finally succeeded in getting Wester atop the part of the boat out of the water. Then the men found the air lock was leaking, and Anderson and Thomas started to swim to shore hoping to get help to rescue Wester.

Anderson made it to shore and there lost consciousness for a short time. When he regained his faculties, he struggled barefoot to the west thumb highway, summoned help, and, believing that Thomas had made it and had become disoriented in the woods, went back in to find him. But Thomas had succumbed to exhaustion and hypothermia and sank just short of the shore. My grandfather was found near the sunken boat.

I was born some sixteen years after my grandfather's death, so all I really know of him are the stories, photos, and letters. Yet when I ponder with uncertainty and mixed emotion the future of Montana, my home, the birthplace of my son, I think about how my grandfather fished the streams that I fish today. I think about how he viewed each day spent astream as a gift, a day he might well not have had. And I think about how he so deeply appreciated the waters he fished for their intrinsic value—for what was within them to be discovered, not simply for what he got out of them. I now realize that for him, Montana could never have been "the last best place," for he understood that place to be the part of the human spirit wherein lies the joy of discovery. He went to that place every time he went fishing, whether he caught anything or not.

One warm summer day, when he is big enough, Emmett will get to wear the worn-out black hip boots that my grandfather gave to my father, that my father gave to me. There is something magical about the union of these tiny boots with the streams and rivers that I, my father, and my grandfather have fished. As surely as water will seep in through the cracks in the boots, so will it flow through my son's very soul, for the waters are an endless source of untold secrets and knowledge. Perhaps the best I can do to ensure that Emmett may enjoy this place as I have is to leave well enough alone, to resist the temptation to teach him too much, thereby robbing him of the satisfaction of having learned by himself. I remain uncertain about Montana's future, but I know that if my son can come to appreciate this world for what is in it to be discovered, and not for what may be taken from it, then he will have found within himself the only last best place.

Christianity and the
Survival of Creation
Wendell Berry

I

I CONFESS THAT I HAVE NOT INVARIABLY BEEN COMFORTABLE IN front of a pulpit; I have never been comfortable behind one. To be behind a pulpit is always a forcible reminder to me that I am an essayist and, in many ways, a dissenter. An essayist is, literally, a writer who attempts to tell the truth. Preachers must resign themselves to being either right or wrong; an essayist, when proved wrong, may claim to have been "just practicing." An essayist is privileged to speak without institutional authorization. A dissenter, of course, must speak without privilege.

I want to begin with a problem: namely, that the culpability of Christianity in the destruction of the natural world and the uselessness of Christianity in any effort to correct that destruction are now established clichés of the conservation movement. This is a problem for two reasons.

First, the indictment of Christianity by the anti-Christian conservationists is, in many respects, just. For instance, the complicity of Christian priests, preachers, and missionaries in the cultural destruction and the economic exploitation of the primary peoples of the Western Hemisphere, as of traditional cultures around the world, is notorious. Throughout the five hundred years since Columbus's first landfall in the Bahamas, the evangelist has walked beside the conqueror and the merchant, too often blandly assuming their causes were the same. Christian organizations, to this day, remain largely indifferent to the rape and plunder of the world and of its traditional cultures. It is hardly too much to say that most Christian organizations are as happily indifferent to the ecological, cultural, and religious implications of industrial economics as are most industrial organizations. The certified Christian seems just as likely as anyone else to join the military-industrial conspiracy to murder Creation.

The conservationist indictment of Christianity is a problem, second, because however just it may be, it does not come from an adequate understanding of the Bible and the cultural traditions that descend from the Bible. The anti-Christian conservationists characteristically deal with the Bible by waving it off. And this dismissal conceals, as such dismissals are apt to do, an ignorance that invalidates it. The Bible is an inspired book written by human hands; as such, it is certainly subject to criticism. But the anti-Christian environmentalists have not mastered the first rule of the criticism of books: you have to read them before you criticize them. Our predicament now, I believe, requires us to read and understand the Bible in the light of the present fact of Creation. This would seem to be a requirement both for Christians and for everyone concerned, but it entails a long work of true criticism—that is, of careful and judicious study, not dismissal. It entails, furthermore, the making of very precise distinctions between biblical instruction and the behavior of those peoples supposed to have been biblically instructed.

I cannot pretend, obviously, to have made so meticulous a study; even if I were capable of it, I would not live long enough to do it. But I have attempted to read the Bible with these issues in mind, and I see some virtually catastrophic discrepancies between Biblical instruction and Christian behavior. I don't mean disreputable Christian behavior, either. The discrepancies I see are between biblical instruction and allegedly respectable Christian behavior.

If because of these discrepancies, Christianity were dismissable, there would, of course, be no problem. We could simply dismiss it, along with the twenty centuries of unsatisfactory history attached to it, and start setting things to rights. The problem emerges only when we ask, Where then would we turn for instruction? We might, let us suppose, turn to another religion—a recourse that is sometimes suggested by the anti-Christian conservationists. Buddhism, for example, is certainly a religion that could guide us toward a right respect for the natural world, our fellow humans, and our fellow creatures. I owe a considerable debt myself to Buddhism and Buddhists. But there are an enormous number of people—and I am one of them—whose native religion, for better or worse, is Christianity. We were born to it; we began to learn about it before we became conscious; it is, whatever we think of it, an intimate belonging of our being; it informs our consciousness, our language, and our dreams. We can turn away from it or against it, but that will only bind us tightly to a reduced version of it. A better possibility is that this, our native religion, should survive and renew itself so that it may become as largely and truly instructive as we need it to be. On such a survival and renewal of the Christian religion may depend the survival of the Creation that is its subject.

II

IF WE READ THE BIBLE, keeping in mind the desirability of those two survivals—of Christianity and the Creation—we are apt to discover several things about which modern Christian organizations have kept remarkably quiet or to which they have paid little attention.

We will discover that we humans do not own the world or any part of it: "The earth is the Lord's, and the fulness thereof: the world and they that dwell therein."[1] There is in our human law, undeniably, the concept and right of "land ownership." But this, I think, is merely an expedient to safeguard the mutual belonging of people and places without which there can be no lasting and conserving human communities. This right of human ownership is limited by mortality and by natural constraints on human attention and responsibility; it quickly becomes abusive when used to justify large accumulations of "real estate," and perhaps for that reason such large accumulations are forbidden in the twenty-fifth chapter of Leviticus. In biblical terms, the "landowner" is the guest and steward of God: "The land is mine; for ye are strangers and sojourners with me."[2]

We will discover that God made not only the parts of Creation that we humans understand and approve but all of it: "All things were made by him; and without him was not anything made that was made."[3] And so we must credit God with the making of biting and stinging insects, poisonous serpents, weeds, poisonous weeds, dangerous beasts, and disease-causing microorganisms. That we may disapprove of these things does not mean that God is in error or that he ceded some of the work of Creation to Satan; it means that we are deficient in wholeness, harmony, and understanding—that is, we are "fallen."

We will discover that God found the world, as He made it, to be good, that He made it for His pleasure, and that He continues to love it and to find it worthy, despite its reduction and corruption by us. People who quote John 3:16 as an easy formula for getting to Heaven neglect to see the great difficulty implied in the statement that the advent of Christ was made possible by God's love for the world—not God's love for Heaven or for the world as it might be but for the world as it was and is. Belief in Christ is thus dependent on prior belief in the inherent goodness—the lovability—of the world.

We will discover that the Creation is not in any sense independent of the Creator, the result of a primal creative act long over and done with, but is the continuous, constant participation of all creatures in the being of God. Elihu said to Job that if God "gather unto himself his spirit and his breath; all flesh shall perish together."[4] And Psalm 104 says, "thou sendest forth thy spirit, they are created." Creation is thus God's presence in creatures. The Greek Orthodox theologian Philip Sherrard has written that "Creation is nothing less than the manifestation of God's hidden being."[5] This means that we and all other creatures live by a sanctity that is inexpresssibly intimate, for to every creature, the gift of life is a portion of the breath and spirit of God. As the poet George Herbert put it:

> Thou art in small things great, not small in any . . .
> For thou art infinite in one and all. [6]

We will discover that for these reasons, our destruction of nature is not just bad stewardship, or stupid economics, or a betrayal of family responsibility; it is the most horrid blasphemy. It is flinging God's gifts into His face, as if they were of no worth beyond that assigned to them by our destruction of them. To Dante, "despising Nature and her goodness" was a violence against God.[7] We have no entitlement from the Bible to exterminate or permanently destroy or hold in contempt anything on the earth or in the heavens above it or in the waters beneath it. We have the right to use the gifts of nature but not to ruin or waste them. We have the right to use what we need but no more, which is why the Bible forbids usury and great accumulations of property. The usurer, Dante said, "condemns Nature . . . for he puts his hope elsewhere."[8]

William Blake was biblically correct, then, when he said that "everything that lives is holy."[9] And Blake's great commentator, Kathleen Raine, was correct both biblically and historically when she said that "the sense of the holiness of life is the human norm."[10]

The Bible leaves no doubt at all about the sanctity of the act of world making, or of the world that was made, or of creaturely or bodily life in this world. We are holy creatures living among other holy creatures in a world that is holy. Some people know this, and some do not. Nobody, of course, knows it all the time. But what keeps it from being far better known than it is? Why is it apparently unknown to millions of professed students of the Bible? How can modern Christianity have so solemnly folded its hands while so much of the work of God was and is being destroyed?

III

OBVIOUSLY, "the sense of the holiness of life" is not compatible with an exploitive economy. You cannot know that life is holy if you are content to live from economic practices that daily destroy life and diminish its possiblity. And many if not most Christian organizations now appear to be perfectly at peace with the military-industrial economy and its "scientific" destruction of life. Surely, if we are to remain free and if we are to remain true to our religious inheritance, we must maintain a separation between church and state. But if we are to maintain any sense or coherence or meaning in our lives, we cannot tolerate the present utter disconnection between religion and economy. By "economy" I do not mean "economics," which is the study of money-making, but rather the ways of human housekeeping, the ways by which the human household is situated and maintained within the household of nature. To be uninterested in economy is to be uninterested in the practice of religion; it is to be uninterested in culture and in character. Probably the most urgent question now faced by people who would adhere to the Bible is this: What sort of economy would be responsible to the holiness of life? What, for Christians, would be the economy, the practices and the restraints, of "right livelihood"? I do not believe that organized Christianity now has any idea. I think its idea of a Christian economy is no more or less than the industrial economy—which is an economy firmly founded on the seven deadly sins and the breaking of all ten of the Ten Commandments. Obviously, if Christianity is going to survive as more than a respecter and comforter of profitable iniquities, then Christians, regardless of their organizations, are going to have to interest themselves in economy—

which is to say, in nature and in work. They are going to have to give workable answers to those who say we cannot live without this economy that is destroying us and our world, who see the murder of Creation as the only way of life.

The holiness of life is obscured to modern Christians also by the idea that the only holy place is the built church. This idea may be more taken for granted than taught; nevertheless, Christians are encouraged from childhood to think of the church building as "God's house," and most of them could think of their houses or farms or shops or factories as holy places only with great effort and embarrassment. It is understandably difficult for modern Americans to think of their dwellings and workplaces as holy, because most of these are, in fact, places of desecration, deeply involved in the ruin of Creation.

The idea of the exclusive holiness of church buildings is, of course, wildly incompatible with the idea, which the churches also teach, that God is present in all places to hear prayers. It is incompatible with Scripture. The idea that a human artifact could contain or confine God was explicitly repudiated by Solomon in his prayer at the dedication of the Temple: "Behold, the heaven and the heaven of heavens cannot contain thee: how much less this house that I have builded?"[11] And these words of Solomon were remembered a thousand years later by Saint Paul, preaching at Athens:

> God that made the world and all things therein, seeing that
> he is lord of heaven and earth, dwelleth not in temples made with
> hands . . .
> For in him we live, and move, and have our being; as certain
> also of your own poets have said.[12]

Idolatry always reduces to the worship of something "made with hands," something confined within the terms of human work and human comprehension. Thus, Solomon and Saint Paul both insisted on the largeness and the at-largeness of God, setting Him free, so to speak, from *ideas* about Him. He is not to be fenced in, under human control, like some domestic creature; He is the wildest being in existence. The presence of His spirit in us is our wildness, our oneness with the wilderness of Creation. That is why subduing the things of nature to human purposes is so dangerous and why it so often results in evil, in separation and desecration. It is why the poets of our tradition so often have given nature the role not only of mother or grandmother but of the highest earthly teacher and judge, a figure of mystery and great power. Jesus' own specifications for His church have nothing at all to do with masonry and carpentry but only with people; His church is "where two or three are gathered together in my name."[13]

The Bible gives exhaustive (and sometimes exhausting) attention to the organization of religion: the building and rebuilding of the Temple; its furnishings; the orders, duties, and paraphernalia of the priesthood; the orders of rituals and ceremonies. But that does not disguise the fact that the most significant religious events recounted in the Bible do not occur in "temples made with hands." The most important religion in that book is unorganized and is sometimes profoundly disruptive of organization. From Abraham to Jesus, the most important people are not priests but shepherds, soldiers, property owners, workers, housewives, queens and kings, manservants and maidservants, fishermen, prisoners, whores, even bureaucrats. The great visionary encounters did not take place in temples but in sheep pastures, in the desert, in the wilderness, on mountains, on the shores of rivers and the sea, in the middle of the sea, in prisons. And however strenuously the divine voice prescribed rites and observances, it just as strenuously repudiated them when they were taken to *be* religion:

> *Your new moons and your appointed feasts my soul hateth: they are a trouble unto me; I am weary to bear them.*
> *And when you spread forth your hands, I will hide mine eyes from you: yea, when you make many prayers, I will not hear: your hands are full of blood.*
> *Wash you, make you clean; put away the evil of your doings from before mine eyes; cease to do evil;*
> *Learn to do well; seek judgment, relieve the oppressed, judge the fatherless, plead for the widow.*[14]

Religion, according to this view, is less to be celebrated in rituals than practiced in the world.

I don't think it is enough appreciated how much an outdoor book the Bible is. It is a "hypaethral book," such as Thoreau talked about—a book open to the sky. It is best read and understood outdoors, and the farther outdoors the better. Or that has been my experience of it. Passages that within walls seem improbable or incredible, outdoors seem merely natural. This is because outdoors we are confronted everywhere with wonders; we see that the miraculous is not extraordinary but the common mode of existence. It is our daily bread. Whoever really has considered the lilies of the field or the birds of the air and pondered the improbability of their existence in this warm world within the cold and empty stellar distances will hardly balk at the turning of water into wine—which was, after all, a very small miracle. We forget the greater and still continuing miracle by which water (with soil and sunlight) is turned into grapes.

It is clearly impossible to assign holiness exclusively to the built church without denying holiness to the rest of Creation, which is then said to be "secular." The world, which God looked at and found entirely good, we find none too good to pollute entirely and destroy piecemeal. The church, then, becomes a kind of preserve of "holiness," from which certified lovers of God assault and plunder the "secular" earth.

Not only does this repudiate God's approval of His work; it refuses also to honor the Bible's explicit instruction to regard the works of the Creation as God's revelation of Himself. The assignation of holiness exclusively to the built church is therefore logically accompanied by the assignation of revelation exclusively to the Bible. But Psalm 19 begins, "The heavens declare the glory of God; and the firmament sheweth his handiwork." The word of God has been revealed in facts from the moment of the third verse of the first chapter of Genesis; "Let there be light: and there was light." And Saint Paul states the rule: "The invisible things of him from the creation of the world are clearly seen, being understood by the things that are made."[15] Yet from this free, generous, and sensible view of things, we come to the idolatry of the book: the idea that nothing is true that cannot be (and has not been already) written. The misuse of the Bible thus logically accompanies the abuse of nature: if you are going to destroy creatures without respect, you will want to reduce them to "Materiality"; you will want to deny that there is spirit or truth in them, just as you will want to believe that the only holy creatures, the only creatures with souls, are humans—or even only Christian humans.

By denying spirit and truth to the nonhuman Creation, modern proponents of religion have legitimized a form of blasphemy without which the nature- and culture-destroying machinery of the industrial economy could not have been built—that is, they have legitimized bad work. Good human work honors God's work. Good work uses no thing without respect, both for what it is in itself and for its origin. It uses neither tool nor material that it does not respect and that it does not love. It honors nature as a great mystery and power, as an indispensable teacher, and as the inescapable judge of all work of human hands. It does not dissociate life and work, or pleasure and work, or love and work, or usefulness and beauty. To work without pleasure or affection, to make a product that is not both useful and beautiful, is to dishonor God, nature, the thing that is made, and whomever it is made for. This is blasphemy: to make shoddy work of the work of God. But such blasphemy is not possible when the entire Creation is understood as holy and when the works of God are understood as embodying and thus revealing His spirit.

In the Bible we find none of the industrialist's contempt or hatred for nature. We find, instead, a poetry of awe and reverence and profound cherishing, as in these verses from Moses' valedictory blessing of the twelve tribes:

> And of Joseph he said, Blessed of the Lord be his land, for the precious things of heaven, for the dew, and for the deep that croucheth beneath,
> And for the precious fruits brought forth by the sun, and for the precious things put forth by the moon,
> And for the chief things of the ancient mountians, and for the precious things of the lasting hills,
> And for the precious things of the earth and fullness thereof, and for the good will of him that dwelt in the bush.[16]

IV

I HAVE BEEN TALKING, of course, about a dualism that manifests itself in several ways: as a cleavage, a radical discontinuity, between Creator and creature, spirit and matter, religion and nature, religion and economy, worship and work, and so on. This dualism, I think, is the most destructive disease that afflicts us. In its best-known, its most dangerous, and perhaps its fundamental version, it is the dualism of body and soul. This is an issue as difficult as it is important, and so to deal with it we should start at the beginning.

The crucial test is probably Genesis 2:7, which gives the process by which Adam was created: "The Lord God formed man of the dust of the ground, and breathed into his nostrils the breath of life: and man became a living soul." My mind, like most people's, has been deeply influenced by dualism, and I can see how dualistic minds deal with this verse. They conclude that the formula for man-making is man = body + soul. But that conclusion cannot be derived, except by violence, from Genesis 2:7, which is not dualistic. The formula given in Genesis 2:7 is not man = body + soul; the formula there is soul = dust + breath. According to this verse, God did not make a body and put a soul into it, like a letter into an envelope. He formed man of dust; then, by breathing His breath into it, he made the dust live. The dust, formed as man and made to live, did not *embody* a soul; it *became* a soul. "Soul" here refers to the whole creature. Humanity is thus presented to us, in Adam, not as a creature of two discrete parts temporarily glued together but as a single mystery.

We can see how easy it is to fall into the dualism of body and soul when talking about the inescapable worldly dualities of good and evil or time and eternity. And we can see how easy it is, when Jesus asks, "For what is a man profited, if he shall gain the whole world, and lose his own soul?"[17] to assume that He is condemning the world and appreciating the disembodied soul. But if we give to "soul" here the sense that it has in Genesis 2:7, we see that He is doing no such thing. He is warning that in pursuit of so-called material possessions, we can lose our understanding of ouselves as "living souls"—that is, as creatures of God, members of the holy community of Creation. We can lose the possibility of the atonement of that membership. For we are free, if we choose, to make a duality of our one living soul by disowning the breath of God that is our fundamental bond with one another and with other creatures.

But we can make the same duality by disowning the dust. The breath of God is only one of the divine gifts that make us living souls; the other is the dust. Most of our modern troubles come from our misunderstanding and misvaluation of this dust. Forgetting that the dust, too, is a creature of the Creator, made by the sending forth of His spirit, we have presumed to decide that the dust is "low." We have presumed to say that we are made of two parts: a body and a soul, the body being "low" because made of dust, and the soul "high." By thus valuing these two supposed-to-be parts, we inevitably throw them into competition with each other, like two corporations. The "spiritual" view, of course, has been that the body, in Yeats's phrase, must be "bruised to pleasure soul." And the "secular" version of the same dualism has been that the body, along with the rest of the "material" world, must give way before the advance of the human mind. The dominant religious view, for a long time, has been that the body is a kind of scrip issued by the Great Company Store in the Sky, which can be cashed in to redeem the soul but is otherwise worthless. And the predictable result has been a human creature able to appreciate or tolerate only the "spiritual" (or mental) part of Creation and full of semiconscious hatred of the "physical" or "natural" part, which it is ready and willing to destroy for "salvation," for profit, for "victory," or for fun. This madness constitutes the norm of modern humanity and of modern Christianity.

But to despise the body or mistreat it for the sake of the "soul" is not just to burn one's house for the insurance, nor is it just self-hatred of the most deep and dangerous sort. It is yet another blasphemy. It is to make nothing—and worse than nothing—of the great Something in which we live and move and have our being.

When we hate and abuse the body and its earthly life and joy for Heaven's sake, what do we expect? That out of this life that we have presumed to despise and this world that we have presumed to destroy, we would somehow salvage a soul capable of eternal bliss? And what do we expect when with equal and opposite ingratitude, we try to make of the finite body an infinite reservoir of dispirited and meaningless pleasures?

Times may come, of course, when the life of the body must be denied or sacrificed, times when the whole world must literally be lost for the sake of one's life as a "living soul." But such sacrifice, by people who truly respect and revere the life of the earth and its Creator, does not denounce or degrade the body but rather exalts it and acknowledges its holiness. Such sacrifice is a refusal to allow the body to serve what is unworthy of it.

V

IF WE CREDIT THE Bible's description of the relationship between Creator and Creation, then we cannot deny the spiritual importance of our economic life. Then we must see how religious issues lead to issues of economy and how issues of economy lead to issues of art. By "art" I mean all the ways by which humans make the things they need. If we understand that no artist—no maker—can work except by reworking the works of Creation, then we see that by our work we reveal what we think of the works of God. How we take our lives from this world, how we work, what work we do, how well we use the materials we use, and what we do with them after we have used them—all these are questions of the highest and gravest religious significance. In answering them, we practice, or do not practice, our religion.

The significance—and ultimately the quality—of the work we do is determined by our understanding of the story in which we are taking part.

If we think of ourselves as merely biological creatures, whose story is determined by genetics or environment or history or economics or technology, then, however pleasant or painful the part we play, it cannot matter much. Its significance is that of mere self-concern. "It is a tale / Told by an idiot, full of sound and fury, / Signifying nothing," as Macbeth says when he has "supp'd full with horrors" and is "aweary of the sun."[18]

If we think of ourselves as lofty souls trapped temporarily in lowly bodies in a dispirited, desperate, unlovable world that we must despise for Heaven's sake, then what have we done for this question of significance? If we divide reality into two parts, spiritual and material, and hold (as the Bible does *not* hold) that only the spiritual is good or desirable, then our relation to the material Creation becomes arbitrary, having only the quantitative or mercenary value that we have, in fact and for this reason, assigned to it. Thus, we become the judges and inevitably the destroyers of a world we did not make and that we are bidden to understand as a divine gift. It is impossible to see how good work might be accomplished by people who think that our life in this world either signifies nothing or has only a negative significance.

If, on the other hand, we believe that we are living souls, God's dust and God's breath, acting our parts among other creatures all made of the same dust and breath as ourselves; and if we understand that we are free, within the obvious limits of mortal human life, to do evil or good to ourselves and to the other creatures—then all our acts have a supreme significance. If it is true that we are living souls and morally free, then all of us are artists. All of us are makers, within mortal terms and limits, of our lives, of one another's lives, of things we need and use.

This, Ananda Coomaraswamy wrote, is "the normal view," which "assumes . . . not that the artist is a special kind of man, but that every man who is not a mere idler or parasite is necessarily some special kind of artist."[19] But since even mere idlers and parasites may be said to work inescapably, by proxy or influence, it might be better to say that everybody is an artist—either good or bad, responsible or irresponsible. Any life, by working or not working, by working well or poorly, inescapably changes other lives and so changes the world. This is why our division of the "fine arts" from "craftsmanship," and "craftsmanship" from "labor," is so arbitrary, meaningless, and destructive. As Walter Shewring rightly said, both "the plowman and the potter have a cosmic function."[20] And bad art in any trade dishonors and damages Creation.

If we think of ourselves as living souls, immortal creatures, living in the midst of a Creation that is mostly mysterious and if we see that everything we make or do cannot help but have an everlasting significance for ourselves, for others, and for the world, then we see why some religious teachers have understood work as a form of prayer. We see why the old poets invoked the muse. And we know why George Herbert prayed, in his poem "Mattens":

> *Teach me thy love to know;*
> *That this new light, which now I see,*
> *May both the work and workman show.*[21]

Work connects us both to Creation and to eternity. This is the reason also for Mother Ann Lee's famous instruction: "Do all your work as though you had a thousand years to live on earth, and as you would if you knew you must die tomorrow."[22]

Explaining "the perfection, order, and illumination" of the artistry of Shaker furniture makers, Coomaraswamy wrote, "All tradition has seen in the Master Craftsman of the Universe the exemplar of the human artist or 'maker by art,' and we are told to be 'perfect, *even as* your Father in heaven is perfect.'" Searching out the lesson, for us, of the Shakers' humble, impersonal, perfect artistry, which refused the modern divorce of utility and beauty, he wrote, "Unfortunately, we do not desire to be such as the Shaker was; we do not propose to 'work as though we had a thousand years to live, and as though we were to die tomorrow.' Just as we desire peace but not the things that make for peace, so we desire art but not the things that make for art. . . . we have the art that we deserve. If the sight of it puts us to shame, it is with ourselves that the re-formation must begin."[23]

Any genuine effort to "re-form" our arts, our ways of making, must take thought of "the things that make for art." We must see that no art begins in itself; it begins in other arts, in attitudes and ideas antecedent to any art, in nature, and in inspiration. If we look at the great artistic traditions, as it is necessary to do, we will see that they have never been divorced either from religion or from economy. The possibility of an entirely secular art and of works of art that are spiritless or ugly or useless is not a possibility that has been among us for very long. Traditionally, the arts have been ways of making that have placed a just value on their materials or subjects, on the uses and the users of the things made by art, and on the artists themselves. They have, that is, been ways of giving honor to the works of God. The great artistic traditions have had nothing to do with what we call "self-expression." They have not been destructive of privacy or exploitive of private life. Though they have certainly originated things and employed genius, they have no affinity with the modern cults of originality and genius. Coomaraswamy, a good guide as always, makes an indispensable distinction between genius in the modern sense and craftsmanship: "Genius inhabits a world of its own. The master craftsman lives in a world inhabited by other men; he has neighbors."[24] The arts, traditionally, belong to the neighborhood. They are the means by which the neighborhood lives, works, remembers, worships, and enjoys itself.

But most important of all, now, is to see that the artistic traditions understood every art primarily as a skill or craft and ultimately as a service to fellow creatures and to God. An artist's first duty, according to this view, is technical. It is assumed that one will have talents, materials, subjects—perhaps even genius or inspiration or vision. But these are traditionally understood not as personal properties with which one may do as one chooses but as gifts of God or nature that must be honored in use. One does not dare to use these things without the skill to use them well. As Dante said of his own art, "far worse than in vain does he leave the shore . . . who fishes for the truth and has not the art."[25] To use gifts less than well is to dishonor them and their Giver. There is no material or subject in Creation that in using, we are excused from using well; there is no work in which we are excused from being able and responsible artists.

VI

IN DENYING THE HOLINESS of the body and of the so-called physical reality of the world—and in denying the support to the good economy, the good work, by which alone the Creation can receive due honor—modern Christianity generally has cut itself off from both nature and culture. It has no serious or competent interest in biology or ecology. And it is equally uninterested in the arts by which humankind connects itself to nature. It manifests no awareness of the specifically Christian cultural lineages that connect us to our past. There is, for example, a splendid heritage of Christian poetry in English that most church members live and die without reading or hearing or hearing about. Most sermons are preached without any awareness at all that the making of sermons is an art that has at times been magnificent. Most modern churches look like they were built by robots without reference to the heritage of church architecture or respect for the place; they embody no awareness that work can be worship. Most religious music now attests to the general assumption that religion is no more than a vaguely pious (and vaguely romantic) emotion.

Modern Christianity, then, has become as specialized in its organizations as other modern organizations, wholly concentrated on the industrial shibboleths of "growth," counting its success in numbers, and on the very strange enterprise of "saving" the individual, isolated, and disembodied soul. Having witnessed and abetted the dismemberment of households, both human and natural, by which we have our being as creatures of God, as living souls, and having made light of the great feast and festival of Creation to which we were bidden as living souls, the modern church presumes to be able to save the soul as an eternal piece of private property. It presumes moreover to save the souls of people in other countries and religious traditions, who are often saner and more religious than we are. And always the emphasis is on the individual soul. Some Christian spokespeople give the impression that the highest Christian bliss would be to get to Heaven and find that you are the only one there—that you were right and all the others wrong. Whatever its twentieth-century dress, modern Christianity as I know it is still at bottom the religion of Miss Watson, intent on a dull and superstitious rigamarole by which supposedly we can avoid going to "the bad place" and instead go to "the good place." One can hardly help sympathizing with Huck Finn when he says, "I made up my mind I wouldn't try for it."[26]

Despite its protests to the contrary, modern Christianity has become willy-nilly the religion of the state and the economic status quo. Because it has been so exclusively dedicated to incanting anemic souls into Heaven, it has been made the tool of much earthly villainy. It has, for the most part, stood silently by while a predatory economy has ravaged the world, destroyed its natural beauty and health, divided and plundered its human communities and households. It has flown the flag and chanted the slogans of empire. It has assumed with the economists that "economic forces" automatically work for good and has assumed with the industrialists and militarists that technology determines history. It has asssumed with almost everybody that "progress" is good, that it is good to be modern and up with the times. It has admired Caeser and comforted him in his depredations and defaults. But in its de facto alliance with Caeser, Christianity connives directly in the murder of Creation. For in these days, Caeser is no longer a mere destroyer of armies, cities, and nations. He is a contradictor of the fundamental miracle of life. A part of the normal practice of his power is his willingness to destroy the world. He prays, he says, and churches everywhere compliantly pray with him. But he is praying to a God whose works he is prepared at any moment to destroy. What could be more wicked than that, or more mad?

The religion of the Bible, on the contrary, is a religion of the state and the status quo only in brief moments. In practice, it is a religion for the correction equally of people and kings. And Christ's life, from the manger to the cross, was an affront to the established powers of His time, just as it is to the established powers of our time. Much is made in churches of the "good news" of the Gospels. Less is said of the Gospels' bad news, which is that Jesus would have been horrified by just about every "Christian" government the world has ever seen. He would be horrified by our government and its works, and it would be horrified by Him. Surely no sane and thoughtful person can imagine any government of our time sitting comfortably at the feet of Jesus while He is saying, "Love your enemies, bless them that curse you, do good to them that hate you, and pray for them that despitefully use you and persecute you."[27]

In fact, we know that one of the businesses of governments, "Christian" or not, has been to reeneact the crucifixion. It has happened again and again and again. In *A Time for Trumpets,* his history of the Battle of the Bulge, Charles B. MacDonald tells how the SS Colonel Joachim Peiper was forced to withdraw from a bombarded château near the town of La Gleize, leaving behind a number of severely wounded soldiers of both armies. "Also left behind," MacDonald wrote, "on a whitewashed wall of one of the rooms in the basement was a charcoal drawing of Christ, thorns on his head, tears on his cheeks—whether drawn by a German or an American nobody would ever know."[28] This is not an image that belongs to history but rather one that judges it.

1. Psalms 24:1. (All biblical quotations are from the King James Version.)
2. Leviticus 25:23.
3. John 1:3.
4. Job 34:14–15.
5. Philip Sherrard, *Human Image: World Image* (Ipswich, Suffolk, England: Golgonooza Press, 1992), 152.
6. George Herbert, "Providence," lines 41 and 44, from *The Poems of George Herbert,* ed. by Helen Gardner (London: Oxford University Press, 1961), p. 54.
7. Dante Alighieri, *The Divine Comedy,* trans. by Charles S. Singleton, Bollingen Series LXXX, and *Inferno,* canto XI, lines 109–11 (Princeton, NJ: Princeton University Press, 1970).
8. Dante, *Inferno,* canto XI, lines 109–11.
9. William Blake, *Complete Writings,* ed. by Geoffrey Keynes (London: Oxford University Press, 1966), 160.
10. Kathleen Raine, *Golgonooza: City of Imagination* (Ipswich, Suffolk, England: Golgonooza Press, 1991), 28.

11. I Kings 8:27.

12. Acts 17:24 and 28.

13. Matthew 18:20.

14. Isaiah 1:13–17.

15. Romans 1:20.

16. Deuteronomy 33:13–16.

17. Matthew 16:26.

18. William Shakespeare, *Macbeth,* ed. by Kenneth Muir (Cambridge, MA: Harvard University Press, 1957), V, V, lines 13, 26–28, 49.

19. Ananda K. Coomaraswamy, *Christian and Oriental Philosophy of Art* (New York: Dover, 1957), 98.

20. Walter Shewring, *Artist and Tradesman* (Marlborough, MA: Paulinus Press, 1984), 19.

21. Herbert, *The Poems of George Herbert,* 54.

22. June Sprigg, *By Shaker Hands* (Hanover, NH: University Press of New England, 1990), 33.

23. Coomaraswamy, *Selected Papers,* vol. 1 (Princeton, NJ: Princeton University Press, 1977), 255, 259.

24. Coomaraswamy, *Christian and Oriental Philosophy of Art,* 99.

25. Dante, *Paradiso,* canto XIII, lines 121 and 123.

26. Mark Twain, *Adventures of Huckleberry Finn,* in *Mississippi Writings* (New York: Library of America, 1982), 626.

27. Matthew 5:44.

28. Charles B. MacDonald, *A Time for Trumpets* (New York: William Morrow & Co., 1984), 458.

Passion, Gifts, Rages
Stephen Bodio

I think we are in some ways dealing with a language failure in listing both baseball and falconry as sports.
—Thomas McGuane

I WAS BORN IN THE CITY, WHERE I LIVED UNTIL I WAS FOUR. THERE, that early, though I could not know it, I was bitten by something and became a naturalist. By the time we moved to what was then still the country, twenty miles south of Boston, I was catching insects, picking up dead birds in the aftermath of a hurricane, and—my parents were artists—sketching the backyard sparrows. When we arrived in the swampy forests of Easton, I kept frogs and toads first, then snakes and baby birds, a perfect example of Edmund Wilson's "biophilic" youth. At eight I began keeping homing pigeons. Having learned to read at three from the pages of 1950s LIFE magazines full of animal dioramas, I became a precocious devourer of books, especially natural history and dog stories. In the halls of the Ames Free Library, I learned that people kept, trained, and "flew" hawks, those remote and dashing killers that sometimes chased our pigeons. And so at thirteen I built a bow net of yardsticks and badminton netting, baited it with a pet store white mouse, and, to my everlasting astonishment and delight, pulled a little kestrel down from the sky.

A week later he flew across the yard to my call, and I was marked for life. As I wrote in *A Rage for Falcons,* "the only thing better than pulling down a hawk from the sky by trickery was to return him there and have him come back to your call because he wanted to." I still play with hawks, thirty years later; I have learned many things from them, and have worked for them.

BIOPHILIA, I EXPECT, is inherent in every human, part of our genes and our earliest culture. Hunter-gatherers must notice everything with the loving eye of an artist, the attentive senses of a good cook. But like many behaviors in us and in our fellow animals, it must be stimulated at the proper time or it will wither. If children do not learn to speak at the proper time, they never will. If they never get to touch animals and plants, they will lose their ability to love them. "Hands-on" is not a myth. I was fortunate to grow up in a time and place before burgeoning human populations and finicky laws denied children free and easy access to wildlife.

All kids, if left to themselves in a decent environment, go through this stage. Sadly, for most of them it is just a stage. What leads a few of us beyond, through obsession to something more healthy—the acceptance of nature as an integral, necessary, and almost unremarked part of our lives? (I once told a new friend that a hawk in the living room seemed more normal and unremarkable than a television set.) Maybe it could be high-end experiences, like that kestrel in the net, modified by something that is rare today—what we might call "apprenticeship."

I AM A WRITER; sometimes I think that, aside from my deep-rooted animal passions, I have begun everything in books. But sometimes I am forced to admit that books cannot do everything. You can learn falconry by reading; up to the age of eighteen, I did. But you cannot learn to be a good falconer from books alone or from such modern techno-substitutes as videos. At eighteen I managed to track down my first real falconer. I drove to his house in rising apprehension; this was the sixties; I had very long hair, and I suspected that he would disapprove. When Ralph emerged from behind his house with a red-eyed goshawk on one fist and a beer in the other, with hair as long as mine, I was relieved. This looked like it was going to be easier than I had feared.

It was, as far as friendship was concerned. But my real work was just beginning. Ralph was a soft-spoken chain-smoker of Sicilian descent who worked nights in the local paper mill in order to have enough time for his proper pursuits, and one of the finest all-around woodsmen whom I have ever met. His family ate mostly wild meat—up to a hundred rabbits and gamebirds in a given year, caught by a goshawk who truly earned her old French title of *cuisinier* (cook) plus a deer or two and plenty of freshwater and saltwater fish. Ralph was an expert with a bow and had built a cross-bow out of old car springs. He hunted for grouse and ducks with an old humpback Browning automatic that had the barrel cut down, and tied his own flies. He could fix a car or a snowmobile, toss off an eighty-yard cast to a striper in the surf, and read a predator's previous week from observing its scat.

But mostly, Ralph could talk to animals. My initial clumsiness and bad manners around birds, must have given him a lot of pain. I scared hawks, his and my own, into tight-feathered, wide-eyed, shrieking fury without even knowing why. I tried to cram ill-fitting hoods onto their heads, intending to calm the birds, and only succeeded in turning them into ducking, dodging, savage balls of erected feathers, monsters that hated the hood almost as much as they hated me. I overfed goshawks and then watched amazed as they stroked off into the trees without a backward look or hunched sullenly atop eighty-foot pines as the January sun dropped below the horizon and our feet turned to lumps of ice. I still wince to think of my ignorance.

And yet Ralph didn't yell at me any more than he yelled at his birds. (I was inclined in those days to yell at everything.) He'd show me, smiling faintly, how he rocked his gloved hand backward no more than a half inch so the bird would move its head forward toward the hood that was slowly rising up its chest, how to cover its head with a swift but somehow unhurried flip at the last moment. "Don't be in a rush," he'd say after covering his completely relaxed bird in a tenth of the time it took me to cram the hood onto a bird that was now bowing and trying to shake off the irritating hat. "And don't tighten it up until she relaxes." He'd feel a breastbone, grin again, and say, "Maybe we ought to rest her for a day." I'd run my fingers up beside his and realize that she was too thin, her keel sticking out like a hollow-ground knife blade, or too fat, the bone almost buried in the curve of her breast. And this despite the fact that I was using a hundred-dollar triple-beam scale and knew the importance of diet and condition.

We'd go out and I'd be in an agony of indecision about where to release my bird, when to release her, *whether* to release her. Once she was up, I'd follow her frantically and call her in if I imagined a chance of her straying. If Ralph were flying a goshawk, he'd release it toward the tree line with a casual flip of the wrist and forge forward without a backward look, watching out for rabbits ahead. If the hawk were behaving properly, following from tree to tree, he wouldn't even look back—"That's what bells are for." If he were flying a falcon, he'd face her into the wind, looking upwind himself (falcons are shy of being watched closely, face-to-face) as she dropped her load of white droppings and fluffed out her feathers— "rousing." When she took off, she would usually turn around and blow downwind, right over the nearby tree-lined New England horizon. Ralph would just stand with his hands in his pockets and wait. He knew that she was well trained and that she would eventually work the wind and come on point hundreds of feet overhead, sailing herself like a kite. He never seemed to worry about a bird unless it stayed out overnight.

And he taught me that branch of falconer's etiquette, too. If a bird were out after dark, it was in danger—from owls and other night predators, from uninformed people who might shoot it or (almost worse) attempt such kindnesses as feeding it pizza or hot dogs or catching it in a fish-landing net. I know of one bird that never flew again after such an experience, having suffered a broken wing that set crooked. Before dawn, you had to be in the place where you had lost it, luring and calling. And every falconry friend you had, in spite of family or work obligations, would be out there too, driving the roads, waving lures, looking and calling.

In short, Ralph taught me to be more polite to a bird than most people in our culture are to other humans. Without these manners, you cannot be a real falconer, not for all the money in the world. As T. H. White wrote in *The Goshawk,* "The thing about being associated with a hawk is that one cannot be slipshod about it."

REAL PASSION GROWS alongside growing expertise. Years came along in which I can remember being ruled by hawks. My first wife, from whom I've been divorced for twenty-some years, recently handed me an old book that had been stored in her attic all that time. "How did you know it was mine?" I asked in amazement.

"It couldn't have been anyone else's." She turned it over to reveal a paint streak of snow-white, odorless droppings. "Who else would have hawk chalk on their books?"

Well, I could think of a few other such maniacs in the early seventies. There was Mark, who drove two hundred miles to show up unannounced on my doorstep with a goshawk and a case of beer. Jim Weaver, who more than any other single individual could be called the Man Who Brought Back the Peregrine, shared his apartment in the Cornell hawk-breeding barn with an aged gyrfalcon, a peregrine's-egg mobile, a buffalo robe, and an Audubon print. Another Jim had a wife who left him for the last time with the admonition that he should go make love to his hawks (although that was not quite how she phrased it). And then there was Darcie, a girlfriend who, I now think, was more attracted to goshawks than to me. She once called back a departing half-trained male to a frozen day-old chick clutched in her bare hand and, with her own blood and the chick's yolk running down her arm, grinned through her tears and bragged, "I got him."

Does this sound extreme for an activity that even Aldo Leopold called a hobby? Well, yes, if you consider falconry a mere time-filler for when you're off work rather than something that you structure work around. But consider those often-misunderstood concepts "hunting" and "play." Sport hunting is not (despite an animal rights brochure I read recently that blandly asserted it was, "of course," sublimated sexual sadism) some sort of aggression against creation. It is a series of rituals that have grown up around the most basic of activities: acquiring food—capturing energy to keep us alive. Some of the rituals have come about because of their beauty, grace, and difficulty; others (like the German custom of giving the fallen animal a sprig of its favorite food), because of the sadness and mystery that accompany taking a life.

Hunters who hunt out of physical need still appreciate these rituals; ones who do so out of "play" or out of a civilized desire to personally touch the roots of the flow of energy may elevate the ritual to the end result. The finest kinds of hunting—fly-fishing, falconry, upland shooting with pointing dogs—are, and should be, elaborate ways of playing with your food and with the universe, ways that also give you windows into the lives of things as alien as insects (in fly-fishing) or into the minds of canine and avian partners. Ideally, you leave the human behind for a few moments and become predator, prey, nonhuman ally.

(Oh, and that food thing. Personally I think that a culinary exam should be part of the elaborate, "If-I-were-king" test for any hunting license. It would remind hunters of the roots of hunting. Hawks leave no lead or steel pellets in their prey, take only a little, and either kill clean or fail. It's not for nothing that the old falconers' toast begins "Here's to those who shoot and miss.")

Obviously, I believe that passion about these activities is good. White's preferred title for *The Goshawk* was "A Kind of Mania." Many years later, I wanted to borrow it for my book *A Rage for Falcons* and ran into the same set of editorial doubts that White experienced. But falconry is a healthy mania. As Father Matthew Fox observed, "'Apathy' is two Greek words meaning 'no passion.' The antidote to apathy and acedia is to fall in love. To rediscover our erotic attachment to what is beautiful in the universe. That is where we get our passion. If we fall in love with creation deeper and deeper, we will respond to its endangerment with passion."

AND WE DID FALL in love. Many of us were attracted to falconry by the sight of a bird falling from the skies, but by the seventies birds were falling in a far uglier manner. DDT had nearly wiped the slate clean of the eastern peregrine and was about to do the same with the western and arctic populations. The bald eagle, Cooper's hawk, and osprey were also in varying degrees of trouble. Alarmed legislators passed a ban on persistent pesticides in 1968, but by then the birds were gone. Even if they could reclaim their old sites—by no means a certain prospect, given growing cities, changing forests, and the expanding great horned owl population—it might take centuries.

Enter the Peregrine Fund. In 1971 four falconers—Jim Weaver, Frank Bond, Dr. Tom Cade of Cornell University, and Bob Berry—formed a nonprofit group to oversee the captive breeding and eventual restocking of the peregrine. They took over an old Quonset hut at Cornell, put it under the day-to-day management of Weaver, and waded in. Over the next two decades, they raised hundreds of birds, which were stocked at every old and many new nesting sites throughout the lower forty-eight states and released under the supervision of hundreds of volunteers. The program continued until its own success made it unnecessary. It was the first, and to date the most successful, restocking of an endangered species. Probably everyone knows this. What the publicity never mentions is that this was done almost entirely by falconers. Not only were the founders falconers, but most of the hack-site attendants during the first decade were too. Where else would you get people with both the expertise and the dedication to spend two months on sunbaked or freezing rock ledges, for little more than food (the average mid-seventies "salary" was $700 for two months), in order to babysit a clutch of obnoxious baby birds?

John Tobin and I were probably as typical as any. He was a Vietnam veteran, an ex-medic, who had just completed his master's in biology at the school where I was engaged in one of my periodic not-very-serious attempts at getting a degree. He had a two-year-old son and a beard so red it was almost orange and was on the short list to become a Massachusetts game warden. I was a free-lance writer and part-time editor who was getting published with some regularity in the sporting and "alternative" press while trying to write fiction. We had in common a taste for whiskey, ancestors in the maritimes, a passion for training goshawks, no money, and a devotion to peregrine restoration that bordered on the maniacal. We were assigned to Mount Tom, near Holyoke, Massachusetts, where a historic aerie had survived the clearing of the forest and the building of a city only to succumb to DDT in the early fifties.

It was a strange summer—exhilarating, exhausting, illuminating, and finally (we thought then) depressing. Our birds, with some others, disappeared soon after they became strong fliers. Before that, we endured bugs (including a near-lethal sting that I, seriously allergic, received from a yellow jacket that was feeding on chicken remains under nest), mud, freezing rain, and not one but two lightning strikes within two hundred feet of our flimsy orange tent. We saved a rare New England diamondback from the terrified park staff, nearly getting bitten in the process. We raised hundreds of half grown-chickens and coturnix quail in cages behind our camp, herds for our screeching charges, and when a flash storm wiped out half of them, we buried them in the mud and packed hundreds of those still alive up a ski lift and then in backpacks to the camp. Each day before dawn we'd sneak the day's supply of freshly killed meat down thirty feet of nearly vertical granite and across a traverse that always contained hundreds of sleepy wasps and might shelter rattlers. We couldn't let the young ones see us lest they associate us with food and end up following humans rather than acting like proper birds. We got severely sunburned from light reflecting off bare rocks and answered what seemed like thousands of dumb questions from hikers, the most common being "Why?"

And somehow we had a great time. Our first reward came after the anxious time when the four birds first flew. After a couple of awkward days during which they flew into rock walls and clung to outcroppings for dear life or got stuck in the center rather than the top of a scrub pine, they suddenly owned the air over the mountain. They showed their mastery by chasing doves, flickers, and butterflies. They were not in deadly earnest yet. If a hang glider passed by overhead, they'd climb to meet it, then circle it companionably; we often wondered what the pilots thought. (This was before city releases made the peregrine project famous.) Once they did the same to a passing wild peregrine, an old bird that swiftly drove them, screaming, to the shelter of the rocks. They were more aggressive with turkey vultures. The buzzards had taken to patrolling the ledges below for chicken scraps, but if any of the peregrine gang were present, they would sail out screaming gleefully and fall hundreds of feet to cut at the terrified scavengers, who would flare and flap and speed off as fast as vulture wings could carry them.

And then, after a week of rain that kept them bored and near the ground, came a clear, blue, high-pressure day. All four young falcons soared up into the blue and never came back. We went through apprehension to fear to sadness. But though they left a hole in our summer, we came to realize we hadn't lost a thing. That summer now stands as a kind of turning point, a time when I realized that there was no going back to a life in which such days were not possible around every bend.

And whenever I see a peregrine in the East, I do still wonder . . .

SO WE LEARNED, as others did, to give back to the birds. What but passion causes anyone to give that much? There are people I know, devotees of television nature programs, who disapprove strongly of my hunting. They do not spend much time in the rural world, nor do they convert their own energy from life to food. They think themselves more moral than I am.

And maybe they *are* more moral, if moral means selfless. I have received more from the birds than they have from me, though they neither know nor care which way obligation flows. Birds have—falconry has—taught me to be polite to an animal, to have manners toward the wild, to listen and move slowly, to watch and keep my mouth shut. These lessons—emphatically *not* morals, but almost Zen disciplines and "ways"—have now permeated my life; I am kinder to dogs, horses, and humans than I was before I learned to carry a bird on my fist, to walk smoothly, to face it into the wind, to keep heedless friends from walking behind its back, not to stare rudely in its face while it ate. I swear that some of my odd, primitive, eighteenth-century ideas—that legal dueling rather than lawsuits would improve manners; that if women were armed we'd have fewer crimes of violence against the weak and a lot fewer rude bigots—somehow come from getting to know these mannered creatures from the skies, these fierce but fair visitors in human society.

Birds have improved my perceptions too. I know that when a falcon "weathering" on the lawn cocks her head momentarily sideways, something significant is passing overhead, often so high that I need binoculars to see it. I can read the cliffs of the West, and I know where the nests of falcons are likely to be. I can go to the woods and almost without conscious observation know when the slope, the height of trees, the nearness of water, the calls of certain songbirds mean that soon I will find the feather-littered "plucking post" of a goshawk or hear her sudden *KUKKUKKUK* of challenge as I approach her nest. I can look down a barrier beach in fall and recognize the rolling flush of shorebird flocks that means an arctic peregrine, a merlin, even a gyrfalcon is making its way toward me. Hawks have molded me more than I have ever influenced any hawk.

IS THIS TOO ABSTRACT? Let me take another tack. I know a place in southeastern New Mexico, once nearly destroyed, that is home to one very rare species that is being reborn. Its location—well, I won't be too specific; let's just say it's a good drive south from the little agricultural and college center of Portales, not too far from Texas. These plains were once home to the legendary "southern herd" of bison, to the great lobo wolf, to the Comanche. For a few years settlers tried to subdue it, to divide it into small farms. When drought came, as it always does here, the broken soil just blew away, forming long ridges where it piled up in the tumbleweeds caught in the mile-long section fences. Eastern New Mexico is the western edge of what came to be called the Dust Bowl. Most of the homesteaders gave up and moved on west, leaving battered graying buildings and maybe a few Siberian elm trees to mark the graves of their dreams.

There are no buffalo out there now, no wolves. Coyotes still howl and giggle, dawn and dusk. There are a lot more deer than you'd think and more doves and cranes and quail and birds of prey than anyplace else I know. The rare trees are hung with nests like Christmas ornaments.

Fewer people live here than in the first two decades of the century. The homesteads that still stand are inhabited by barn owls and ghosts. When you walk on the prairie at dawn, the sun comes up out of the ground the way it does out of the ocean. At such a time, the sight of a band of Comanches might scare but not surprise you.

Once, flocks of pinneated grouse, better known as prairie chickens, lived here. The latest research indicates that they were nomads that came in when the buffalo left, living on the fertile margins of grazed and ungrazed land. They have spiky black headdresses and dance like the plains tribes. When the pioneers broke the sod, the grouse population first boomed with the new food sources, then crashed as their last nest sites disappeared. Nobody seemed to understand that birds who once followed the great herds need edges. Though they hung on through the Depression and the Dust Bowl, their numbers continue to diminish.

But native open country grouse—the sage grouse, the sharptail, and the greater prairie chicken, as well as these "lessers"—are the noblest of all falconry quarry, the most difficult and beautiful and (when you can catch one) the most delicious. To hunt them, you walk or ride your horse in the sky; you are often the tallest thing you can see. You follow wide-ranging pointing dogs that run in quarter-mile casts ahead of you. When they "make" game, they turn to stone. You cast your gyr or peregrine to the wind. She circles and works in it until she stands overhead, "waiting on," sometimes a thousand feet above you, looking as tiny and insubstantial as a swallow. You run in, and the grouse burst up and race for the horizon. The hawk falls through the clear autumn air, her bell slots whistling with a demon's scream, and hits with a burst of feathers. Or misses, rebounds, and tail chases over the horizon. Later, there may be Mozart and braised grouse breast and wine, or whiskey and worry and early-to-bed.

Grouse brought my friend Jim Weaver to this place; first, as rumors, twenty-some years ago, then, as quarry in a nomad's true home and favorite camp, through eighteen years of raising young birds at Cornell, and as many banding young arctic birds in Greenland. He would return here for rest and recuperation after countless hours in his plane checking the hack sites and their attendants, or after mapping populations of rare hawks in Zimbabwe.

A couple of years ago, with peregrine reintroduction an official success, he came here for good. He is buying land, reseeding native grasses, banding all the raptors from barn owls to Swainson's hawks to migrant prairie falcons. He is restoring the land's capacity to hold water. Although he does not share the fashionable equation of cows with evil, he has removed them from many overgrazed pastures. Until and unless the land recovers, he'll keep them off. He spends days on his tractor, dawn to dusk in his fields, planting, building fences, putting in water points, studying the land. He is showing his neighbors by example and hard work, rather than by preaching, that you can graze and grow grain and still provide a habitat for wildlife. He has inspired in the more thoughtful among these farmers a new interest in their most unique "crop," the prairie chicken, not to mention other more common game animals. They are beginning to realize that if your product is more diverse, your topsoil won't blow away—and then you won't have to blow away either when the lean dry times come again.

Which is why Jim and I are not hunting this year. It has been a dry year, and young bird survival was low. So we stand beside his mile-long dirt driveway at dusk, with no hawks, no guns, and no dogs. We are as still as the almost freezing air—silent, waiting, watching. The sun is almost down.

In the last moments of light, I see a flicker, a vibration of molecules almost, on the horizon. It turns into a flock of birds, resolves into individuals, tacks like a bunch of ducks. They set wings, curve down, drop into the stubble against a background of darkly luminous sky, raise their heads for a moment, calling, and then disappear.

The light goes. A coyote yaps, and I hear sandhill cranes, their eerie bugling falling from above, though I can see nothing in the darkening sky. I'm grinning like a maniac because it has just occurred to me that all these things—our friendship, the prairie chickens' restored habitat, this ranch, and everything on and above it—are still more gifts from the hawks.

Walking in Tierra del Fuego
Dan Gerber

Sometimes there is no sun or moon in the sky, but there is no
absence of the essence of seeing that sees the sun and moon.
   —*The Secret of the Golden Flower* (the classic Chinese
   book of life), trans. Thomas Cleary

HOW DO WE MANAGE OUR DESPERATION, OUR RAGE, AS WE SEE OUR
world being inexorably diminished by thoughtlessness, greed, apparent
necessity, and egotism? How do we maintain our balance so that we can
address the question of this progressively diminished earth with at least
some clarity, compassion, and intelligence? Does it behoove us to view
the problem through the eyes of those with whom we find ourselves in
opposition, who have interests that seem to and do conflict with our
vision of preservation, those whom we think of as "the enemy"?

What does stewardship mean in a world in which change is not only the condition but the definition of life? Does it mean keeping, or trying to keep, things as they are at this moment, or reshaping them to some former state which was itself only a plateau in the constant process of becoming? As John Muir observed, "The world, though made, is yet being made; . . . this is still the morning of creation." Can we actually preserve anything, any one thing or place, while the greater environment, the context in which it lives, has been and is being irrevocably altered? Can we do that without making our world a wasteland punctuated occasionally by an artificially sustained oasis of the supposedly natural world?

Is there some sacred state of The Way Things Are Now we should try to maintain, or rather should we keep a component of flexibility in our stewardship of the world's continual process of becoming? Are there actual enemies out there, or are those "enemies," those with attitudes radically divergent from our own, simply the natural progression of a burgeoning population? Man is only an element within nature, but he is within it and not a separate order. If he despoils the natural world, it isn't the assault of an enemy; it is the disease of a body attacking itself. Beyond the abortion debate and the apparently futile endeavor to bring voluntary birth control to the propagating masses, no one seems willing to actually address the idea of controlling populations through legislation. The right to reproduce, to overproduce, is viewed as sacrosanct, and anyone who would posit the idea of a legal means to control our rampant population growth would almost certainly be silenced and labeled a Nazi. Thus, we seem doomed to battle the effects of a diminished earth rather than addressing its principal cause.

Several years ago, with my son and two other friends, I hiked across southern England from Eastbourne to Chichester on a trail called the South Downs Way. The path traversed both private and public land, most of it open high meadows which looked out from verdant ridges over rolling hills, forest plots, and prosperous farms. To me it seemed idyllic, the sort of bucolic splendor that must have inspired the pastoral etchings of Samuel Palmer and his group. Yet wherever we stopped in the villages and pubs along the way, the people with whom I talked saw the Downs as diminished. After expressions of amazement that we were actually walking ten days to a place we might easily reach by car in one, they would tap their pipes, set down their pints, wipe the foam from their upper lips, and, after agreeing that this was indeed beautiful country, shake their heads ruefully and say, "Ah yes, but the Downs aren't what they were, ya know." The source of their chagrin was that in their memory the Downs had been almost entirely high grazing land and that now so much of it was under the plow. This observation became as much a commonplace as talk of the weather. The countryside remained for me as quaint and lush as I had originally observed it to be, but I felt disquieted by a sense of impending doom, that I might be among the last to enjoy this land as it was now.

I carried this sadness as palpably as the pack on my back until we reached Chichester and the South Downs Museum. There I studied a diorama of the Downs depicting the progression of uses to which the land had been put since the fourteenth century. What struck me was the fact that never, over the course of the past six centuries, had the nature of the Downs remained unaltered for more than fifty years. It had been successively forest, farmland, grazing pastures, and cultivated fields. And I realized that what the villagers had been lamenting was not necessarily the beginning of the end of the Downs. Rather they were lamenting the cusp of a change from what the Downs had been in their memory.

I remember looking at photographs taken around 1920 of the farm and forest land of western Michigan where I grew up. I studied some of those pictures intently, trying to pin down their exact locations. In one I might recognize a particular hill in its relation to the captioned lake, or a unique bend in a particular road. I pinpointed those places intellectually, geographically, but there was something oddly remote about them. Though I could verify the locations, they weren't the landscapes in which I had wandered as an awed young animal and discovered what I had then believed to be "the natural world." Finally, it occurred to me that what made the places in those sepia photographs seem unfamiliar to me was the fact that in 1920 or thereabouts there were no trees. The forested hillsides and lake edges I had believed to be ancient sanctuaries of wild beauty had, twenty years before my birth, been stripped bare to build and to heat the somewhat grander houses of the generation that followed those who had stripped the fields to plant the crops by which they might survive. How much more "natural" the land appeared now, softened by dense growths of pine, maple, hemlock, beech, and oak, and how much grander or, in the view of my ancestors a century earlier, how much less hospitable it must have been when it was dominated by primordial white pine.

I'm fairly certain that my great-great-grandfather, who came to Michigan in the 1840s hoping to establish a tanning business, didn't give much thought to stewardship and would have had little cause to do so. The sparsity of the human population alone ensured the abundance of the land. The journal of one of his sons reveals that my great great-grand-father was an anomaly among the settlers of his generation, who, for the most part, regarded trees solely as a threat, a nuisance, or an economic opportunity. He loved huge trees and was said to have hugged them and to have praised their size and beauty vocally. It wasn't an altogether altruistic love, however; he depended on hemlock and tamarack bark for the tannic acid he used in curing hides, and since he was an industrious man already involved in harvesting trees for their chemical properties, he also founded a lumber mill.

SOMETIMES OUR LOVE OF a place, our appreciation of it and our human impulse to share that love and appreciation, contributes to the erosion of what it is we most love about it. Twenty years ago I discovered Key West and almost instantly it became my second hometown. It was like no other place I had been. It had an aura of mystery and a slight wind of threat, a residue of its miscreant heritage as a haven for pirates and salvagers. A decade or two earlier it had harbored a coterie of artists and writers, drawn by its simultaneous remoteness and accessibility and, perhaps more importantly, its indifference to their presence. At the very end of America, on the way to nowhere, no one stumbled on it passing through. It was a foreign country for which you needed no visa and had to undergo the scrutiny of no border guards. It had a naval base, a shrimping industry, a dedicated cadre of sport fishermen, and not much to recommend it to ordinary vacationers in the way of elegant accommodations, good restaurants, or bathing beaches. But writers write out of their enthusiasms, which is what I, along with a number of other writers similarly attracted, did. We evangelized Key West in our stories. Hordes of vacationers and those in search of the last good place, all of whom had as much right as we to enjoy it, responded. The developers swooped in to accommodate them, and property values and prices soared so that many of the natives could no longer afford to live there. Key West isn't what it used to be, but what is? A friend of mine, one of those writers most responsible for inadvertently popularizing Key West, nailed down the whole dilemma of change and development when confronted with his responsibility in the "ruination" of Key West. "Yeh," he said with a deep sigh of weariness, "everywhere I go people are always saying, 'Oh, but you should have been here a couple of years ago.'"

Each of us wants to be the last one allowed into paradise and to lock the door behind us. But there is no door. My own love of the natural

world and my desire to participate in it was largely kindled by my early
reading of Thoreau. Has my presence in nature and the trips I have taken
to enjoy it, from a simple walk in the woods near my house to dozens of
journalistic expeditions to wild places, and the resources consumed in
doing so contributed to the demise of what it was I was seeking? And is
Thoreau indirectly responsible for having encouraged me?

Though I prefer those places touched only lightly by human influence,
I love storied places as well, places in which human life and the landscape
have struggled and reached a harmony of sorts. I love wormy old barns
and stone walls built from the rocks of the fields they enclose. "The story
of any country," Willa Cather wrote, "begins in the heart of a man or a
woman." And I love wild places, not only because they are wild, but
because they expound some vital aspect of my mind when I look on them
or even in the turmoil of everyday life when I reflect on them.

But I can't escape the fact that I'm a human being and that my presence alters, however subtly, the environment I enter. Through my life and
work as a writer, I have probably given more attention, conscious and
unconscious, to the natural world than have most people, and I have
probably cultivated a deeper affinity for it. But I need to be careful not to
let myself translate that affinity into license, into a belief that I own a
more compelling right of access to what we call nature than the man or
woman who, in their preoccupation with making a living, have concentrated their attention elsewhere, even if they happen to work for the paper
company or the mining company I perceive as a threat to the continued
well-being of that world I cherish.

When I go to the woods, what I am seeking and what I experience,
when I am truly aware of my mind and not preoccupied with its contents,
isn't just the wind through the pine boughs and the croak of the raven. I
go to find a window in the relentlessly confusing context of my life, that
I might be reminded for a moment who I am and where I came from, that
I am not ultimately defined by the names, titles, and manifestations of
personality so intriguing to that insistent biographer in my head who
wants me to be one solid thing he can point to. If we are not imprisoned
in the poverty of a one-dimensional Newtonian vision, the earth isn't one
thing either, and our care for it must be akin to our nurturing of a child
whose life is forever unfolding.

I need to know there is wildness in the world, even if I were to never
see it. Even if I were confined to a cell, I would need to know it was out
there. It isn't essential to my enjoyment of fishing that I catch fish, only
that I know there are fish in the water. I need to know there are wolves,

bears, and sharks, our true brother predators, sharing this world, and not just chickadees, though I love chickadees too. It isn't necessary that I *see* wolves, but it's vital to know that if I were to apply my attention diligently, there's a chance I might see them. And if there are people who don't understand this, I have no logic to persuade them.

We cannot individually save the earth, but it is possible that we may each save some small part of it. For the past seven years I have been one of a group of seven hundred people banded together to prevent 3.68 acres of wetlands bordering the Crystal River in northwestern lower Michigan from being filled in, fertilized, and tamed into four fairways of a golf course. I can't pretend to any objectivity in this matter. I have canoed that stretch of water many times since childhood and am convinced the earth will be irrevocably diminished if this desiccation is allowed to happen. And my dismay has been compounded into outrage by the old-boy network of venal businessmen and politicians who have sought to subvert the process established to protect it. The developer, the governor, and a U.S. senator, who was the developer's college roommate, brought influence to bear on the director of the Environmental Protection Agency to remove the case from the jurisdiction of its midwestern regional office, where, after exhaustive study and review, it had been conclusively denied. The director of the EPA then appointed a three-man ad hoc panel of water quality experts to resolve the matter, but when that panel concluded that the regional office had been correct in denying the permit, the director overturned his own agency's ruling and granted the developer permission to fill in the wetlands. The Friends of the Crystal River, joined by the Sierra Club Legal Defense Fund and several other environmental organizations, subsequently filed suit against the EPA. A federal judge has ruled that the EPA had chosen to act outside the authority of the law and granted an injunction against the golf course. The developer has filed an appeal, and the battle, involving twenty-seven lawyers by last count, continues.

Faced with the perfidy and implacability of this kind of cronyism, my first impulse is to reach for a gun or a stick of dynamite. But that would hardly be a compassionate response. Or would it? How do you respond to minds that see the intrinsic worth of nothing, that see the natural world only as a storehouse to be raided?

NOW, FROM THE HILL on which I live, my gaze follows the slope of a meadow of purple knapweed, down over the tops of a hardwood forest, then leaps out over the brilliant waters of Lake Michigan to the Manitou

Islands, and comes to rest in the empty horizon connecting them. There's a salient of land to the southwest which, with a palm tree or two in the foreground, could be Diamond Head. Some days I imagine this as Oregon or the northern coast of California, and, when the ghost of the fog moves out, it could be Italy or the aquamarine waters of the Caribbean, depending on my mood or the music in my head. It is arguably the most prodigiously beautiful view in the Midwest, and you would expect, after the sun has gone down, when the lake has become a New Mexican mesa and the islands, buttes rising above it, that it would be punctuated by the lights of a thousand condominiums. But it isn't. I can walk one mile down the hill from my house, through the forest, through cedar swamps, and over sawgrass hills to the white sands of a public beach that rims the jutting shoreline thirty-five miles to the south and encompasses the Sahara-like Sleeping Bear Dunes. I can do this now, and my great-grandchildren, and yours, will be able to do this, largely because of the stewardship of one man, a U.S. senator from Michigan named Phil Hart, who had the vision to save a piece of this coast from becoming the grist of developers and the exclusive domain of a few thousand wealthy vacationers. Wealthy vacationers are free to enjoy this pristine beach and the seventy thousand acres of forests, hills, and ski and hiking trails of the Sleeping Bear Dunes National Lakeshore, but so is anyone who craves the illusion, at least, of a little solitude.

Our stewardship of the earth is a love story, a give-and-take we cannot win but one we must not lose. It is, as the noted philosopher Erazim Kohák points out, by our care for a thing, rather than our need or desire for it, that we realize its intrinsic worth. In Buddhism, the bodhisattva, the awakened being, doesn't find her way by acquiring something but rather by subordinating her desires for her own realization to her commitment to fostering the conditions through which all other beings may achieve realization before her. And it seems to me that this is a true reflection of our present mission on earth. "Here," we might say, "let me care for this meadow, and if it is attended to so that you may enjoy it, then thereby I may enjoy it too." We can't take whatever we think is good about our world and keep it inviolate for ourselves. Cut off from sustenance, the give-and-take of its surroundings, it would wither by the same process of suffocation through which any truth we might cling to becomes a delusion by virtue of our clinging.

Finally, I find myself asking, what is nature? And the answer that comes back to me is this: It is our experience of a consciousness in the world itself, uncircumscribed by conventional thought, liberated as Frederick Turner puts it, from "the vicious circle of expectations governing perceptions which in turn confirm expectations." It is Blake's "seeing through, not with, the eyes." It is not merely a place relatively undominated by human influence, though it may be that too. We may take ourselves to the wildest reaches of the Brooks Range, but if we don't leave our everyday concerns behind, our concerns, and not the Brooks Range, are what we will experience. Max Oelschlaeger points out that Western culture has "refused to reconsider the absolute presupposition that nature was anything more than a stage upon which the human drama was performed" and that the land ethic "explicitly recognized humankind as a self-aware participant whose choices had profound impact on the course of evolution."

Often when I walk out from my house into the hills surrounding it, I discover after twenty minutes or so that I have taken the house with me, have taken the unanswered letters and telephone calls, the windows that need caulking, the slights I suffered last week, the things I should have said but didn't, the things I plan to say next week but probably won't. My feet have been taking a walk without me. Every step has been clouded by the metronome beat of "yes, no, yes, no." Words like *ground squirrel, cinquefoil, osprey,* and *dove* flit across my consciousness in response to beings that appear, but I don't see them. It doesn't matter whether the ground I'm walking over is planted alfalfa or wild knapweed, whether the trees are virgin or second growth. If I am not aware of them, not conscious of their consciousness, nature doesn't exist for me, though I may be walking in Tierra del Fuego.

Nature is the great emptiness, the source, out of which our culture and all its flowering comes, and in order not to lose sight of this, not to become orphans lost in the minutiae of our daily lives and, like the rich man's son starving outside his father's gate, to forget who we are, it is vital that wildness be preserved for its own sake, which is to say, for our sake.

Thoughts of a
Fly Fisherman—or Two
Joan Salvato Wulff

IN THIS YEAR OF THE FILM VERSION OF NORMAN MCCLEAN'S *A River Runs Through It* (1992), I feel acknowledged. The famous opening words, "In our family there was no clear line between religion and fly fishing" touch a responsive chord in me. My parents had become disenchanted with their respective churches before they were married, and there was no religious upbringing for me of the organized kind, only an awareness of an all-knowing "God," who, it turned out, was my conscience.

In an ever-growing way, the woods and waters of the outdoors became my church, a place where I could examine my thoughts and feel I was connected to all living things. This feeling has remained throughout my life. It is especially strong when, fly rod in hand, I am wading a river for trout or salmon or stalking the saltwater flats for bonefish and permit. It is where I want to be, where everything makes sense, where there is nothing but truth. There will be no disenchantment with this church.

These outdoor genes I've inherited came from my dad, Jimmy Salvato. Trained to be an accountant, he followed his heart instead and in 1927 opened the Paterson Rod and Gun Store in Paterson, N.J. He loved to hunt upland game birds and moose, and was a founding member of the hunting and fishing conservation clubs in northern New Jersey. Those clubs had winter feeding programs for deer and game birds, and as I grew up I realized that hunters were the most likely people to take care of the animals and birds they later harvested.

Dad was also an active member of the Paterson Casting Club, and his favorite fly-rod species was largemouth bass. Mother was not an outdoorswoman, but she was "game" for occasional adventures. My first exposure to fishing was on an evening with the two of them on nearby Greenwood Lake, when I was younger than five. Mom was at the oars, and Dad was casting deer-hair bass bugs in among the lily pads.

Mother was not at ease rowing a boat, and all evening long, Dad kept reminding her that she was either too close to the lily pads or too far away. I sensed her frustration, and, too young to know that women didn't fish, a very strong thought took form: "It was better to be the fisherman than the rower!"

On the first of Dad's catches, I was given the fly rod to hold. I remember the thrill (and sixty years later, it still happens every time) of having that bamboo rod come to life as every move the bass made was telegraphed to my then-inexperienced hands. When the fish was close enough for me to get a good look at it, I froze in fascination at the size of this strange-looking creature that lived in black water under lily pads . . . and relaxed the tension on the line. As I watched, the bass bug came out of its jaw, and the largemouth sank slowly out of sight. Dad reassured his tearful daughter by saying that he would have put the bass back anyway and that he'd catch another, which he did.

The conscious knowledge of that evening's experience was that it was better to be the fisherman than the rower. The unconscious knowledge was that a wild creature could be seen and held and put back where it lived, all through the magic of using a fly rod.

Being a girl who wanted to take part in a man's world was a challenge. When I was ten and my brother, Jim Junior, was eight, he was taught to shoot and cast. I was left out. Because I wanted to fly cast, I finally found a way to get Dad's attention and was "allowed" to take part in the activities of the Paterson Casting Club. And I also learned to shoot a twenty-two caliber rifle.

That was the beginning, in 1937, of my lifetime involvement with casting and fishing. Winning national casting titles, especially the fly-casting titles, brought me national publicity. Fly casting was like a passport for me, opening doors that surely would have been locked otherwise and giving me reason to be in many of the beautiful places on this earth. Even so, as a woman in a man's world my physical (female) limitations forced me to work harder to keep up with male companions. I thought the rewards were worth the discomfort of the awkward costume and the heavy tackle. I fished because I loved it, never expecting it to reward me financially, never dreaming that fly fishing could one day have status in our primarily urban society. I was wrong in thinking that because the sport involved wild creatures it could never gain that acceptance. I hope I remain wrong.

A second outdoorsman, Lee Wulff, entered my life in the mid sixties and gave focus and form to my inherent but undeveloped instincts for conservation. Lee was an extraordinary man: an original and controversial thinker, a leader, a man ahead of his time. Once logic convinced him that a course of action was "right," he never gave up on it, although he most often stood alone. He thought it was an obligation to actively give something back to the sport and protect the resources we love and enjoy. He served on and became chairman of the New Hampshire Fish and Game Commission and was a director and eventually chairman of the Atlantic Salmon Association. Lee and others who were equally dedicated started the Federation of Fly Fishers, the Theodore Gordon Fly Fishers, and the Catskill Fly Fishing Center. When he died at the age of 86 in 1991, he was engaged in an all-out crusade to have the Atlantic salmon designated a game fish.

The concept of catch-and-release first came to us in print through Lee's *A Handbook of Freshwater Fishing*. In the introduction he wrote, "There is a growing tendency among anglers to release their fish, returning them to the water in order that they may furnish sport again for a brother angler. Game fish are too valuable to be caught only once." And the last sentence in the book reads, "The fish you release is your gift to another angler and, remember, it may have been someone's similar gift to you."[1]

He inserted the "good game fish" philosophy into all of his writings, lectures, and films. He would say "more and more anglers are releasing their fish" when they were not! But, as I said, he was persistent, and finally in 1964, Jack Anderson, then supervisor of Yellowstone Park, set aside the first catch-and-release area in the park. New York State followed, setting aside four miles on the Beaverkill River near Roscoe. Over the next twenty years, relatively little water was designated as catch-and-release around the country due to the opposition of catch-and-take fishermen. However, in the last ten years, more and more stretches of prime water have become subject to special regulations, and among fly fishermen the concept has caught on like a religion. Everyone does it, "special regs" or not.

With this acceptance, with fly fishing being an "in" activity, the problems that have always been there for the few are compounded because of the many. What are we going to do about them? The needs are simple: clean water, maintenance of wild stocks, a fair sharing of the resource among (too many) anglers through catch-and-release when feasible, and also, perhaps, the metering of time spent fishing. Among our conservation organizations are Trout Unlimited, Federation of Fly Fishers, Theodore Gordon Fly Fishers, and the Atlantic Salmon Federation, the watchdogs of our rivers and streams. They do a magnificent job, and even if they don't win every battle for clean water, fish passage, and so on, they never give up.

For too many anglers, a fish is a fish is a fish, but to those of us who know the difference, wild fish are our most precious resource. And of course they are always at risk, from pollution, elimination of spawning grounds, and dissolution of their genes when hatchery stock is introduced in their waters. Lee felt that hatchery fish should be stocked in rivers and streams that cannot sustain wild fish and should be a put-and-take fishery. As such, hatchery stock would be fin clipped and the users required to pay for the fish they take through the purchase of a special "trout stamp," which would, in turn, pay for the hatcheries. Lee tried to sell this idea to New Hampshire but failed, even though the concept was accepted by hunters for pheasants there and in other states.

How can we spread the available fishing among an ever-larger number of users? We can issue licenses that are good only on odd days of the month or the first or last two weeks of the month. In heavily used areas, we can have a lottery as we do with big game management. In a land where freedom is a birthright, how can you tell someone they can't fish on certain days? If we are free to create problems, we are free to solve problems. Everyone who can reach the public must make anglers aware of the fragility of the resource. And we must do this before we've reached bottom. It is in our nature to rescue something only at the last minute, never to think ahead, never to learn from others' mistakes.

Those who care have a big job cut out for them. But it is doable. In the fishing schools I conduct, I have faced the dilemma of whether or not to continue to entice new people into our already crowded field. But for a river to survive in today's world, it must have friends. Now, too, there are saltwater areas that need friends, where game fish (marlin and sailfish specifically) are being taken for commercial use. The more anglers we have, the larger will be the number of good ones, the caring ones, the ones who will join in stewarding the resource.

Those words, *caring* and *stewarding*, describe the segment of the population from which our newest allies come. Women are entering the outdoor field as never before. They are attracted to fly fishing for the same reasons as are men, but they bring their nurturing natures with them. A woman looks at a river she loves as she would a child: Is it well fed and healthy or underweight and hurting? She thinks of the fish she releases as going on to grow bigger or to produce babies. And just as she does with her family, she thinks of the future, looking ahead to long-term goals while achieving short-term goals. She is well suited to being a tireless worker for conservation.

There is one other thought I wish to offer. The word *sanctuary* means, to most of us, a place where birds, game, and fish are not accessible to users. Lee taught me to think of it in a larger context, specifically with regard to fishing. In the old days when there weren't too many of us and there was no spinning tackle, fishing was a sport of great limitations. You could only throw bait so far on conventional revolving spool reels, and fly lines were either dressed to float on the surface for dry fly fishing or left undressed for use with wet flies and streamers just below the surface. The methods by which we fished gave fish a sanctuary in the hard-to-reach areas.

When spinning tackle was imported from Europe after the Second World War, it revolutionized sport fishing. The good news was that anyone could cast a backlash-free spinning reel and put a sinking lure wherever a fish might be. The deep areas of streams and lakes were suddenly accessible to all. The bad news was that, in about ten years, some of our finest rivers and streams were all but depleted of wild trout. From 1947 to the eighties, we could look to the cause as "spinning." But now, in waters reserved for fly fishing, we non-spin anglers are dredging the bottom with fast-sinking lines for trout and steelhead, putting weight on our leaders and in our flies to ensure success. Once again, the sanctuary has been invaded.

I am privileged to have known fly fishing when it was undeveloped and to have watched it grow and become the sophisticated sport it is today. But I worry that fly fishing as an experience may lose its quality in my life-time. We have become too efficient, too deadly. But paradoxically, I have faith in fly fishermen as a group. Success is the bottom line in this sport, as it is in others, but fly fishermen are a cut above the average and have shown themselves capable of seeing disaster in the making, capable of making the right decisions to protect the resource.

Is it unthinkable that to protect wild stocks, areas could be designated to be fished by surface techniques only? Is this any more unthinkable than catch-and-release was in the thirties? Every time I fly fish I think of my children and theirs. My joy in this sport is so great, so real, that I am filled with an indescribable longing to have them share it. They are not ready. When they are ready, which will probably be after I'm gone, will it still be there for them?

Solutions to problems often get complicated, as individuals and groups want the solution that is in their own best interest. One of Lee's many wonderful ideas concerned the management of Atlantic salmon stocks. Lee was always telling the Canadians how to manage their salmon. I once asked him why he thought he had a better solution than did the man-agers, business interests, or other sportsmen. His answer was succinctly beautiful. "It's simple," he said, "I always look at it from the fish's point of view."

And so must we.

1. Lee Wulff, *A Handbook of Freshwater Fishing* (New York: Frederick A. Stokes, 1939), xv, 263.

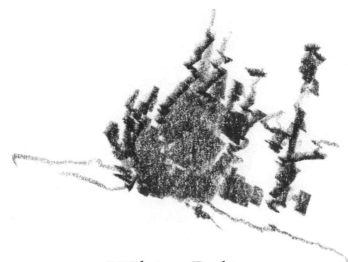

White Pelicans
Jack Turner

I AM LOUNGING ON THE SUMMIT OF THE GRAND TETON, SURROUNDED by blocks of gneiss and a cobalt sky. It is midmorning in July: warm, still, and so clear the distant ranges seem etched into the horizon. To the east, the Absaroka, Gros Ventre, and Wind River; to the south, the Salt, Snake, and Caribou; to the west the Big Hole and the Lost River; and to the north, the Centennial, Madison, Gallatin, and Beartooth. Directly north, and closer, is the still-snowy summit of the Pitchstone Plateau, and beyond it is the fuzzy blur of a geyser somewhere near Old Faithful. To the northeast are slices of Yellowstone Lake. Despite the breadth of view I always feel this summit is a place of great simplicity. I have just climbed the Exum, or south, ridge of the Grand Teton with clients. They are taking photographs. Since I have climbed the Grand for thirty years, I have my pictures, and since I am fifteen years older than my oldest client, I am tired. So I lounge and enjoy the clarity and count shades of blue as the sky pales into the mountains. Then I hear a faint noise above me and my heart says, "Pelicans."

The sounds are faint, so faint they are sometimes lost—a trace of clacking in the sky. It is even harder to see them. Tiny glints, like slivers of ice, are occasionally visible, then invisible, then visible again as the sheen of their feathers strikes just the right angle to the sun. With a small pair of binoculars, we see them clearly: seventeen pelicans soaring in a tight circle. I have seen them here before, as well as from the summit of Symmetry Spire and from the long ridge of Rendezvous Peak. But it is rare—in part, I think, because the conditions for hearing and seeing them are so rare. Perhaps they are often above us, but with the wind and clouds and the ever-present anxiety of the climbers, we fail to notice them. I wonder if glider pilots see them here and if they soar together in the blue.

The American white pelican (*Pelecanus erythrorhynchos*) is a large bird, often weighing twenty pounds, with some individuals reaching thirty pounds. It is one of seven pelican species worldwide. The only other pelican in North America, the brown pelican (*Pelecanus occidentalis*), is smaller and restricted to the coasts. The white pelican's wingspan reaches nine and a half feet, equal in length to the California condor's. Of North American birds, only the trumpeter swan is consistently larger. Though it is huge, a pelican, like all birds, consists mostly of feathers, flesh, and air. The beak, skull, feet, and bones of a twenty-five-pound pelican weigh about twenty-three ounces. Its plumage is a brilliant white except for the primaries and outer secondaries, which are black, and pale yellow plumes on the crown of the head during breeding season. Sometimes there is pale yellow on the chest. The eyes are the color of fine slate.

The summit of the Grand Teton is 13,770 feet high, and the pelicans above us are at the limit of unaided human vision. In good light a flock of white pelicans is easily visible at a mile. So they are at least a mile above us, or around 19,000 feet. This seems high for any bird, but geese have been photographed at 29,000 feet, ravens are a nuisance on the South Col of Everest at 26,000 feet, and I have watched flocks of Brahminy ducks from Siberia cross the ridge between Everest and Cho Oyu, a ridge that is nowhere less than 19,500 feet in height. So although 19,000 feet is impressive, and no one knows how high pelicans can or do fly, the more interesting question is this: What are they *doing* up there? Soaring, clacking—yes, but why? I don't think anybody knows, and this mystery, along with the inevitable speculations, are a large part of why I find their presence so appealing.

For many years I've asked biologists and birders about pelican sounds. They are unanimous: they have never heard a pelican make a sound. The popular bird books do not mention pelican sounds, and most of the technical literature reports that pelicans are mute except when breeding. Then the authors go on to admit they have spent little time around breeding pelicans. There are good reasons for this. The white pelican so dislikes human presence during its breeding period that if approached by humans the pelicans will abandon their nests and congregate on nearby water. Their eggs, or the chicks, are then exposed to the sun, the cold, and the depredations of the ever-present gulls. An hour or less is sufficient to wipe out the breeding colony. If repeatedly harassed, pelicans will abandon a rookery, and they do not return. For these reasons, monitoring the white pelican population is usually done from airplanes now, increasingly with aerial photography. In one sense, this is commendable; in another sense, it is sad, for fewer and fewer people know less and less about pelicans. The hard data is known—the average length of the bill, the average time of arrival and departure during migration, the average number of eggs—and no doubt it will increase, but our understanding of pelicans, a way of knowing that requires intimacy, is nil.

We could, of course, let pelicans come to us. This is the difference between seeking and stalking and just sitting and waiting. It is an old difference, as old as hunting, but it is a method hard for us to choose because we are, as a nation and as a civilization, a people of seeking and stalking, though exactly why this is so remains fugitive.

I used to visit an old Tibetan Sherpa in Khumbu who had served on perhaps fifty Himalayan expeditions. His name was Dawa Tensing, and he lived in a village just north of Thyangboche Monastery on the trail to Everest. He was famous for saying, "So many people coming, coming, always looking, never finding, always coming back again. Why?" Once in all sincerity he asked me, "Is America beautiful? Why you always come back here?" It took a long time for Dawa's "Why?" to sink into my thick skull, and it took even longer to prefer his question to the closure of an answer. I suspect now that if we wish to know pelicans intimately, we must begin by a preference for questions and a preference for sitting and waiting. Perhaps it would be better if ornithologists became glider pilots, mountaineers, and fisherman, lived in the great thermals, lounged on the tops of great peaks, fished great rivers, and waited for pelicans to come to them.

If we sit quietly in the places of pelicans, I believe they *will* come to us. I have been sitting in a cabin in a national park for portions of ten years now. Although I do not feed any animals, the eagles watch me from a nearby snag, a red squirrel sits by my elbow while I shave, martens and weasels peep in my window, and deer and elk nip the weeds by the porch.

Moose sometimes sleep on the porch—and scare the wits out of me when I go out at night to pee.

Dogen's famous lines in the *Genjo Koan* are always suggestive, even when removed from their context:

That the self advances and confirms the myriad things is called delusion;
That the myriad things advance and confirm the self is enlightenment.[1]

The Japanese word here translated as *enlightenment* can also be translated as intimacy. Perhaps it would be best to sit and wait, to allow pelicans to advance and confirm us, to allow them to choose their degree of intimacy with us: no banding, no radio collars, just watching and waiting.

A few people have spent time sitting with pelicans, and, *of course*, they heard pelican sounds. In 1962 George Shaller spent 367 hours sitting in a canoe watching pelicans breed. He heard lots of pelican sounds. Other researchers have noted that pelicans hiss when angry, snap their mandibles together as a warning, and while mating make sounds described as piglike, low-toned grunts, subdued croaking, deep-voiced (not loud) murmuring groans, and grunting quacks. Audubon's description is memorable. It was, he said, a sound "like blowing through the bunghole of a cask."

So although pelicans do make sounds, they are, relative to other birds, quite silent. There may be phylogenetic reasons for this. The newer species of birds are the most vocal and produce the greatest variety of sounds, while pelicans are very old: they have been around thirty-five to forty million years. We have one fossil record from the Pliocene, and we know pelicans have been in the American West since the Pleistocene. Ornithologists have discovered prehistoric nesting sites on mountains that were once islands arising from the Pleistocene lakes that covered much of the Great Basin.

The silence of pelicans, along with their great age, contributes to their dignity. Everyone who studies pelicans agrees on their dignity. And this is no doubt augmented by the fact that the pelican is not a popular bird. The Hamilton Stores in Yellowstone offer no pelican postcards or posters or stuffed pelicans or pelican candles or coffee mugs—merchandise that nibbles at the dignity of other animals.

After fishing Yellowstone's water for thirty-two years, I believe that white pelicans are fond of their fishing kin. Their reason is probably a good pelican reason, a sustained meditation on "anything that spends that much time trying to catch trout can't be all bad." Although other pelicans eat rough fish, especially carp, 98 to 100 percent of a Yellowstone pelican's diet is *Salmo clarki lewisi*, otherwise known as the black-spotted trout or, more formally, as the westslope cutthroat. On my off days I am consoled by the firm belief that the karma of those who subsist on trout is superior to those who subsist on carp, and that Yellowstone pelicans are virtuous pelicans.

There may be some condescension in a pelican's view of fly fishermen. Pelicans know how to fish. They have been found with the bones of four-pound trout in their bellies, and they have been observed struggling with twenty-four-inch fish. Sometimes they are so bloated by success that they have to vomit so they can lose enough weight to fly. On an average day, a Yellowstone pelican will eat over four pounds of cutthroats. If the average fly fisherman had to catch four pounds of trout a day to survive, there would be fewer *Homo sapiens* than pelicans—and lots of carcasses surrounded by $3,000 worth of high-tech fishing gear. One reason fishermen should love pelicans is that they are good guides, probably superior to the $300-a-day human variety.

Unlike the brown pelican, the white pelican does not dive for fish. It fishes with its bill and the flabby, stretchy gular pouch that hangs beneath it. The pelican is clever with this pouch, using it as a dip net to catch fish, fluttering it to regulate its temperature (it is filled with blood vessels), and, in one case of a pelican in captivity, catching balls with it and throwing them back up into the air. Since this bill is about a foot long, the pelican must feed near the surface of the water, probably the top two or three feet. If fishing alone on a river, the pelican is attracted to fish feeding near the surface, and this often means fish that are feeding on emerging aquatic insects and hatches. Although biologists stress that pelicans are always in flocks (except for stragglers during migration) and that they are timid, anyone who fishes Yellowstone knows that they are often solitary—sort of like fly fishermen. The Yellowstone River is a great dry-fly river—what better place for a bird that must feed near the surface? If you go to the estuary below the lake during the gray drake mayfly hatch in late July, you will occasionally see pelicans floating amidst a blizzard of fly lines and mayflies, performing upstream and downstream ferries like skilled kayakers to avoid all the people standing in the river. The novice fly-fishers try to match the huge duns; the pelicans and their followers attend to the spinner fall.

Buffalo Ford, a picnic area with a small island offshore that divides the river and provides good holding water for trout, is another favorite place of pelican and fisherman. I have seen pelicans work this water the way an angler works a dry fly or an emerger. They land above the good water, float into the deep pool at the head of the island, and then along the side of the deep trench of the main current that flows between the east side of the island and the far shore; after reaching the tailwater below the island, they lift off and fly back to the head of the good water. They do this again and again—just like the rest of the folks fishing the Ford.

Like wading fishermen, the pelican often courts disaster. Indeed, each time a pelican lands on the river it looks like a disaster. They drop the backs of their huge wings, throw out their feet, and steady themselves for a controlled crash—just like landing a 747. Every time, they almost nose over; every time, they just make it. Then, to regain their composure, they tuck their bills into their chests with a priggish English-butler look and casually paddle off after more trout, buoyant as a well-greased fly. As the poet Onitsura says:

> The water-bird
> Looks heavy,—
> But it floats![2]

Because I guide in the Tetons all summer, I have little time for fishing; but when work slows I fish the Yellowstone River, and afterward, on my way home, I stop at the Lake Hotel. I tell myself it is for dinner, but this is just an excuse to sit in the lounge, listen to the string quartet that plays during the summer months, and watch the light on Yellowstone Lake. The owners recently remodeled the lounge in civilized colors: pale green, rose, mauve, and cream. I like to sit in a wicker wing chair, sip margaritas, and listen to young musicians play music that does not remind me of machines. Last year the first violinist was a young woman who played beautifully. Her skin was a color found only inside seashells. Bent to her violin, she swayed in oblivion, concealed in the solitude of her music, fully present but lost, as luminous, self-contained, and remote as a star.

Just visible above her shoulder, through the bay windows at the end of the lounge, was the lake, speckled with whitecaps. In the distance stretched its southeast arm. The slant of evening light and the ever-present storm clouds darkened its western shore, while sunlight revealed light rock or fresh snow on the peaks of the Absaroka. Further, almost concealed by cloud, were Colter Peak, Turret Peak, the Trident, and the Two Ocean Plateau. Further still was the Thorofare, the wildest, most remote place in the lower forty-eight states. At the tip of this southeast arm, just west of where the Yellowstone River enters the lake and roughly a half mile off the western and southern shores, are the Molly Islands. If you were to stand on this shore you would see two spits of sand named Sandy Island and Rocky Island. They are small, low, and sparsely dappled with Scouler willow, nettles, sky pilot, and cinquefoil. Until recently, these remote islands were the only white pelican rookery in Wyoming, the chosen home of strange white birds thirty-five million years old.

The first recorded sighting of a pelican in Yellowstone was by the Stuart party in 1863. Like good Americans, they promptly shot one near what is now Pelican Creek. This set the tone for our relations with white pelicans for the next century. The population was nearly wiped out in the late twenties when it was discovered that the pelican carried a parasite that infected the cutthroat. This, in addition to their high consumption of trout, led to the slaughter of the pelicans. This was not an isolated act of stupidity. In 1918 the Utah Department of Fish and Game went to Hat Island, which was then a breeding colony in the Great Salt Lake, and clubbed and shot to death hundreds of pelicans and herons. Of the original twenty-three breeding colonies in the American West, only five major sites remain. Many, like the Molly Islands, are small. In 1980 there were only 285 nests on the Molly Islands.

The islands are so low they are vulnerable to flooding. According to the topographic map, Sandy Island is only six feet above the lake, and Rocky Island is only nine. When Shaller studied the colony in 1962, the lake rose 2.3 feet in June due to runoff from a heavy snow pack and wiped out "at least eighty" pelican nests. It is conceivable that a heavier runoff could completely flood the islands and cause the pelicans to abandon the colony. That there are over a hundred thousand breeding white pelicans in North America would not diminish our loss. For years there has been an effort to have the white pelican listed as endangered. The U.S. pelican population is vulnerable, especially in Wyoming, where it is listed as a "Priority 1 species," one needing "immediate attention and active management to ensure that extirpation or a significant decline in the breeding population" does not occur.

On the Molly Islands, pelican chicks hatch when the bison calves drop. (They are exceptionally ugly: nothing looks so like a dinosaur as a pelican chick.) Soon thereafter, in a striking example of natural timing, the cutthroat spawn; the small streams around Yellowstone Lake are choked with millions of cutthroats laying billions of eggs in shallow, pelican-heaven water. Trout eat the unprotected eggs of other trout, and larger trout eat little trout, and all of them are gobbled up by grizzlies, California gulls, and pelicans in a wild frenzy of sex and gluttony. It's a good time to be a pelican chick.

At ten to eleven weeks the chicks begin to fly, and soon afterward they make their first sighting of the Teton Range fifty miles to the southwest and clearly visible from above the southeast arm. From this direction the so-called Cathedral Group of peaks—Teewinot, Mount Owen, and the Grand Teton—resembles a pyramid. If you were a soaring bird, you would want to go there.

White pelicans soar. Like the large pelagic birds, pelicans have wings with a high ratio of length to width. They are built to soar, and they soar well; thirty-five million years of constant feedback and fine-tuned design make a difference. All authors writing on pelicans mention their soaring, and most have watched the birds disappear upward into the blue "at the limit of human vision."

Of all places available to them, mountains provide the most opportunities for soaring. Pelicans can soar up slopes where the prevailing winds meet an obstacle, such as a mountain, for instance. Air flows over a mountain like water flows over a boulder in a rapid. Just as beyond the boulder there is a hole followed by smaller standing waves, so are there standing "wave trains" of air currents beyond the mountain. Pelicans can soar up each wave of a wave train. Since our prevailing summer wind is from the southwest, the wave trains behind the Grand Teton stretch toward the Molly Islands.

Pelicans also soar in thermals. As the ground warms, patches of warmer air rise, puff out at the top, peel off, and are sucked back into the vortex that keeps rising again and again through the center of the thermal. The stronger the rise, the stronger the thermal, and the tighter the circle a soaring bird can cut. The Teton Range has strong thermals, which is why glider pilots are here. The pelicans above the Grand Teton always soar in tight circles, carving into the wind for lift, then dropping around for the tail wind, then around further and into the wind again for more lift. Thermals tend to stack up in a long "thermal street" and drift downwind. A pelican can climb in one thermal, cut out and glide to the next, climb again, cut out again—all with virtually no energy expenditure. In the summer the Grand Teton's thermals stack up in a line heading straight toward the Molly Islands.

Pelicans also soar in thunderheads. Thunderheads suck cold air down from the upper atmosphere. When this air hits the ground, it spreads out, displacing warmer air, which, in turn, goes upward, creating more good soaring places. So pelicans wander the edges of great storms in their silence. I envy them this freedom, even though it has its risks.

The Grand Teton has some of the most dazzling thunderstorms, with lightning to match, of any place on the planet. Pelicans are killed by lightning. In one account thirty-three were knocked out of the air in Nebraska. In another, twenty-seven were killed by lightning in Utah. The same thing must happen over the Teton Range. Ten years ago my guided party was hit four times by ground currents while descending the Grand Teton. We watched green bolts of lightning ricochet through glaciers like bullets. Yet I still climb mountains and pelicans still soar in thunderheads. After thirty-five million years they must know about lightning and its risks, just as mountaineers do. Since this does not change our behavior why should it affect pelicans' behavior?

So there are many good reasons for pelicans to be above the Grand, but exactly why they are there still remains a mystery. The pelicans we see above the Teton Range in July are not migrating. The pelicans of the Yellowstone region winter in Mexico and the Sea of Cortez. Then in late March to early April, they fly to the Great Salt Lake. Then in late April to early May, they fly to the Molly Islands. Perhaps the pelicans overhead are returning from a foraging mission. Perhaps they are nonbreeding adults on a lark. Perhaps someone will put a radio collar on one and find out, though I hope not. I am not interested in what scientists find out about these birds, and I do not approve intruding into their lives. What interests me is not that pelicans soar or that soaring is useful.

I believe that pelicans *love* to soar, hence their total lack of caution regarding danger—always a sign of love and obsession. My father will fish for anything with anything, cranking in a tiny perch as happily as a four-pound brown trout, in total disregard of the weather. That's love and obsession. Passions, obsessions, and acceptance of risk must all have evolutionary value, but what is this value for pelicans—or for us?

The pelican's love of soaring is only hinted at in ornithological literature, but it is there. In his *Handbook of North American Birds*, Ralf Palmer uses the word *indulge* in the cryptic grammar of scientific description: "Often indulge in high-soaring flights." And again: "While soaring in stormy weather may indulge in aerial acrobatics with much swooping and diving."[3] This is not exactly the language of reductive mechanistic science. Does this mean pelicans are—sometimes at least—up there for pleasure? Do they play in thunderheads for fun? Do they fly in thunderheads knowing full well the danger? What does it mean to attribute emotions to animals? To a bird?

Consider Doug Peacock's cinema footage of the grizzly he named Happy Bear.[4] Happy Bear likes to sit on his butt in small meadow streams in the spring when the streams are still frozen and break off chunks of ice, bite them, push them underwater with his huge paws, then bite them again when they pop up. He does this a lot. I don't think we can say why

Happy Bear is doing this without using analogies and metaphors from human emotional life.

Or consider the gulls in Guy Murchie's *Song of the Sky*:

> Many a time I've seen sea gulls at the big Travis Air Base near San Francisco flapping nonchalantly among the huge ten-engine B-36 bombers while their motors were being run up. The smoke whipping from the jets in four straight lines past the tail accompanied by that soul-shaking roar would have been enough to stampede a herd of elephants but the sea gulls often flew right into the tornado just for fun. When the full blast struck them they would simply disappear, only to turn up a few seconds later a quarter mile downwind, apparently having enjoyed the experience as much as a boy running through a hose— even coming around eager-eyed for more.[5]

Simply disappear. Like careening into the curl of a huge wave on a surfboard. Like paddling a kayak into Lava Falls.

It is not popular now to attribute human attributes to wild animals. Some say that it erodes their "otherness." But all knowledge is a matter of analogy and metaphor and as such is forever imperfect and respectful of mystery. Even our knowledge of our spouse and friends is fragile and often mistaken. The mystery increases when we consider strangers, much less Bushmen. We may feel fairly secure in our understanding of a dog or cat, but a vole? And we often fail to appreciate the analogies and metaphors we appropriate from wild animals: the lion-hearted hero, the wolfish cad, the foxy lady. It is no more odd to say that pelicans *love* to soar and do so in *joy* and *ecstacy* than it is to say what we say of human love and joy and ecstasy: that our heart *soars*.

I do not believe the wild is something other. When I see pelicans riding thermals in the mountains, I feel their exultation and love of open sky and big clouds. Their fear of lightning is my fear, and I extend to them the sadness of descent. Increasingly, I believe the reasons they are soaring over the Grand Teton are the same reasons why we climb mountains, sail gliders into great storms, and stand in rivers with tiny feathers from a French duck's butt on a barbless hook at the end of sixty feet of $60 string thrown by a $1,000 wand trying to catch a fish. It may be in love and joy, ecstasy and passion that we are closest to what we conceive of as other. In passion all beings are at their wildest. And in passion we, like pelicans, make strange noises that defy scientific explanation.

If pelicans soar above the Grand Teton in joy and ecstasy, what do their sounds mean? I can find only one reference in our extensive literature on birds to the clacking pelicans make at high altitude. In his *Life Histories of*

North American Petrels and Pelicans and Their Allies, Arthur Cleveland Bent quotes P. L. Hatch as saying:

> This immense bird usually signals his arrival in the early part of April by his characteristic notes from an elevation beyond the range of vision except under the most favorable circumstances. The sound of those notes is difficult to describe, but unforgettable when once certainly heard from their aerial heights. I have sometimes scanned the heavens in vain to see them, but am generally rewarded for my vigilance and patience if the sky is clear, and if cloudy, also, when I watch the rifts closely with my field glasses.[6]

Why do they utter these unforgettable sounds only when they are so far up in the sky—at the limit of our vision? In *A Field Guide to Animal Tracks*, Olaus Murie says of the sounds of coyotes that "if the coyote could reflect and speak he would say that this is his song, simply that."[7] Simply that. The song of coyote emotion.

Is the clacking a pelican song? Do pelicans clack in ecstasy? I know climbers who whistle, sing, and yodel when they are up in the sky. The reasons for this are also fugitive. Some whistle, some yip, some clack in the sky, some make love to their violin. Why saw and pluck in ecstasy at strings of gut stretched over holes in burnished wood? Why sing cantatas and masses and chorales?

The expression of emotion is a release, often a release from the difficulty and suffering that inevitably attends all life—the Buddha's First Noble Truth. Life is hard, even a trout-eating pelican's life, but pelicans must experience occasionally what we experience occasionally: a soaring of body and heart. The 102d Psalm is "a prayer of the afflicted when he is overwhelmed." The sixth line beseeches God: "I am a pelican of the wilderness."

1. Translated by Hakuyu Taizan Maezumi, *The Way of Everyday Life* (Los Angeles: Center Publications, 1978).
2. R. H. Blyth, *Haiku*, vol. 4. (Tokyo: The Hokuseido Press, 1982), 1259.
3. Vol. 1 (New Haven: Yale University Press, 1962), 270.
4. *Peacock's War*, Bullfrog Films, 1989.
5. From *A Treasury of Birdlore*, Joseph Wood Krutch and Paul S. Eriksson (New York: Doubleday & Company, 1962), 31.
6. (New York: Dover, 1964), 291.
7. (Boston: Houghton Mifflin, 1954), 96.

Third on a Match
(Notes from the Trenches of the Final World War)
William Hjortsberg

EVERY TIME I RECYCLE, I THINK OF WORLD WAR II. IT'S AN automatic mnemonic response, a cerebral detonation like those triggered by Marcel Proust's evocative madeleine. I was born ten months before the Japanese attack on Pearl Harbor, and my earliest memories are flavored forever by the upheavals of that mysterious and distant war. As a toddler on the home front, mimicking Mom weeding the Victory garden, hanging on her apron in the kitchen when she canned fruit and vegetables to supplement the ration coupons, mine was a purely domestic view of the conflict.

Nearly everything was saved: newspaper and cardboard, bacon fat poured off into jars, old flashlight batteries in a shoe box on the closet shelf. My personal contribution to the war effort was helping with empty tin cans after my mother peeled off the paper labels. Now every time I crush an aluminum can and drop it into the recycle box by the garbage, I remember the swell of a four-year-old's pride as he climbed a kitchen chair and turned the crank on the wall-mounted opener. Both lids and bottoms were removed and slid carefully, for the serrated edges were razor-sharp, inside the corresponding cans. The really fun part was stamping each cylindrical package flat on the faded linoleum, jumping up and down in my buckle-front Buster Browns, a tiny warrior putting the boot to an imaginary enemy.

GARBAGE IS A GOOD yardstick of wealth. The more you can afford to throw away, the richer you must be. By that measure, even the down-trodden of our fair republic are maharajahs. America is hemorrhaging trash like an overstuffed hog at sticking time. Used hypodermics and other intriguing medical waste wash in with the tide on our eastern beaches. The highest elevation on Staten Island is built entirely from refuse. Someday, according to the master plan, it will be a park. Other future parks have been riding around the country on barges and railroad trains, looking for landfills that aren't already full.

Haiti is the poorest nation in the western hemisphere and conse-quently has almost no trash. Everything there has value, so nothing is ever thrown away. Some time ago, Coca-Cola ran an international survey to determine how frequently their bottles were returned for reuse. The United States was at the very bottom, with one and a half returns for every bottle sold. Haiti topped the list. Each bottle capped in Port-au-Prince had an average predicted life span of seventeen returns. And there's even reincarnation: after inevitable breakage the poorest Haitian shoeshine boys carry their polish in the jagged bottoms of broken Coca-Cola bottles.

Haitian beaches are litter free; no discarded aluminum or styrofoam lies along the sides of Haitian roads. Once I watched another tourist toss away the tinfoil wrapper from a stick of gum. A boy of around six imme-diately ran forward to pick it up.

"What do you want with that?" I asked him in my broken French.

The barefoot kid grinned with pure urchin pleasure. "A paper mirror," he said proudly, folding and unfolding his treasure as he walked away, staring at his wrinkled reflection.

AS ONE PRIVILEGED to live in a relatively unsullied part of the country, I find I have to check my temptation to blame the ills of the world on the excesses of modern urban society. Rural Montana boasts its share of abandoned farm machinery and front-yard car gardens. Most of the old ranches sport one or more dumps tucked away in draws and coulees, hidden from view behind sage-covered hills. Although now prohibited by law, many of our stream banks have been riprapped with abandoned automobile carcasses strung along lengths of cable like giant necklaces of junk. I've never gone on a wilderness camping trip when I haven't packed out a cache of rusted cans left behind by earlier sojourners. Everywhere, pastures are overgrazed, forests clear-cut and slashed with roads, streams polluted by thoughtless mining. Montanans are no better at safeguarding their natural heritage than the much-disparaged "dudes" living elsewhere. It's easy to be lulled into a false sense of complacency under that majestic Big Sky, but the Titanic sank just as fast for the first-class passengers as for those in steerage.

"BOB-WIRE WON THE WEST," or so the saying goes. Death by strangulation, I think, whenever I find another spiny strand coiled like some lethal serpent beneath the junipers. Old fences come down, and the wire, as often as not, ends up tossed aside, out of sight, out of mind. A decade ago, when I kept horses, I removed endless barbed wire, replacing it with jack-fence. More of the damned stuff, ancient and rusty, was yanked from under bushes and out of thickets. Mine was not a labor based on aesthetics. If you've ever seen a wire-cut quarter horse, trembling with terror as the flies gather around a bloody foreleg nearly severed at the pastern, you would relegate all barbed wire, along with its inventor, to the far reaches of Dante's hell. There, waiting for all eternity, it would wrap like a thorny constrictor around those doomed for contaminating the natural world with fences, pesticides, chemicals, radioactive waste.

THERE IS NO SUCH thing as ownership. This is not a political statement. The grave is all of the earth we can ever lay claim to. In spite of contracts, titles, and deeds, any sense of possession is but an illusion fostered by our irrational belief in personal immortality. When it comes to death, we all secretly think it only happens to the other guy. The truth is more severe.

For most of my life, I've been a collector. In high school, I haunted the used bookstores crowding Manhattan's lower Fourth Avenue. A passion for reading initially propelled me down into those basement stacks, but I soon discovered that a little bit of searching uncovered Hemingway and

Faulkner first editions for the same two bucks the reprints cost. Thus a collecting habit was born.

I seem to be acquisitive by nature. If I had nothing and lived alone as a hermit on some deserted beach, the available spaces of my driftwood shack would soon be filled with colorful shells and any interesting flotsam that caught my eye along the tide line. For a long time, I harbored a private guilt about such tendencies. They seemed somehow shameful, conjuring up images of Silas Marner greedily hoarding his gold. Now I look at things differently. I know I won't be buried in the manner of an Egyptian pharaoh with all my antique toys and oil paintings and first editions stacked beside me in the tomb. I am merely the custodian of my own eccentric museum. The task is to preserve the past, treasuring what is rare and beautiful, for how else can we hope to ensure that the future is not a wasteland?

THE GRIZZLY BEAR is an indicator species. While the cockroach and the Norway rat may thrive living alongside mankind in his garbage-strewn environment, *Ursus horribilis,* an infinitely more noble creature, requires solitude and the pristine wilderness. Driven from his traditional river-bottom and prairie homeland to the remote fastness of the northern Rockies by ever-increasing human incursion, the grizzly, for all his wisdom and power, is a creature as fragile as the endangered land he inhabits. If there's no more wilderness, the griz is gone as well. It's that simple. More precisely, if civilization forces the grizzly bear from a certain area, it's a sure indication that 250 other species in the same ecosystem will soon follow him on the path to extinction.

Islands are the indicator species for the earth. Our tiny green planet is but another spinning island adrift in the vast reaches of eternal space. Darwin formulated his theory of evolution by observing certain species of lizards and birds found only on the Galapagos Islands off the coast of Ecuador. The dodo, a bird so stupid its name has become a synonym for imbecility, once lived happily on the island of Mauritius in the Indian Ocean. It didn't have an enemy in the world. Then the Dutch arrived in the seventeenth century, with their dogs and their pigs and their own insatiable appetites, and very soon the only thing deader than the door-nail was the dodo. Whether a rocky dot in the middle of the ocean or our own beloved Spaceship Earth, the moral is the same: when things get tough on an island, there's no place left to run.

THE REPUBLIC OF HAITI occupies one-third of the island of Hispaniola in the Caribbean. No more telling litmus informs the hemisphere than this tragic nation. As a French colony formerly known as Saint-Dominique, Haiti was valued more highly by her masters than all of Canada. It was the age of "King Sugar," and the topsoil in fertile Haitian valleys was up to sixteen feet deep. High pine-covered mountains with cool climates were ideal for the cultivation of coffee. France made huge profits through a rapaciously cruel slave program. Sweat, misery, and the sting of the lash eventually gave birth to the only successful slave rebellion in the history of the world.

Under the leadership of Toussaint L'Ouverture, who was to die far from the Caribbean in a dank French prison, and inspired by the brilliant generalship of two other former slaves, Jean Jacques Dessalines and Henri Christophe, the ill-equipped black revolutionary army defeated twenty thousand of Napoleon's crack troops, veterans of the Rhine and the Pyramid campaigns. Yellow fever claimed more victims than the battlefield, including the French commander in chief, the emperor's brother-in-law, General Leclerc. By 1804 the impossible had happened, and Dessalines tore the white center section from the French tricolor and raised a new red-and-blue flag over the Haitian Republic, the second independent nation in the Americas.

For almost two hundred years, the history of the island has veered between high tragedy and the darkest form of opéra bouffe. Proclaiming himself emperor, Dessalines ruled despotically for two years until his assassination. At that time, Haiti was divided in half; Alexandre Pétion, a mulatto revolutionary general and Jeffersonian democrat, took control of the south, while Christophe, crowned King Henri I, reigned as a tyrant in the north. Ironically, it was the north that prospered.

Christophe maintained a monoculture economy, running the great sugar plantations as efficiently as his former French masters. His subjects continued to toil as virtual slaves. The profits funded the construction of Sans Souci, Christophe's magnificent palace, and of the extraordinary mountaintop citadel, La Ferrière, a fortress with stone walls nearly a hundred feet high built at the cost of thousands of lives.

Only a steeply winding, single-track donkey trail leads up to this incredible edifice. Standing on the ramparts, surrounded by huge bronze Napoleonic cannons lying randomly about like the abandoned playthings of a willful giant, you cannot help but think of the platoon of crack Haitian troops that turned, when King Henri wished to impress some visiting foreign dignitary with the discipline of his army, and marched at his command without hesitation, rank after rank, off the edge to their deaths. And when the misty clouds part, you can see all the way across to the harbor of Cap-Haitien, over eroded, barren hills clustered with the thatched roofs of mud-walled huts as humble as any to be found in the far reaches of Africa. Here at your feet lies an entire nation that has marched into the abyss.

Henri Christophe committed suicide in 1820 after a paralyzing stroke left him unable to wield the sort of authority that compelled his loyal subjects to march off cliffs at his whim. The kingdom of the north merged with Pétion's southern republic, where democratic institutions and land reform prevailed. The big estates were broken up and the property divided among the peasantry, each family receiving a small plot. The idea was to make every man self-sufficient. As with so many good intentions, this social experiment sowed the seeds for future environmental disaster.

Pétion's land reform condemned the island to a market-garden economy with no single large cash crop for export. Haiti slid inexorably into endemic poverty. At the same time, the population exploded. Today, nobody knows exactly how many Haitians there are. Estimates vary, with the government offering one set of statistics, the World Health Organization another, and neighboring Dominican Republic (which broke away from Haiti in 1844) yet a higher figure. There could be as many as twelve million—a Malthusian nightmare.

Because Haitian country people cook over charcoal, almost every tree in the nation has been cut down and burned. Piled like tumbleweed along the lone two-lane highway between the capital and Jacmel, pathetic bundles of twigs, all that is left of the once lush forests, await the charcoal kilns. Even the excess limbs of fruit trees are lopped off to feed the cooking fires, leaving the desecrated landscape dotted with surrealistically truncated mango, mammee, soursop, and star apple groves. The precipitous Haitian hills now look as if vast swarms of gargantuan locusts grazed them clean. Massive erosion has washed most of the nation's rich topsoil away into the sea. What was once a fertile paradise has become a wasteland.

"READ ALL ABOUT IT . . ." The signs are not good. Every other headline brings word of fresh disaster: oil spills, radiation leaks, global warming, holes in the ozone layer.

A French adventurer who recently rowed a small boat single-handed across the Pacific reported that not a day went by that he didn't see plastics and other human trash floating in the sea. Scientists have discovered particulate traces of air pollution trapped in the (perhaps-not-so) permanent polar ice cap of Antarctica. Hunters are advised that they may no longer safely eat the ducks they shoot: pesticide residues in the bird's skin and fat have reached toxic levels. And this thirty years after Rachel Carson warned us of these problems in *Silent Spring.* Is nobody listening?

The population of the United States is 5 percent of the world's total, and yet we use 25 percent of the available natural resources. Only a hypocrite would point the finger of blame elsewhere when South American rainforests are being slashed and burned in order to create grazing land to raise the cheap beef we demand for our Big Macs. And who can fault the Third World for craving their fair share of fax machines, CD players, air-inflated running shoes, digital watches, color TVs, microwaves, air conditioners, all-terrain vehicles, and VCRs? We can't tell everybody else that the party is over when we're still unwrapping our presents and loudly blowing the noisemakers. Not when what we throw out as trash is equal to the gross national product of most emerging nations.

There are no easy answers to these enormous problems. Perhaps there are no answers at all. Still the effort must be made even if the task seems hopeless. Out in the backyard is a good place to start. Every time we start a compost pile, or strip and refinish an old oak rocker that some damn fool has painted baby blue, or pull a rusting coil of barbed wire out from under the junipers, we begin to be part of the solution. There really is no other choice. We're all involved in a very subtle form of warfare where the only enemy is us, as that great philosopher Pogo once observed. As the millennium approaches, it's like being on the front lines, hunkered down in the trenches, third man on the match. Got a light?

The Elephants of Tsavo:
The Failure of Stewardship
Patrick Hemingway

ONE OF THE MAIN TASKS OF STEWARDSHIP HAS ALWAYS BEEN THE keeping of records. How do you catch a bad steward? Almost always he has cooked the books. To trip him up you must audit his accounts. What follows is a sort of audit.

There used to be a sign that greeted visitors to the Serengeti: "Everything here is new and fragile. Treat it as such." What rubbish. Africa is old and tough. Today little remains of the iron grip that Britain, France, Germany, and Portugal had at the opening of the twentieth century on its land and people. It is the one continent, with the exception of its extreme northern and southern portions, where man has been forced to live in some sort of balance with the natural world. A temporary victory over one of its major human diseases, malaria, allowed a hundred and thirty years of a thin urban skin of modern industrial society that is now rapidly vanishing under the twin solvents of social chaos and epidemic disease.

Humanity is not perishing in Africa, but modern industrial society certainly is, and along with it, in East Africa at least, one of its most misguided creations, the national park.

Charles Elton, the man who first used the word *ecology*, showed that the cover on travel routes, which allows animals to disperse and move safely throughout a large geographical range, is necessary for their survival. He pointed out that the hedgerows of the traditional English landscape provided that requirement for its birds and small mammals.

The traditional landscape of rural East Africa was similar to England's in its pattern of vegetation cover, but on a scale that allowed not just for birds and small mammals but also for the largest of all land mammals, the elephant. Good agricultural soil in the region tended to occur only in scattered patches, and fertility could only be maintained by shifting cultivation—the natural vegetation was allowed to reestablish itself on a former patch of cultivation for periods of as long as twenty years or more.

Tourists from the developed countries may still enjoy Tsavo, well washed, well fed, well clothed, and traveling comfortably in a minibus, capturing images with their through-the-lens 35-millimeter reflex cameras of the pink elephants of Voi or Bachuma station as those not quite believable survivors from the Pleistocene come in to water for their evening drink and bath. I doubt it though. They have more likely been diverted to other places, smaller and more easily guarded, like Amboseli or the Kenya Mara, where it is still possible to create in the short term the illusion of a vast continent teeming with wild animals, the last stronghold of a vanishing Eden.

Beryl Markham in four chapters of *West with the Night* has described what was going on in what is now Tsavo National Park during the time between the two world wars. Her account is one-sided, though, in that she tells us only of the white hunters and their clients. The black hunter, the real key to the matter, is only mentioned as a tracker for this team. He was not just a part of white men's elephant hunting, "the essence of which is discomfort in such lavish proportions that only the wealthy can afford it," but the most important ingredient in the fifteen-thousand-year-old man and elephant, yin and yang of the Nyika, the thornbush belt that lies inland of the narrow strip of coastal forest and cultivation in eastern equatorial Africa.

Though we will never know for sure, what evidence there is points to the origin of both man and the elephant in Africa, and if man was indeed responsible for the extermination of elephants on the other continents to which both species emigrated, such was not the case in Africa, where both survived together down to the end of World War II. I arrived on the scene seven years later in November of 1952 by what seemed an endless journey by freighter starting in Brooklyn, down to Mobile, Alabama, across to Walvis Bay, around the Cape of Good Hope, and finally disembarking at Mombasa. It took a little time to clear my four-wheel drive jeep pickup, and then I was driving up the road to Nairobi.

Because I was late getting away from Mombasa, I decided to spend the night in Voi, where there was a hotel of that very personal sort usually run by a retired British official and his wife, both with fluent Swahili and good with labor, as the colonial phrase put it. After checking in, in order to pass the hour or so before supper, I followed a dirt track for a few miles into what I later learned was Tsavo Park. There was no gate, no entrance fee, no nothing. I came around a bend and there was an elephant in the middle of the road. It spread its ears, screamed, and started forward. I threw the pickup in reverse and backed as quickly as I could, and he turned and ran away. A little farther on, a small bunch of zebra tore across the road in front of me in a cloud of dust, with a scruffy-maned lion close on their heels. I had probably inadvertently spoiled his chance for a kill. I had already read the famous *Man Eaters of Tsavo* by Colonel Patterson, and it thrilled me to think that the lion I had seen was a direct descendant of the beasts that had become so daring during the construction of the Uganda Railway as to snatch their human prey from the inside of railway carriages where the terrified construction workers had gone for safety. Very happy to be in East Africa, I turned the car around and went back to the hotel, which was smothered in bougainvillea and golden shower vines, its cool cement floors shiny with red wax, its waiters in the dining room very black, tall, and dignified in their red tarbushes, white kanzus, and bare feet.

Although I didn't know it at the time, the antipoaching campaign of Bill Woodley and David Sheldrick had already started to give the elephants around Voi a sense of security and safety within the borders of the new national park, even if there was nothing to show a greenhorn Yank like myself that I really was in a national park and not the "Heart of Darkness."

Three years later, at the end of the long dry season, and after an East African orientation program that had seen me acquire a personal gun bearer, Mumu Hamisi—Mumu's last employer had been Sidney Waller whose old age, decline, and death at Voi had reconciled poor old Mumu to undertake once more the task of showing a young person the ropes, a working knowledge of Swahili, and a bolt-action Cogswell & Harrison

.375 Holland and Holland magnum—I was back at the border of Tsavo Park.

I was sharing a camp with the Percivals, father and son. Young Percival, Dick, was older than I was, an artillery officer who had served in Burma against the Japanese. My dad was very fond of old Mr. Percival. He had used him in part for the character of the white hunter in *The Short Happy Life of Francis Macomber* and as Pop in *The Green Hills of Africa,* but he did not like Richard Percival. I thought I knew why. Dick had come to America on a visit after the war, staying with friends of his father, who had guided on safaris most of the American playboy millionaires of the 1930s. Dick had had a very abrupt introduction to the lifestyle of the rich in Palm Beach. He was changing into a pair of swimming trunks in the pool house, when his hostess walked in and without any sign of embarrassment remarked that Dick was very well equipped. My dad was a long-time, loyal friend of this woman's husband and although he knew very well that she was a bitch, hearing Dick tell the story in his clipped Brit accent annoyed him, as we Americans can be annoyed on occasion by our British cousins and vice versa. A general statement my dad was fond of in such circumstances was that all Englishmen's feet smell. Another was that Britons never will be slaves because they always have been. Luckily for me, he had kept these "home truths" to himself during his second, recently ended long safari with old Mr. Percival.

We were camped at Bachuma station, but that was not where we had started out, some three weeks before. Old Mr. Percival was in his eighties, and he had hunted elephant in the Kenya Nyika since before the first World War. He had served as a mounted scout in the campaign against von Lettow Vorbeck along the Kenya-Tanganyika border and was as familiar with those waterless wastes as any white man could be. We had started our hunt with a good plan based on his knowledge.

First we camped at Maktau, a station on the railway spur that linked Kilimanjaro with the Uganda Railway. Then we moved to Kasigau, an isolated mountain in the middle of the Kenya side of the border. From there we were able to cover all the country almost to the Umba River over in Tanganyika. In all this vast country, we had seen no fresh sign of elephant whatsoever.

We ended up in this final camp, where both the highway and the railroad marked the western boundary of the park and our hunt had been reduced to the simple strategy of driving along a dirt road parallel to the park boundary early every morning to check where elephants had crossed out of the protected area during the night. We would follow these tracks if they were those of big bulls—and most of them were—hoping to catch up with them before they headed back to the place where they were safe in the park.

Our patience was rewarded. After several days I shot the first and biggest elephant of my life, just under a hundred pounds a side, weighed in on the railway scales at Bachuma station. The Percivals had given me the first chance as their guest, and Dick got a second elephant a couple of days later, not as big as mine, but quite respectable.

I enjoyed that camp as much as I've enjoyed any place in my life. Set in a clearing in the thick thornbush on the side of a hill, it overlooked for as far as I could see the vast area we were free to move in at that leisurely pace that is one of the principal charms of hunting a trophy elephant. After the initial outing at first light to try to pick up a good track to follow, if there were none we were free to return to camp to rest, read, and listen to the wonderful stories Mr. P had to tell. All of this was heightened by the certainty that when good tracks did turn up we would have to work like hell to catch up to the big elephant that had made them.

What was so strange was that there were no elephants anywhere in the big block of country open to hunting in the middle of Tsavo Park. That land had been left out of the park because of political considerations, it being too inhabited by people and developed in one way or another to make it practical to apply the national park policy of complete protection of all wildlife.

It has long been a popular belief that elephants have very good memories. Memory is one component of intelligence, and I know from twenty years' observation of elephants in the field that they are very intelligent animals. They belong to that select group of mammals, along with chimpanzees and bottle-nosed dolphins, whose brains have developed to rival our own. Like the bottle-nosed dolphin, the elephant lives in a perceptual environment very different from ours, a world of smells and sounds. Accounts of elephants until very recently often mentioned the rumbling of their stomachs. We know now that these noises, which go on almost continuously in an elephant group, are made in the trunk and are a means of communication similar in purpose to the noises made by bottle-nosed dolphins.

The most startling example of elephant intelligence I ever personally witnessed was two old bulls who had made a pet of a blind cape buffalo cow. Cape buffalo, although they form herds and are social animals, are utterly unable to deal with a handicapped individual. These two elephant bulls had actually modified their feeding and resting behavior to enable their buffalo pet, a cud-chewing ruminant, to lead what was for her a normal life. It was an amazing sight to see one of those old bulls run his trunk affectionately along the back of that blind buffalo cow, just as a duck hunter in the blind might caress the head and back of his Labrador retriever.

During the three years since I had first visited the Tsavo National Park, the Mau Mau Emergency had come and gone. Bill Woodley, the park warden who had initially been put in charge of antipoaching activities there when he was just a teenager, was now a seasoned veteran of antiinsurgency warfare. The situation was in many respects like that in the American West in 1876, when Phil Sheridan decided to end the problem of the Sioux and Northern Cheyenne who had refused to come into the reservations. Men like Custer, Terry, Crook, and Miles, who learned their military trade in the harsh realities of the Civil War, and who had faced the grim task of bringing their own people to heel within a framework of unified government, were not about to have any doubts about doing the same with a native people. Bill Woodley and David Sheldrick knew how to round up the Liangulu and Kamba elephant hunters, whom they saw as a threat to the integrity of the area put under their command, and they did so in short order.

By the time these black hunters had served their terms in jail, in 1958, I had started a small safari firm of my own called Hemfar, after its cable address. All the safari companies, in both Kenya and Tanganyika, had been asked by the Kenya authorities to try to find places in the tourist hunting business for these convicted poachers who had served their time. I got one of the very best to work for me as a tracker and gun bearer. His name was Denge Abajila, and his capture by Woodley's antipoaching team and subsequent imprisonment is described in Denis Holman's book *The Elephant People*. Denge was a very fine young man, utterly without bitterness about his capture and jail sentence. Hunting elephants with him I saw with my own eyes the incredible ability he and the other top Liangulu hunters had in tracking elephants. I have no doubt had he been raised in other circumstances, he would have become as great a physical scientist as Bohr or Schrödinger. After all we only know the ultimate concepts of matter and energy by the tracks they leave.

Holman's account of the Liangulu hunters is what you might expect from a hardworking journalist very much dependent on the Tsavo Park wardens for the information he needed to write his book. The native hunters appear as a semicriminal group of reprobates whose principal motive for killing elephant was to get money in order to buy palm wine and girls and get themselves drunk and laid as often as possible. I don't doubt that their hunting was less pure than some pristine form of hunter–food gathering with all the idealistic overtones of Jean Jacques Rousseau about man being born good and corrupted by society. True, it was tied into a complex web of Asian commerce, but it was something more complicated and indeed more precious than Holman's account would lead someone who had no personal experience of the region and its native peoples to believe.

Human beings have passed through three cultural stages. First were the hunter-food gatherers, then the nomadic pastoralists, and finally the settled farmers. By the time the Old Testament was written, the hunter-food gatherers had been completely forgotten and we hear only of Cain and Abel, but the human mind was created by hunting, not by sheep herding, farming, or shop keeping. What I thought I had a glimpse of in the black hunters of Tsavo was the life that made us what we are. These were men who could make fire, clothing, and weapons from the bush around them, from the plants and animals as they came across them, one-on-one with their environment. Their way of doing things was at least a hundred thousand years old, and it seemed to me they were being snuffed out in an instant. I came to feel as well that this was an ecological disaster.

The area of Tsavo Park, both east and west, was only about a fourth the size of the vast Nyika of southeastern Kenya. In the Nyika, before the park was established and more importantly, made safe, elephants were spread more or less evenly throughout it. The Liangulu saw to that. No place was entirely safe for the elephants in all that huge area. They had to be especially careful of black hunters in using permanent water sites and even temporary ones. They could use them only at night and never too predictably or too often. Their wits were always matched against those of the black hunters. Armed with a sense of smell that could detect a human footprint even a day old, they knew when to take a warning and move on. Never stay any place too long. Never give the black devils who preyed on the good gray people a chance to see a pattern, to make a prediction.

It was a hard life for the gray people and the black people too. They forced each other to the very highest point of fitness, and the twin currents, gray and black, yin and yang, meandered together down through a hundred millennia to the Phoenicians, the Greeks, the Persians, the Arabs, the Portuguese, and finally the British, where they were ending in the blink of an eye, as things often do in our universe.

Elephants are smart. They know where they are safe as well as we do.

They are not capable of short-term increases by higher birth rates or lower death rates. Sudden increases or decreases can only come by immigration and emigration. By 1965, all the elephants of the Kenya Nyika had moved in to join the elephants that were there when the whole thing started. Where there had been one elephant in the park, now there were four. The sustainable yield of food had not increased one bit. The standing bulk of woody perennial vegetation, especially the bark of the larger trees, had always been a safeguard for the elephants of the Nyika in the occasional droughts that were a recurring and natural characteristic of this country. The elephants could use a part of it in drought as emergency food, and the vegetation would recover when the drought broke.

Because of their size, strength, tusks, and trunk, elephants can feed on the entire range of Nyika vegetation from a bunch of grass to the giant baobab trees. I have had a chance to see the vegetation of the Sonoran desert in North America, where the climate is very similar to that of the Kenya Nyika, and although at first glance the two plant formations look very similar, there is one great difference. In the Nyika, the plants grow on a mosaic of soil types which is much more complex than anything that can be found in Arizona, Baja California, or Sonora. Alternating periods of wet and dry climate have sorted the soil particles derived directly from weathering from the rock below into soil chains, the finer-grained soils at the bottom of the drainage profile and the coarser ones at the top, on the ridges. The complex soil mosaic is conservative. Whatever short-term changes may take place in the overlying vegetation, what grows will have to accommodate itself to the soil it is growing on. Starting around 1965, there were some spectacular short-term changes all right.

In ten years, by 1975, the horde of immigrant elephants, completely undisturbed by man in their frantic search for food, had reduced the core area of the park to, in the jargon of plant ecology, the stage of primary succession, the sort of thing you get after a volcanic eruption. I spent an hour one day toward the end of that decade watching a hungry elephant feeding on what was left of the perennial tufted grasses, the darlings of the people who would restore the North American grasslands to their pristine glory. This clever elephant would delicately, like an Asian farmer planting rice, grasp each grass plant by its dry stalks, then curling the tip of the trunk around it, that tip that can take a single peanut from your outstretched hand through the bars at the zoo, pull the whole plant out of the ground. Then he would tap the roots against his tusk to shake the dirt out and shift the whole plant to his mouth, chewing and swallowing the entire plant. This was grazing with a vengeance!

As I drove through areas that had once been almost impenetrable thornbush, the only thing standing were the giant baobabs, dead, stripped of their bark, gnashed and torn by the tusks of elephants until they looked like some strange artifact of an atomic explosion. But this was not an atomic disaster or one of those insidious cases of industrial pollution like the PCBs dumped in the Hudson River or the mercury left in the Swedish forests by the pulp mills at the turn of the century; the soil was still there and its complex and conservative mosaic. Given time, the vegetation might very well reestablish itself in all its original variety and special adaptation. I say "might," for vegetational succession does not always repeat itself any more than history does. What it was not was stewardship. What it really was, I think, was some sort of vast natural experiment of the explosive sort, like throwing gasoline on a carpet on the floor of a large old-fashioned Victorian building, touching a match to the carpet and sitting back and watching the building burn to the ground. Sure the whole thing could be rebuilt, provided the original architectural plans had been kept somewhere in a safe place and someone had made a complete video inventory of the rooms and their contents.

When it was clear that the building really was on fire, a call was put in to the fire department in the form of a research project, funded by the Ford Foundation and directed by Dr. Richard Laws. Dick Laws, whom I got to know very well and who will always have my unqualified admiration and respect, was a very different sort of person than the people who so far had been dealing with the elephants of Tsavo. For one thing, he was a mammologist whose training had been a thorough mixture of theory and practice in understanding and dealing with large mammals in one of the harshest environments in the world, the Antarctic. When he left the Tsavo Research Project, he was named to replace the retiring director of the British Antarctic Survey, Sir Vivian Fuchs. In collaboration with Ian Parker, a very talented young man in the private sector, he had developed an organization in Uganda that could kill, commercially process the meat, hide, and ivory of, and collect scientific data from as many as fifteen elephants a day and keep that pace up for a month at a time without stopping. One month's hard work could produce a valid statistical sample of three hundred elephants of all ages and both sexes that for the first time in human history really clarified the biology of the elephant. I will never forget that phrase of his which I would enter now and then on a form on a clipboard as that incredible team of hardworking competent people, white and black, went about the dirty, bloody, but very efficient work of showing how elephants could be used and studied. The phrase was "motile in seminal fluid." It referred to the behavior of a sperm sample taken from the vas deferens of a freshly shot male elephant and smeared on a glass microscope slide, to which was added a drop of solution taken from the bulbo-urethral glands of the same beast. That solution was full of energy in the form of sugar, and when it hit the sperm they started to thrash if the elephant from which they were taken was sexually mature.

Laws had studied under Marshall at Cambridge, one of the great students of the physiology of reproduction in mammals and one of the fathers of the Pill. Laws was no amateur. He knew his profession and was so hardworking that it was a piece of luck that he had a person like Ian Parker to back him up. Ian was the right stuff, as good as anyone we ever sent to the moon. Completely honest and fearless, he had a way with machines that took your breath away. The first time I saw him in action was at a project he and Laws were doing together upstream from Murchison Falls in Uganda a few years before the Tsavo crisis. He was using an old Piper Pacer on an airstrip he had cleared that ended abruptly at a high bluff above the Nile and too short at the other end in a pile of giant boulders, a kopje, as they call it in Cape Dutch. It was a sight to see him take off, hold the little plane stationary with the breaks as he throttled up to full power, releasing the brakes and tearing down the slope till he shot over the cliff to the river. He would drop suddenly to just above the surface of the water and then gain altitude enough to clear the vegetation fringing the other side of the river. Try it some time. The trick is to do it right on the first try.

The picture of the elephant as it gradually developed from the work of Laws and Parker, most of it done in Uganda, before the Tsavo Research Project began, was in some ways very much like that of humanity. Elephants reach sexual maturity at about the same age we do, and they live about the same period of time. They are capable of having about the same number of children in a lifetime. Socially they are a collection of small, tightly knit matriarchal groups, each headed by a grandmother, her grown-up daughters, and their teenage and dependent children, with the mature males in looser associations of unrelated individuals, some of whom split off and join a matriarchal group when one of its females is ready to breed.

The elephant's social structure was the key to the success of the method Laws and Parker used to collect their samples of elephant populations. Either a fixed-wing light aircraft or a helicopter was used to spot a family group from the air. Once located, the same aircraft drove the elephants into range of the killing team. These three men used NATO .308

automatic rifles equipped with twenty round clips loaded with military-style hard-nosed ammunition. Each team member carried several spare clips in addition to the one in the rifle. The team would kill the matriarch first, aiming only for the brain. The first round of firing would see her almost instantly dead on the ground and the rest of the family group packed tight around her, offering easy targets until the whole family was piled in a heap within a matter of a few minutes. Very quickly the trucks carrying the work crews would come in to skin, dismember, and butcher the carcasses. Nothing was wasted, the method as efficient as a meat-packing plant in Sioux Falls.

It is doubtful that this type of elephant study will ever be done again, especially as it involved killing large numbers of elephants, deliberately wiping out in a matter of minutes whole family groups at a time so as not to spread terror and confusion any further than was necessary, the very opposite of traditional "elephant control," the rather haphazard killing of individual animals, mostly males, in order to "teach the elephants a lesson" when they deliberately took to raiding human crops and cultivation.

The elephants that were killed by the team headed by Laws and Parker had already been condemned to death because the lands they had occupied in the past were being taken over for human use. The only choice was between a relatively quick death, which would at least provide reliable information that would help protect the species in places where humans could tolerate their presence, or an extremely slow and distressful end, being harried from one corner to the next of lands that no longer held a place for them.

Human population growth is the one real threat to the large animals of Africa. It has already virtually eliminated them from the densely populated areas of West and Southern Africa, and no doubt this will eventually be the case in the rest of that continent south of the Sahara. So far the plan to return large areas of the northern Great Plains of the United States back to the buffalo that once roamed there has generated little enthusiasm among the permanent human residents of Nebraska, the Dakotas, Wyoming, and Montana, but the success of such a scheme here at home might point the way for similar schemes in Africa. It is simply not true that hunting, legal or illegal, or the ivory trade, has eliminated elephants from most of their former range in sub-Saharan Africa.

When the Tsavo Research Project started in the late sixties, Laws and Parker had already developed the means in Uganda to reduce elephant populations quickly. Had the authorities in charge of Tsavo ordered them to do so, in two years they could have brought the resident population in the park down to a size which would have prevented the habitat destruction that eventually resulted. There were many reasons why the authorities never gave those orders. One rather silly one was the "Buy an Elephant a Drink" public relations slogan that the Kenya National Parks used in their fund-raising campaign in Europe and America. Before the nature of the immigration crisis was fully understood, many conservationists thought the solution was the creation of more widely spread artificial watering points for the elephant, such as artesian wells and dams. Ian Parker, who had a biting tongue, told me he couldn't see why they just couldn't coin a new slogan: "Buy an Elephant a Bullet." Of course, building artificial watering points to better distribute the elephant population was a sound idea, provided that the surrounding vegetation, which had never been subject to such grazing pressure before, could stand up to the increased use and that the overall stocking rate of elephants in the park was first reduced.

The more serious reason the order to reduce the number of elephants in the park was never given was the breakdown of the relationship between David Sheldrick, the park warden, and Richard Laws, the scientist. Looking back on it after all these years, I think this had something to do with the way most administrators and politicians think of scientists and the way most scientists usually act with people other than scientists. When administrators and scientists start to fight, it is always the scientists, in the short term at least, who lose. They are simply kicked out of the area under the administrators' control and that is that. It reminds me of the story of the Roman admiral who was forced by established religious practice before committing his forces to battle to consult the oracle of the sacred chickens. We shouldn't laugh at this. We also, in our country, require our leader to consult the sacred chickens in Congress before we go to war. Grain was put before these important fowl, and the favorable divination was that the chickens would eat the grain. In this case, they would not eat, and the admiral had them thrown overboard with the remark that "if they will not eat, let us see if they will drink!"

I visited with Dick Laws at his house in Voi when he was packing up to leave, at the headquarters of the research station that the Ford Foundation's money had built on his recommendation. He and his family were very shaken by the treatment he had received from the trustees of the Kenya National Parks, who had followed the recommendations of their senior warden. It was, however, the one check in a brilliant career. After the Falkland Islands war between Great Britain and Argentina, Dr. Laws was given a knighthood for his service to his country.

David Sheldrick in later years was judged by the Kenya parks trustees to have developed a somewhat obsessive relationship with the area he had served so long, and old "Saa Nane" was transferred to another post. He died shortly afterward. His widow, Daphne, who had once won a French literary prize for the book she wrote about the orphaned animals of Tsavo that she had rescued when their mothers had been killed by poachers, chose to stay on as the caretaker of another group of such orphans in what is known as the animal orphanage near the gate of the Nairobi National Park. This institution is a great favorite with the German, French, American, Scandinavian, and Japanese tourists, who come to it in large numbers during winter in the northern hemisphere. As perhaps the last Kenya-born white settler on public display in that country, she is almost as great an attraction as the orphaned animals themselves.

I wish I could give an account of Tsavo and its elephants for the last seventeen years since I left Africa for good in 1975. Most of the elephants I've seen recently on public television have been in every place but Tsavo, mostly in areas next to Tanzania, like the Mara or Amboseli. There has been the occasional story in the papers about tourists being gunned down in southeastern Kenya by gangs of Somali poachers armed with the latest in Russian and American automatic weapons. Are these the same Somalis who did such a good job under the leadership of Woodley and Sheldrick in ridding the park of the poaching menace in the late sixties? Surely not, they would be too old. Their children perhaps. Or are they adventurers who have left their families behind to starve in Mogadishu, wolfish young individualists from the Horn of Africa, where political stewardship has taken a beating lately in a deadly mix of great power rivalry and clan warfare?

At one stage in the rapid disappearance of woody vegetation down the throats of starving elephants in Tsavo, somebody came up with the idea, attributed first to Leibniz and later made fun of by Voltaire in *Candide,* that all was for the best in the best of all possible worlds. What was happening was really a blessing in disguise. The elephants were punching useful holes in the ecosystem, and the disappearance of the woody vegetation would turn Tsavo Park into a grassland paradise for zebra, hartebeest, and other plains game species. The picture of East Africa as a land of rolling plains dotted with flat-topped acacia trees chock full of herds of wildebeest, zebra, lions, and so forth is a media creation going back as far as the turn of the century, when George Eastman, inventor of the Kodak box camera, made the discovery that certain very special areas in Kenya and Tanganyika photographed much better than they looked in real life, like some clotheshorse fashion models. There are only two areas in East Africa that look like the media version: one is the Kapiti Plains just before you get to Nairobi, and the other is the world-famous Serengeti. Both these areas owe their appearance to very special soil conditions that inhibit the growth of trees and shrubs, and the distribution of rainfall is such that the grasses that grow there at least part of the year can support the large herds of grazing animals that the media have led tourists to expect.

The Tsavo Park has no such special soil conditions or distribution of rainfall, and once the elephants had done away with the woody vegetation, the area became a wasteland, even before I left it for good. Gone were the beautiful lesser kudu, the gerenuk, the giraffe, and the dikdik. On the rock-piled kopjes there were no longer any hyrx, the little people who built their houses of rock, nor were there any klipspringer or steinbuck. Just tree stumps, bare ground, and dust, the dust blowing in the wind.

Patagonia:
The Next Hundred Years
Yvon Chouinard

WHEN I WAS A YOUNG MAN MY PASSION WAS CLIMBING MOUNTAINS, and I earned a living working as a blacksmith forging pitons. The only pitons available in the late fifties were from Europe and were made of iron. The theory was that, because the malleable iron was inexpensive and molded well into rock cracks, the pitons could be left in place for the next person.

My pitons were made of aircraft-quality chrome-molybdenum steel and could be driven even into crackless, rotten seams of granite. They could be repeatedly placed and taken out without breaking, and so were instrumental in opening up the multiday routes on Yosemite's El Capitan, where a typical climb took eight or ten days and hundreds of piton placements. In keeping with John Muir's philosophy, I tried to leave as few signs of our being there as was possible, unlike Europeans who left pitons, slings, and cables in place for future parties.

I never intended for my craft to become a business, but every time I returned from the mountains, my head was spinning with ideas for improving the carabiniers, crampons, ice axes, and other tools of climbing. My partner and I seemed to have a gift for good design, and the blacksmith shop soon grew to be a machine shop, and then into Chouinard Equipment Company. Our guiding principle of design was a quote from Antoine de Saint-Exupéry:

> Have you ever thought, not only about the airplane but about whatever man builds, that all of man's industrial efforts, all his computations and calculations, all the nights spent working over draughts and blueprints, invariably culminate in the production of a thing whose sole and guiding principle is the ultimate principle of simplicity?
>
> It is as if there were a natural law which ordained that to achieve this end, to refine the curve of a piece of furniture, or a ship's keel, or the fuselage of an airplane, until gradually it partakes of the elementary purity of the curve of the human breast or shoulder, there must be experimentation of several generations of craftsmen. In anything at all, perfection is finally attained not when there is no longer anything to add, but when there is no longer anything to take away, when a body has been stripped down to its nakedness.[1]

Later on I applied the same philosophy of industrial design, simplicity, and absolute reliability to the making of clothing for climbing when we started a sister company, Patagonia. Designing from the cornerstone of a functional need focused our efforts, and customers appreciated our "hand-forged" Stand Up Shorts®, *cagoules*, and corduroy knickers. As the business grew, Patagonia also became a supplier of clothing for many other outdoor sports, such as white-water kayaking, back-country skiing, fly-fishing, and sailing.

In the late sixties, we began to see that the repeated use of our hardsteel pitons by increasing numbers of climbers was in fact causing a great deal of harm to the rock. Still, we didn't want to democratize the climbs by leaving all the gear in place, so we developed a new way to secure anchors in the rock. These aluminum chocks could be placed in constrictions in the cracks to provide a secure anchor yet could be put in and taken out with just the fingers. Clean climbing became the accepted style throughout most of the climbing world, and Chouinard Equipment Company was the recognized leader in innovative tools for climbing rock, snow, or ice.

In 1978 I wrote a book on ice-climbing techniques. In the last chapter,

I said that ice climbing had become so sophisticated that, with existing tools and techniques, a skilled climber could scale any given slope of snow or ice in the world. To add sport to progress, I wrote, we have to go back. We should start doing away with these tools and replace them with greater skill and courage. I felt that the whole idea of climbing should move away from goal-oriented technology to a place in which personal qualities like creativity, boldness, and technique were supported rather than suppressed by the tools of the trade.

I lost the desire to make ever-more complex tools merely to make climbing safer and easier. I also had increasing difficulty relating to the new indoor sport climbers, who saw climbing as a strictly gymnastic endeavor in which mountains or crags were unnecessary and sticking one's neck out was unacceptable. I began loathing the very equipment I was making, preferring to go out and do easier climbs without gear rather than harder ones with all the gear. Then, as climbing became more and more "mainstream," liability lawsuits began, and I knew finally it was time to get out of the game. The assets of Chouinard Equipment were sold to some of its former employees in a Chapter 11 proceeding, and the company ceased all operations.

Meanwhile, Patagonia was growing at such a rate that in 1991 we calculated that in eleven years it would be a billion-dollar company. We were growing the business by traditional textbook ways: increasing the number of products, adding retail stores, opening more dealers, and developing new foreign markets . . . and we were in serious danger of outgrowing our britches. We had nearly outgrown our natural niche, the specialty outdoor market. Our products were carried in most of the outdoor stores we wanted to be in. To become larger, we would have to begin selling to general clothing and department stores. But this endangered our philosophy. Can a company that wants to make the best-quality outdoor clothing in the world become the size of Nike? Can a three-star French restaurant with ten tables go to fifty tables and retain its three-star rating? Can a village in Vermont encourage tourism (but hope tourists go home on Sunday evening), be pro development, woo high-tech "clean" companies (so the local children won't run off to jobs in New York), and still maintain its quality of life? Can you have it all? I don't think so.

As a society, we've always assumed that growth is both inevitable and positive: "bigger is better," "you grow or you die." When our economies sour, as they inevitably do, we simply look for new technologies, new resources, and new consumers. In America we have always been able to go west whenever we needed more breathing space or more virgin groves of trees to cut or more prairies to till. Now we hunt new export markets and new Third World sources for raw materials. Free trade is replacing the microchip as our new savior. But Third World resources are close to exhaustion, and many world economies, burdened by debt, are no longer viable dumping grounds for our manufactured goods.

When the nineties and the recession arrived and President Bush began asking everyone to spend, the country's response was different. We didn't think spending would get us out of our problems. The government can offer consumer tax "rebates" and give incentives to help ramp up the manufacturing sector, but someone has to want to buy the product.

In Western Europe, and among the trendsetters in the United States and elsewhere, it was clear that many people were no longer interested in shopping as entertainment and no longer were accumulating wealth as a sign of status. Just a few years ago the definition of an upscale family was a television in every room; now, it's no televisions. Movie stars have been seen driving to environmental fund-raisers in Toyotas and taking off their furs and pinky rings before going inside ("stealth wealth"). Maybe everyone got out of bed one day and discovered we were nauseated by the thought of going to the mall and buying more junk we didn't need. Maybe we got tired of being called consumers instead of citizens.

What if this new attitude catches on? What if America, Japan, and France decide that the right thing to do is to reduce consumption? A European only consumes a quarter of what an American does now, so it's entirely plausible that America could realize a big drop in spending habits. Even a 10 or 20 percent reduction would be catastrophic for the economy.

The world's economies are certainly threatened by more than a change in attitude. Most intelligent people around the world have stopped denying that we have enormous problems with overpopulation, pollution, climate changes, and diminishing resources. However, we are still denying that we ourselves are the causes. We say "shame" on those Mexican or Kenyan parents who have eight or ten children, yet our two North American children will, in their lifetimes, consume fifteen times more than the same number of Third World children.

We continue to delude ourselves into thinking that technology is the answer, even though over and over again it's been proven that technology doesn't create jobs, that instead it eliminates them. Technology cures our diseases but doesn't make us healthier; it doesn't even fulfill its promise to free us from our labors and give us more leisure time. All technology has really done is allowed more of us to be temporarily on this earth—perhaps for only a short time longer.

For years I was tormented by the realization that my own company, dependent on the consumer economy, was responsible for making some of this overabundance of goods. Although I'd tried in the past to limit this runaway growth, I'd always failed. So now I was faced with the prospect of owning a billion-dollar company, with thousands of employees making "outdoorlike" clothing for posers. I needed to do some soul searching so I could reconnect to my original philosophy of simplicity and quality.

My wife and I flew to Florida to meet with a business consultant who we hoped would help us with our future planning. Before he could help us plan, he wanted to know the reasons why we were in business. We told him the history of the company, how I considered myself a craftsman who had just happened to grow a successful business. I told him I'd always had a dream that, when I had enough money, I'd sail off to the South Seas looking for the perfect wave and the ultimate bonefish flat. We told him the reason we hadn't sold out was that we were pessimistic about the fate of the world and felt a responsibility to do something about it. We told him about our tithing program, how we gave away a million dollars in the last year to over two hundred individuals and organizations, mostly in the environmental field, and that our bottom-line reason for staying in business was to make money that we could give to such causes.

The consultant thought for awhile and then said, "Oh I think that's bullshit. If you're really serious about giving money away, you would sell the company for a hundred million or so, keep a couple of million for yourselves, and put the rest in a foundation. That way you could give six or eight million away every year, and if you sold it to the right buyer, they would probably continue tithing as well because it's good advertising."

Needless to say, my wife and I were rattled. It was as if a Zen master had hit us over the head with a stick. But instead of finding sudden enlightenment, we were shocked and confused. Only after several months of soul searching did we realize that once again we had fallen into the trap of thinking about the result and not the process. A million or ten million dollars a year won't go far toward solving the world's problems; however (back to the Zen lesson), if you want to change government, change the corporations, and government will follow. If you want to change corporations, change the consumers. Perhaps the real good that Patagonia could do was to use the company as a tool for social change, as a model to show other companies that a company can do well by taking the long view and doing the right thing.

I have a little different definition of evil than most people. When you have the opportunity and the ability to do good and you do nothing, that's evil. Evil doesn't always have to be an overt act, it can be merely the absence of good.

I've always believed that the key to government doing the right thing is that it base its planning and decisions on the intention that the society will be around for a hundred years. The Iroquois nations extended their planning out even further, seven generations into the future. If our government acted this way, it would not clear-cut the last of the old-growth forests or build dams that silt up in twenty years. It would not encourage its citizens to have more children just because doing so results in more consumers. My wife and I realized that if we really believed in the rightness of such planning, then Patagonia as a company must walk what it talked.

When I think of stewardship or sustainability, I think back to when I was a G.I. in Korea and saw the farmers pouring night soil on their rice paddies, which had been in continuous use for over three thousand years. Each generation of farmers assumes responsibility for seeing that they leave the land in better condition than when they took possession of it. Contrast this approach with that of modern agri-business, which wastes a bushel of topsoil to grow one bushel of corn and pumps groundwater at a rate 25 percent faster than it's being replenished.

A responsible government encourages farmers to be good stewards of the land and to practice sustainable agriculture. But why should only the farmer or the fisherman or the forester have the responsibility to see that the earth remains habitable for future generations of humans and other wild things?

We label our governments evil, yet a society gets the government it deserves. As we deny that as individuals we are the cause of our problems, we also deny that we are the solutions. No one wants to be the first to take the "hit." It won't be the timber worker who refuses to cut another old-growth cedar, or the real estate broker who votes to put a moratorium on development in his town, or the young couple that chooses to have only one child. So where do we begin?

Doing risk sports for most of my life has taught me one very important lesson: never exceed your limits. You strive, you push the "envelope," and you live for those moments when you're right on the edge, but you

never go over. We must be true to ourselves; we must know our strengths
and our limitations and live below our means. I decided to try to simplify
my own life, reduce my consumption of material goods, eat lower on the
food chain, and work toward mitigating the damage I was causing to the
earth. This was a start. But I also realized that if Patagonia tried to be
what it is not, if it tried to "have it all," it would die. In the clothing field,
the fastest-growing companies usually have the shortest life spans. Patagonia was over the "edge," and in order to take it back to the size it
should be, we had to downsize. We started by laying off 20 percent of our
employees and cutting back on projects worldwide. We also made a commitment to only grow at such a rate that we would still be here a hundred
years from now.

The American Dream is to own your own business, grow it as quickly
as you can until you can cash out, and retire to the golf courses of Leisure
World. The business itself is the product. Long-term capital investments
in employee training, on-site child care, pollution controls, and pleasant
working facilities are all just negatives on the short-term ledger. When
the company becomes the fatted calf, it's sold for a profit and its resources
and holdings are often ravaged and broken apart, disrupting family ties
and jeopardizing the long-term health of local economies. The notion of
a business as a disposable entity carries over to all other elements of society. As we at Patagonia strive to make a sustainable product (hoping to
make a sustainable business for a sustainable planet), we find disposabil-
ity to be our greatest nemesis.

When you get away from the idea that a company is a product to be
sold to the highest bidder in the shortest amount of time, all future decisions of the company are affected. The owners and its officers see that
since the company will outlive them, they have responsibilities beyond
the bottom line. Perhaps they will even see themselves as stewards—pro-
tectors of the corporate culture, the assets, and, of course, the employees.
A corporation is only an empty legal shield without its people. A company that intends to be around for a long time must live within its
resources, care for its people, and do everything it can to satisfy its community of customers. No business can be done on a dead planet. A company that is taking the long view must accept that it has an obligation to
minimize its impact on the natural environment.

As we reassessed our operation, we realized that all of Patagonia's
facilities should be involved in recycling and composting and have edible
landscaping, low-energy-use power, and insulation. We should use re-

cycled paper everywhere, even in our catalogs, encourage ride sharing, eliminate paper cups, and so forth. Could we go further? Absolutely. In Denmark it's illegal to sell nonrefillable pens. So should we eliminate all packaging. We would have to to get away from buying cotton from Egypt, shipping it to Japan to be made into fabric, then to Jamaica to be sewn, then to California to be warehoused, and then to stores in New York. We needed to move toward local economies.

At the same time that we were making these long-term plans, we began an environmental audit to investigate the impact of the clothing we make. The results are still preliminary, but to no one's surprise the news was bad. Everything we make pollutes. Synthetics like polyester and nylon, because they are made from petroleum, are obvious villains, but cotton and wool are no better. To kill the boll weevil and other insects, cotton is sprayed with pesticides so poisonous they gradually render cotton fields barren; toxic defoliants are used to permit mechanical picking. Cotton fabric is often treated with formaldehyde and various resins that control shrinkage and make it "stay press." Wool relies on flocks of sheep and goats that often denude environmentally fragile land.

"Sustainable manufacturing" is an oxymoron. It's nearly impossible to manufacture something without using more material and energy than results in the final product. For instance, in modern agriculture it takes three thousand calories of fossil fuel to produce a net of one thousand calories of food. To make and deliver a 100 percent cotton shirt requires as much as five gallons of petroleum. The average so-called 100 percent cotton product is only 73 percent cotton fiber, the rest being chemicals and resins.

Other than shutting the doors and giving up, what Patagonia can do is to constantly assess what we are doing. With education comes choices, and we can continue to work toward reducing the damage we do. In this process, we will face tough questions that have no clear-cut answers. What good does it do to make an organically grown T-shirt if the price is so high that no one buys it except rich people who just add it to their ongoing disposable clothes collections? Should we add a bit of synthetic fiber in a cotton fabric if it makes a pair of pants last twice as long? Which is better to use, toxic chemical dyes or natural dyes that are less colorfast and will fade?

In the final analysis, we have concluded that the key word that lets us out of this "no exit" dilemma is *quality*. The most responsible thing we can do is to make each product as well as we know how so it lasts as long as possible. So we build clothes that don't shrink and don't need dry cleaning or ironing, that have nonbreakable, lock-stitched buttons and heavy-duty thread and stitching.

Quality is not only about how long a button stays on a shirt. It's also a whole way of doing business. For example, two years ago there were 375 items in the Patagonia line. Today we are doing the same amount of business with only 280. Next year there should be even less. Our goal is to offer only viable, excellent products that are as multifunctional as possible so a customer can consume less but consume better. A ski jacket should work perfectly well for all disciplines of skiing, but it doesn't have to look like a ski jacket. You should be able to wear it on a sailboat or in a winter rainstorm in Paris. We shouldn't build in obsolescence. If the fashion this year is paisley shirts with five-inch collar points, we shouldn't make them, because the customer will just throw them away in a year when the fashion changes. If we use high-tech materials for a more durable and functional product, we fully weigh their benefits compared with the total cost to the environment. Our environmental assessment program is not only the responsibility of the environmental desk, it is to be a part of every position in the company. Our catalog is not sent to anyone who hasn't requested it, and we respect the privacy of our customers by not selling our mailing list to other mail-order companies.

We plan to be a long-lived company, and as such we try to be good neighbors. We try to make our facilities and retail stores architectural "gifts" to the neighborhood. Whenever possible we restore older buildings rather than build new ones.

At Patagonia, employee benefits are not given as part of the company's responsibility to take care of its employees from cradle to grave, but rather, each benefit is chosen because it is mutually beneficial and makes good business sense. For instance, child care is provided because women should have every opportunity to succeed and because it makes sense to not lose these valuable people when they decide to have children.

A stable-growth company is forced to primarily hire from within. Since there is less upward mobility, there should be more horizontal movement. This means spending as much money on employee education as on research or promotion.

The "corporate culture" at Patagonia reflects who we are, and we guard that culture zealously. We need to seek out and hire "dirt bags"; these are the passionate outdoor people who are our core customers. We believe that it is easier to teach these people business than to turn a businessman into a passionate outdoor person. When the surf's up, you go surfing; you don't plan to go next Tuesday at two o'clock. Why should you care what hours your employees keep as long as the work gets done?

Even after doing this we will still be polluters. So we take at least 1 percent of our total sales and use it to protect and restore our natural environment. This is our voluntary "Earth Tax." Accepting a leadership role is not something we take lightly at Patagonia. When you choose to be a publicly visible company, everyone is aware of your successes and failures. We hope someday to be an example that other companies will follow, and we continue to strive to be that example.

On my desk is an oval box made of cherry wood that was shaped to fit a curved last, then finished with copper nails. The box was designed by the Shakers, who designed furniture and household goods to fit their philosophy of simplicity and sharing: that the path toward life's meaning is more clear if you get the clutter out of the way.

Technocrats tell us we can't go backward, we can't refuse technology, because then we won't progress. We are told that life is increasingly complex, that's the way it is, and that a company must keep growing otherwise it will die. If this is all true, then we are doomed.

Going back to a simpler life based on living by sufficiency rather than excess is not a step backward; rather, returning to a simpler way allows us to regain our dignity, puts us in touch with the land, and makes us value human contact again. This direction is as pleasing to the soul as the lines of my Shaker box are pleasing to the eye.

1. Antoine De Saint-Exupéry, *Wind, Sand and Stars* (New York: Harcourt Brace Jovanovich, 1968), 41–42.

The Day Lee Brodsky Died
John Nichols

I WAS SITTING IN THE CAFÉ HAVING BREAKFAST, WHEN BARBARA arrived and sat down at the table across from me. She was flushed, and her hair was a bit more tangled than usual.

"Did you hear who died last night?" she said, and I shook my head, no I had not.

"Lee Brodsky," she said. "He just died in his sleep. Isn't that sad?"

What I usually wind up saying when somebody gives me that kind of news is, "I just saw him in the post office yesterday, or maybe a couple of days ago."

Barbara got up and went over to the counter to order. She said, "So we all better be nice to each other, because you just never know."

I recalled, "He was always smoking cigarettes. He never took much care of himself, did he?"

Lee Brodsky ran one of the bookstores in town. It was a nice little shop. I didn't go in there too often, but I patronized it enough. I liked chatting with Lee, a big guy who wore thick glasses. Though physically clumsy, he had an acerbic wit. I remembered his ex-wife, but after the divorce, she and the children left town. That was a while ago.

Barbara returned to her table. "He'd just had a pacemaker installed," she remarked glumly.

I smiled and said, "I guess it didn't work so hot, did it?"

Barbara shook her head and gave me a rueful grin. She looked melancholy and rather beautiful. I folded my newspaper and put it in my knapsack, added the mail I had finished reading, and paid at the counter. Outside, I got on my bicycle and pedaled home, thinking about Lee Brodsky all the way. Already, I had decided to take the day off. Put simply, I guess my reasoning was: life's too short.

I continued thinking about Lee as I made sandwiches and put a few lite beers and some ice cubes in my cooler. I remembered his computer, which had never functioned properly at the store. It took forever to buy a book because Lee was always futzing with inventory stats that rarely came up correctly on the screen. I always teased him about it, and he took my ribbing in stride.

I carried a shotgun and the edibles out to my truck, then returned for the canteen, a box of 16-gauge shells, and a couple of topo maps that were folded up and pretty worn. A few minutes later I was headed south on the main highway to Ranchos, where I turned east toward the mountains, my excitement growing, feeling free.

I don't get very emotional when friends or acquaintances die. I expect it. To me, death has become an intimate and normal part of life, and I don't consider it a tragedy. I've had a bad heart for a long time, and over the years I have learned to respect my own mortality. But I like the natural cycles. I think we often cling to life in an unseemly manner. Perhaps when I'm up against the wall, I'll go down on my knees, begging for another month, more years, a few added decades. And maybe I'll finagle expert medical care to prolong my days; nobody knows the future. But for the moment, I regard death as an honorable conclusion, and I don't fear it much.

The day was sunny, bland, with vibrant blue skies but no wind—not my favorite mood. I like real, raggedy-ass weather, rife with ominous clouds, rain, wind, hail, and snowflakes. The autumn world, radiant in dampness, makes me gloat.

Leaving the highway, I rattled up a dirt road alongside the Little Rio Grande. An old green truck approaching from the other direction slowed down and stopped. Behind the wheel was my old friend Bobby. Beside him sat his buddy Raoul, sucking on a Bud. Their truck was loaded with vigas. Bobby is a stone alcoholic, but I like him a lot. He once stabbed a guy in a bar fight, and I gave the judge a character reference letter. Bobby is killing himself, but he sure works hard. He has a wonderful garden—corn, squash, cucumbers, and *habas* galore. He can wield a shovel all day in the hot sun, cleaning our irrigation ditch. Long ago he smacked his wife around, so she left him and took the kid. His face is puffy and sour from booze, his eyes are bloodshot. But he is usually chipper and always kidding around. His energy is skewed, outlaw, intriguing.

We shmoozed a couple of minutes, half-English, half-Spanish. They had cut their logs up at Cerro Vista and didn't see any grouse. Bobby offered a beer, but I declined. I had my own, and anyway, I never drink before hunting.

He reached out the window, gave me the bro handshake, and we both moved on.

I miss Bobby. Before I got divorced and moved out of the old neighborhood, our paths crossed from time to time. We traded gossip. A couple of winters ago I bought wood from him. His mom and dad are good friends.

I shifted into first for the climb up to the meadows at Turkey Park. Off to the left at the summit sat a truck, an Airstream trailer, a couple of canvas tents, two visible ATVs, and a half dozen blue-tick hounds milling around. One of the chunky visitors waved, and I guess I waved back. Bear hunters. I don't much like them. Not for moral reasons, understand, I just don't cotton to their style, I dislike their attitude, I'm appalled by their methods. Yes, I hunt too, though I'd never touch a bear—or any big animal, for that matter. I go after grouse and, occasionally, doves. Also I fish. That's the extent of it. For the most part, I do these things alone. To me, hunting is a private affair.

Five miles beyond Turkey Park, I pulled over at the mouth of Saloz Canyon. Down by the creek stood another trailer with nobody around. I started walking at 1:00 P.M., climbed over a couple of bulldozed humps blocking the road, and proceeded a ways above the creek. A dozen grasshoppers jumped up and hovered, crackling in the air. I marched right through them, smiling. Truth to tell, my feet felt weightless, I was almost dancing.

The instant I begin leaving civilization, my mood changes. Call it corny, but I'm happy. I travel light. I carry the shotgun, and a canteen, ten extra shells, and a sweatshirt in my backpack, that's all. I feel lithe and secretive and expert at my trade, almost a professional.

I crossed the little river by hopping gracefully from stone to stone—me and Edward Villella! I could smell mint and paused to pluck a couple of leaves. I sniffed deeply, popped them into my mouth, and chewed. Two trout scooted under a rotten log. Blue darning needles were everywhere.

A quarter mile south my curiosity really kicked in; time to investigate a new place. I stopped at a patch of raspberries intermingled with tall elephant weeds smashed askew. Few ripe berries remained on the bushes. Something had stripped off the fruit—my friend, the bear.

Proximity to wildness always makes me tingle. I could imagine that big brown hulk scraping its claws through those succulent brambles.

The slope down to the river was pretty steep, so I traversed it with care, then jumped across the water and climbed the opposite hill along a feeder creek. On the map this trickle had no name, so I gave it one: Ursus Creek. The altitude lines were real tight, a steep climb. I figured that up a ways I would bump into old logging roads, I always do. Usually, I don't have to bushwhack very far.

Game trails take you anywhere. Yours truly (AKA Natty Bumppo) found a good one and followed the cookie crumbs: an endless supply of fresh elk droppings. Every now and then I halted and listened. Maybe I would hear an elk bugle. But it was a little too early for the rut, I guess. I know next to nothing about elk even though I bump into them on almost every outing.

Again I opened the map and studied the lines. I love doing that, transposing from the printed page to a three-dimensional forest around me. I adjusted my angle of ascent. My heart was pounding. I had been off the pills for almost a year but felt pretty confident. Still, the ticker was really chugging along at a hyper pace. An aspirin a day keeps my blood thin and is all that stands between me and a stroke.

When I spotted a faded red ribbon tied to a branch in the middle of nowhere, I flinched. Man, I hate those ribbons. I don't know the codes, but some of them are tied by archeological survey teams who go through prior to a timber sale. There are yellow ribbons, blue ones, pink and red. Occasionally, they are put there by guys who tramp about searching for goshawk nests or spotted owls. But usually what those tags mean is log-ging and the holocaust left in its wake.

But not here. Moss lay underfoot, also kinnikinnik rich with red berries, scrub oak leaves, ponderosa cones, holly. Or maybe it wasn't holly, but rather barberry. I'm no expert, and even though I have traveled this country with guidebooks in hand, I often forget.

I veered up a steep rise, on top of which, according to the map, was a plateau. And sure enough, the ground leveled off. As it did, directly in front of me lay a bear cave. A big hole was tunneled out underneath a mammoth slab of rock. I leaned over and peered inside the den. There wasn't much sign around the entrance. Apparently, nothing had used it during the summer.

The area was scuffed from elk passing through. I found a bright blue Steller's jay feather and stuck it under the strap at the back of my cap. My pounding heart took a long while to quiet down, but it stayed in rhythm, which is all I can ask. Impatiently, I took a sip of water. I don't like to drink in the mountains, but I'm told you are supposed to. It seems you can get seriously dehydrated without ever feeling it.

Once in motion, I don't like to stop until dark. Usually, you have to walk a ton of miles to find grouse. I like that. And the motion alone—always moving—translates into an almost trancelike endeavor.

Another steep incline began west of the cave. But the forest floor wasn't too cluttered. I move slowly over good terrain or bad, marching through the woods like a little old man. Once I am warmed up, however, I can hike for hours. Today, I had started around eighty-five hundred feet; by now I was up to ten thousand.

Finally, I reached an old logging road probably dating back to the 1920s. For decades, most roads like it in the high country have been closed off to vehicles. And what do you know—ho!—directly in front of me stood a huge pile of fresh bear shit. I let out a whoop 'cause it gave me a thrill. Made me a trifle nervous, too. And it was full of raspberry seeds.

I walked south but hit a dead end immediately. So I found a game trail and followed the elk droppings. I also spotted a few white nubs from a grouse, which perked me up. I pinched them, but they were dry and old.

A surveyor's stake almost tripped me. Like a good monkey-wrencher, I tugged it out of the ground and flung it off a ways . . . with a tip of the hat to Ed Abbey, that bawdy old curmudgeon who's gone to his just reward. Those things piss me off—the stakes. Humanity should leave my forest alone!

I located another road. Down the center of it marched ten- to twenty-foot-tall aspen saplings, almost all of them bent or broken over between five and eight feet high by elk cleaning their antlers before the rut. My feet squashed gopher mounds crisscrossing the road. A stump was torn apart and scattered every which way.

The signs of nature's creatures mucking about always make me chuckle.

I descended through a mature aspen grove to Jaroso Creek, which is not even two feet wide. But it's pretty, all slate-colored stones and a padding of vitriolic-green moss. In small pools, aspen leaves floated. I found the breast feather of a grouse and some coyote scat.

Whenever I locate fresh leavings, I always stop and look around, as if the perpetrator is going to be waiting right there for me to gawk at. Fat chance, I know, but I cannot help it. I once saw a fox, and I have spotted coyotes. A friend of mine ran into a bobcat. Someday I know I'll surprise a mountain lion.

A raven squawked and I glanced up: two large black birds glided over, aiming west. In all the feathered kingdom, ravens most suit me to a T. Why? Because I identify.

That's why.

A chickadee called. Some juncos twittered while flitting about in a small spruce. A red squirrel started scolding; another chattered back. I plucked a couple of bright-red thimbleberries and ate them. Kind of tart, not as tasty as raspberries, but okay.

Next, I popped fat rosehips into my mouth and chewed off the meat from around the pits. The world's best source of vitamin C, I have been told.

Hey, I could live off the land *easy!*

In due course I traveled a road rich in clover, which the grouse adore. Then I waded through thimbleberry and stretches of yarrow blossoming an almost iridescent white. I am a connoisseur of light. Ahead of me, then, I spotted something odd in a sapling beside the road and halted.

A small porcupine had climbed five feet up the tree. It was just sitting there, contemplating its navel, or maybe taking a nap. I spoke without getting a reaction. The animal had no quills; its backside was a dark concave bowl. I wondered if it had shed the quills, or if perhaps they hadn't grown in yet. Maybe it had lost them to an attacker.

Putting my face about ten inches from the porcupine's wizened little snout, I said, "Yo, what's your name? And what are you doing out here in broad daylight?"

That triggered some action. The pudgy beast climbed higher. But the tree was so frail it bent over, and pretty soon the porcupine presented a ridiculous sight, almost touching the ground.

"Good-bye," I said and sashayed obnoxiously away. Every small confrontation in the forest is an adventure that lifts my spirits.

A hundred yards farther along, I came across that porcupine's baby sister. She was sitting in the middle of the road, immobile. Same deal, no quills. She was up on her haunches, front paws tucked under her chin as if silently praying. I spoke my usual insouciant rap and finally prodded her a bit, but she did not want to move. She seemed groggy and was obviously hunkered down for the duration. So, still in my St. Francis mode, I bid adieu and continued hunting.

There's a fork where the canyon splits, and thimbleberry is everywhere, a thick golden russet carpet. I wondered why the leaves here had turned so early when a mile to the west they were still green. Just another mystery. I paused to admire a mountain ash sporting clusters of almost Day-Glo bright-yellow berries.

Why hadn't I brought the camera?

In one area, seeps abound along the road, and you wind up wading through a miniswamp. I tried to walk on clumps of grass, spongy hummocks, but my sneakers were quickly soaked. Willow stands higher than my head almost blocked off the road, and broad-leafed cow parsnips were abundant. Many of them had dry seed heads. When I grabbed the stalks and shook, beige seeds flew off in all directions—whoosh!

Soon enough, the path dried out. A thin line of aspen saplings took over the middle line. I traipsed through a profusion of purple and yellow asters, then everything was gone except for pine needles, a few wild strawberry plants, and low-lying geraniums.

By 6:15 I had turned up another canyon, circling northeasterly, beginning to head back. I was rambling at ten thousand five-hundred feet, but ready to descend. It was growing darker. I stopped because a tiny green hummingbird sat on the tip of a dead branch jutting up off a large tree lying across the path. We stared at each other. I hate to anthropomorphize, but I do it all the time anyway.

"Hello, hummingbird."

It buzzed down off the branch and began feeding at Indian paintbrush blossoms around my legs. It flew at about knee level, wings almost touching me or the gun barrel. I remained perfectly still as the bird sucked nectar from about ten bright orange flowers, then zipped up the road, out of sight.

Yes, I laughed in delight!

Below me was another seep, stubby willows, a few alders. I took a couple of steps and flushed a grouse, fired without aiming, and killed it. *Wow!* Usually, I miss. Then quickly I got hold of myself, replaced the spent shell, and waited to see if another grouse would jump. When nothing happened, I walked forward cautiously, picked up the bird, and slipped it into my knapsack.

At such moments I fight a battle with my emotions. I am incredulous, also triumphant. But I do not wish to be unseemly. I have a code about dignity. Too, I always feel guilty. I am uncomfortable with the fact that I like to kill. Of course, I would never touch the hummingbird or a porcupine, and I revere all living things. Yet I accept this blood sport as an important ritual that enhances my well-being. Still, no justification ever truly absolves me or eliminates the ambivalence.

It was almost dark. Suddenly I realized I was dog tired. A blister on my left foot ached. The fatigue was so great I had an urge to weep, but the tears would have been for joy. I love that kind of exhaustion.

I sat on a log and sipped water while looking around, deliberately taking note, savoring. There were spruce trees and tall firs and plenty of aspens. All leaves were gleaming. A breeze rustled through, a squirrel chattered. I heard wings overhead but was too pooped to look up. Probably jays or Clark's nutcrackers or a flicker.

At the bottom of the canyon I proceeded north along the river. In a meadow, slogging through high grass and mucky water, I almost stepped on a wren. Typically, the small bird popped out almost from underneath my foot. At that exact moment, a hawk cried and flapped off a treetop, crossing the open meadow. It was silhouetted briefly against the dark sky, but I couldn't identify it for sure. Large, a buteo, probably a redtail—gone.

I took a deep breath and said, "Thanks, Lee."

Then I jumped a deer and almost shit a cupcake! It bounded from high grass and alders to my left, leaped across the path, and went up a steep hillside, crashing through oak and snapping rotten aspen branches on slim trunks lying across the terrain. I heard the hoofbeats and breaking twigs long after the doe had disappeared.

I reached the truck at 7:30, almost dark. Dogs were yapping down by the creek where I had seen the trailer, and a radio played rock and roll. The intrusion was irritating. Above the trees along the opposite ridge hung a half moon surrounded by a fuzz of cloud. Maybe rain tomorrow—?

I popped open a beer, unwrapped a sandwich, but did not dawdle. I wanted out of there, turned around, hit the old rodeo. Vermillion sunset clouds lit up the sky, then the color faded. Odd diminutive birds fluttered back and forth through my headlights. They seemed wounded, delicate, mysterious.

Ten minutes farther down the road, I stopped at my favorite beaver pond for one of my favorite rituals. The moon was reflected, still rising. Some bird clucked. I killed the engine and listened to the tranquility. Concentric circles appeared on the water whenever a trout touched the surface. Gratefully, I let the scene play out for about ten minutes, then moved on.

When I reached the highway, I clicked on the radio and tuned it to a Duke's baseball game, and opened another beer. Top of the fifth, the Duke's were ahead, but then the Las Vegas Stars scored a run. "C'mon, Dukes!" The play-by-play was almost drowned out by static.

At home, exquisitely pooped, I sat in front of the TV plucking the grouse while John McEnroe won a tennis match. I stripped the feathers into a shopping bag and found one hippoboscid fly, an odd, flat, green parasite that zips about with an oily silverfish motion. After the bird was cleaned, wrapped, and stashed in the freezer, I went outside and sat on my rear stoop and thought about things, feeling dreamy and lazy and content. The moon was up there, high above my woodpile. I listened to all the usual serene village noises: a dog barking, a far siren, a door closing. A faint wind rustled in silvertip poplar leaves.

Well, it is true: I rarely weep for the dead. Instead, I bless them for how intrinsically they focus in my heart all life, urging me to rejoice.

A Modest Proposal: The Sequel
Robert F. Jones

There was a time when meadow, grove and stream,
The earth, and every common sight,
To me did seem
Appareled in celestial light,
The glory and the freshness of a dream.
It is not now as it hath been of yore;—
Turn whereso'er I may,
By night or day,
The things which I have seen I now can see no more.
    —William Wordsworth, "Intimations of Immortality"

I TRAVEL A LOT TO THE WILDER CORNERS OF THE WORLD. OR PERHAPS
I should say, to what once were its wilder corners. They are wild no more.
Turn whereso'er I may—from East Africa to Central America, from my

home in Vermont to the Rocky Mountains or the once-verdant islands of the North Pacific coast—meadows are disappearing under asphalt or the plow, groves topple to the unmuffled yowl of chain saws, and crystalline streams, where not too long ago I fished alone (for silver trout and brighter dreams), now run dark with eroded, clear-cut earth, glistening here or there with evanescent tendrils of diesel oil. The most common sight on this fin de siècle planet of ours, to me and many others who have loved it in all its wild, fresh, glorious diversity, seems to be ruin. You can bet on it: the things we have seen we now can see no more. As Joni Mitchell observed: "Don't it always seem to go that you don't know what you've got till it's gone? They paved paradise, put up a parking lot."

But it's too easy merely to lament these losses, even to write odes or lyrics about them, and thus feel righteous for being on nature's side. The problem is graver than that. Scientists believe there have been five "major extinction spasms" on the planet over the course of the 3.5 billion years since life began. These great setbacks to evolution, one of which (at the end of the Paleozoic era some 245 million years ago) wiped out 96 percent of the earth's sea-dwelling species along with the dinosaurs that dominated the land, were caused by natural phenomena: meteor impacts and/or climate changes. Edward O. Wilson, the Pulitzer-prize-winning Harvard scientist who is one of the world's leading authorities on everything from the lives of the ants to the death of nature, believes we are now in the midst of the sixth such spasm—this one attributable entirely to man. In *The Diversity of Life* (Cambridge, Mass.: Harvard University Press, 1992), Wilson describes how human population pressures, particularly in the developing nations of the so-called Third World, are destroying other species of life at a disastrous rate. Human beings are literally overwhelming nature. By the year 2020—less than a human generation from now—no fewer than 20 percent of the earth's existing species of plants and animals will be extinct, by Wilson's *conservative* estimate.

No one knows with anything like certainty just how many species—from microbes and molds through insects and flowers to eagles and elephants and whales—there are on our once-green and rich planet. Estimates range from ten to thirty million to as high as a hundred million. Tropical forests contain more than half of the species of life on earth, and already half of those fecund woodlands have been cut down for human use. Exotic hardwoods have been harvested to panel posh homes and offices from Tokyo to Manhattan to Oslo. The grain fields and grazing lands that replace the forests will erode in a generation or two, leaving bare lifeless bedrock. By 2020, even the half of the woodlands that remains—some eight million square kilometers—will be cut in half again, or perhaps by as much as 90 percent. Wilson estimates conservatively that because of this runaway destruction of the earth's tropical forests, the planet is losing twenty-seven thousand species a year: seventy four a day, or a little more than three species an hour (even while we sleep).

And extinction is forever.

Humankind is clearly the cause of this disaster. As Wilson notes: "Human beings—mammals of the 50 kilogram weight class and members of a group, the primates, otherwise noted for scarcity—have become a hundred times more numerous than any other land animal of comparable size in the history of life. By every conceivable measure, humanity is ecologically abnormal."

When I was born in 1934, the population of the United States was about 123 million; of the earth, just over 2 billion. In 1992, as I write this, those numbers have increased to 245 million and 5.4 billion, respectively. By the year 2000, demographers project figures of 268 million and more than 6 billion, and by 2025—when nearly all of the environmental damage will have been done (we should live so long!)—the United States will contain nearly 313 million human beings, while the planet sags under the weight of more than 8 billion. By 2050, only two generations down the road, the world total could reach 15 billion. Too many fucking people.

If things are bad now—not just in terms of waning biodiversity but in the rapidly eroding quality of human existence itself—they will only get worse in the years ahead. The conditions of life we associate with the developing nations of Africa, Latin America, and south Asia—famine, overcrowding, lawlessness, pestilence, corruption, and brutality—will almost inevitably become part of our own lives. Visionary artists in various media have already given us glimpses, as through a glass darkly, of what the future might hold if we continue to proliferate as wantonly as we are right now: in books like Aldous Huxley's *Brave New World*, George Orwell's *1984*, and Russell Hoban's *Riddley Walker* and, more viscerally, through the busy, nightmarish scenes of such films as *Blade Runner*, *Brazil*, and *The Terminator*.

Ironically, it is the well-meaning philosophy of humanism that has led us to this sorry pass. By placing man at the center of the universe and by bending every technological and scientific effort, especially in the realm of medicine, to the end of prolonging individual human lives, humanism and its works have ensured our domination of the planet and all the millions of other creatures on it. Yet even as we blithely, mindlessly, inexorably destroy the hard-won balance of nature, each of us smugly proclaiming him- or herself a "people person," we remain, as far as we know so far, the only animal capable of reflecting on nature or even of conceiving of such an entirety. At a time when humankind's numbers have never been higher, when we dominate the earth with our wasteful, wastrel ways as no other animal has before, we continue to prate about "the sanctity of human life" as if it were something rare and therefore precious. It certainly is to the self-preoccupied individual who proclaims "Screw off, Jack, *I'm* all right!" But in terms of species survival, we've long since passed the point where individual lives are rare and precious. After all, as humanistic liberalism teaches us, no single individual regardless of gender, race, creed, sexual preference, or place of national origin is any better or worse than another. All people are created equal. Given a decent chance in the way of nutrition, education, and opportunity, each of us can be just as successful as the other.

Meanwhile, to provide this heaven on earth for each human being, we dim the skies with poisons, fell forests, and befoul rivers and even the oceans. Deserts spread like skin cancers across the face of the continents, and other species die, unnamed, unmourned, forever. What, if anything, can be done to correct this tragedy in progress?

The last time human beings were in ecological balance with the planet was in the seventeenth century. At that time, 1650 to be precise, the human population was only five hundred million worldwide (less than that of sub-Saharan Africa today, and only half that of China). What a time that was! Shakespeare was not long dead, John Donne had caught the bard's falling star, Robert Herrick was out a-maying with the fair Corinna, while Andrew Marvell and his coy mistress tore their "pleasures with rough strife,/ Through the iron gates of life." The interior of Africa, with its teeming herds of Pleistocene wildlife, remained a ghastly blank, punily nibbled at around the edges by Arab and European traders in ivory and slaves (many of whom paid for their temerity with death by fever or worse). The interior of North America too was still virtually pristine, the realm of Stone Age Indian tribes living in symbiosis with some thirty million bison and plentiful antelope, deer, elk, wild sheep, and bears both black and grizzly; the skies darkened in spring and fall to the seemingly limitless flights of the passenger pigeon. Those few intrepid (and often greedy) Europeans who tussled with the Indians usually ended up with a stone-headed arrow or spear through their vitals and their scalps drying on a lodgepole.

In Central and South America, Spain's so-called conquest had not made much of an impact except on the Aztec and Incan civilizations (which were looted and wiped out). Most of the tropical forest still stood intact as it had for eons, with its millions upon millions of life forms still breeding, changing, and speciating, all the while fueling the great photosynthetic engine of the planet by absorbing sunlight and giving back oxygen—the very fuel of life itself in all its variety.

The mid-Pacific cultures of Polynesia, Micronesia, and Melanesia were still intact as well, along with all the sea's riches of marine life. In south Asia, tigers, leopards, rhinoceroses, gaur, nilghai, musk deer, gibbons, and orangutans, along with wild elephants and many smaller species, still lived in self-sustaining numbers while humankind waged its greedy wars and led its silly, messy, short, brutish, and nasty individual lives harmlessly in their midst. At the poles, Antarctica lay "undiscovered" save by myriads of marine and avian animals along with the rich stew of microscopic life that fed them, while in the Arctic a few hardy Inuit thrived in harmony with nature's hot/cold heart, blessedly ignorant of snowmobiles, satellite TV, liquor, and money—or of measles, tuberculosis, and gonorrhea.

We will never return to a world like that, no matter how hard we try. Even if by some miracle we could undo history, retool the human mindset that it's produced, and somehow reduce human numbers to five hundred million again without further damaging the nonhuman life that remains on the planet, it would not be the same. We know too much now about our own human propensity for messing things up. Perhaps that was the inarticulate subtext of Wordsworth's ode, "Intimations of Immortality." We are indeed the spoilers.

Sometimes, in my more bitter moods, I wake at night with the three-o'clock willies, remembering the things I've seen through more than half a century wandering this earth: too many trout streams destroyed; too many grouse covers exchanged for cheap housing tracts; vast reaches of African or Asian or American or Australian game lands laid waste to make room for the crops and factories and tin-roofed hovels of the never-ending onslaught of people; vistas of dying reefs and the dead white carapaces of sea urchins, beneath the sea's surface in the Florida Keys, or off the so-called Coral Coast of East Africa, or in the South Pacific, or the Caribbean; an empty cigarette packet resting on a sludge of diesel waste blown by Russian trawlers on a reef near Havana where thousands of fish—sergeant majors, wrasses, French angels, parrotfish of rainbow colors—once teemed. At these times, I imagine a few things that might at least keep our numbers in check, and might even reduce them somewhat. I present them here as my modest proposal, or proposals, for I can imagine a number of alternatives.

None of these ideas is new, nor are any politically correct. Most of them fly in the face of humanistic decency, and sometimes even I shudder on thinking them. But an old German folk song, learned at my mother's knee, gives me courage: "Die Gedanken sind frei . . ." Thoughts are free, no one can forbid them. At least not yet.

Require licenses for having children. After all, we require licenses for many other things: driving a motor vehicle, flying an airplane, practicing medicine or law, selling alcoholic beverages, hunting, fishing, even marriage itself. We're used to the idea of licensing by now; it's an old friend, even (or perhaps especially) in places like Africa, South America, and Asia, where "baby licenses" are most needed. License requirements should be at least as strict as those applied by New York's Sullivan Law for getting a pistol permit: applicants must have a well-paying job, live in a decent neighborhood, never have been arrested for even a minor infraction, be of sound mind and body, and append three vouchers in writing from respectable fellow citizens (lawyers, police officers, or politicians). As in the hunter safety courses now mandatory in all of the United States, prospective moms and dads would be required to attend a series of parenting classes, culminating in a battery of stringent tests—oral, written (no multiple-choice or true/false questions), and "hands-on." For this last, they would be observed by hidden monitors over a long, rainy weekend in a crowded one-bedroom apartment as they care for a pair of carefully selected and coached teenage "problem children"—the sort who watch MTV with the volume at full blast, leave dirty clothes and dishes lying around everywhere, whine incessantly, pick sullenly at their food, and when asked if they'd like to do something—anything—reply, "Not really." Those wishing to have children could repeat this parent safety course up to three times if they failed the first time. But three strikes is out. A final failure would result in mandatory sterilization at government expense.

Provide free birth control for all. The U.S. Food and Drug Administration dragged its feet for thirty-five years before finally approving Depo-Provera, a synthetic version of progesterone, that, if injected in 150-milligram doses once every three months, prevents conception in all but 0.3 percent of women using it.

Another alternative is the Norplant implant, small rods placed under the skin of the upper arm that prevent conception for up to five years and are effective in all but 0.05 percent of cases. The United Nations and various national governments in countries with runaway birth rates could inject or implant these devices at no cost to the women involved and perhaps even offer bonuses to women who elect this procedure. The same goes for vasectomies.

Pay bonuses for abortions. For that 0.05 to 0.3 percent of women who get pregnant anyway, the World Health Organization, with contributions of money and medical manpower, could provide free, safe abortions around the globe. With a little extra financial cost—much less than it would take to provide famine relief to millions of starving children—the WHO could pay hefty bonuses to these women, perhaps even implant them with sterility rods.

Encourage alternative means of sexual gratification. The human sex drive is powerful, often overriding reason or even the fear of death, as witness the number of men shot out of the saddle each year by irate husbands or Frankie-and-Johnnie scenarios of women's revenge on men they feel have done them wrong. Fortunately, the sex drive is infinitely mutable (see Krafft-Ebing). Since only heterosexual congress produces offspring, perhaps the UN and Madison Avenue could join forces to produce tastefully persuasive advertising worldwide—in newspapers and magazines, on radio and TV—extolling the joys of homosexuality (both male and female), onanism, sadomasochism, and bestiality. Even fetishism could be encouraged. I recall a case in France some years ago where a polite, well-dressed gentleman of the Indochinese persuasion would chat up middle-aged women on the Paris-to-Lyon express train, offer them bonbons laced with a sedative, and then diddle them as they lay half-conscious with a long, almost-prehensile big toe. Whatever turns you on.

Reverse societal attitudes concerning life and death. Rather than discouraging dangerous activities and the consumption of substances deemed hazardous to health, governments, religious leaders, and trend setters around the globe might promote such things. The aim, after all, is a reduction of the human population and its deleterious effect on the planet. The more bungee-jumping and helmetless motorcycle riding, the better. With a little "hidden persuasion" in the right places, Russian roulette might supplant golf and tennis as a popular weekend diversion. Speed limits on the world's highways could be abolished, freeing traffic cops to shoot more innocent bystanders. The Food and Drug Administration and similar agencies in other countries could busy themselves establishing mandatory minimum levels for carcinogens in all foods and drugs. Seatbelts and airbags could be banned in all vehicles; tax-free unfiltered cigarettes could be made available to everyone

(especially schoolchildren). As more and more farms fail, plowshares
might be hammered into weapons and distributed at cost to the young.
Knife fighting and spearsmanship could replace rope climbing and vol-
leyball in high school gym classes. By banning all health foods and rec-
ommending high-fat diets, along with excessive consumption of beer or
wine with meals (including breakfast), a sizable slimming in human numbers might be accomplished. Free ice cream and nitrate-laden hot dogs at
every ball game!

Let AIDS and other epidemics save the planet. It's a horrific idea—almost
unthinkable—yet many people familiar with the peak-and-valley dynamics of animal populations have wondered if this latest visitation by the biblical horseman Pestilence is not just a natural corrective to human
overpopulation. When any species becomes too abundant for its habitat,
some blight usually comes along to pare the population back to its environment's carrying capacity. Tularemia in rabbits, mange in foxes, various epizootics in waterfowl. Epidemics have ravaged human populations
throughout history: the Black Death (bubonic plague) killed from a third
to a half of Europe's population in the fourteenth century, and more
recently the Spanish influenza pandemic of 1918 wiped out twenty million
people worldwide. But none of them, so far, has caused more than a
momentary check to human population growth. Tragic as it may be to
millions of individuals, it seems highly unlikely (given a planetary human
population of nearly six billion) that AIDS will reduce human numbers
significantly.

"Many persons concerned about wildlife had high hopes for AIDS at
first," a woman wildlife researcher told me in East Africa a couple of years
ago, "as a kind of deus ex machina, cruel as it is to say so, that would solve
Africa's overpopulation problem. But I'm afraid that it's not to be. AIDS
can't catch up with the birthrate." The World Health Organization
recently estimated that HIV, the virus that causes AIDS, is spreading in
Asia—at least in some nations—with the rapidity it showed in black
Africa in the early 1980s. More than a million people in India are infected,
the WHO says, and the Indian Health Organization projects 20 to 50 million infected by the year 2000, out of a total Indian population of 860 million. Already, more Indians test HIV positive than all the current cases in
Europe and about as many as in the United States. But by the time the
projected big numbers come into play, preventive measures and improved
treatments, perhaps even a cure, will probably have reduced the AIDS
impact on world population to a mere blip on the growth charts. No deus
ex machina can save nature. Only humankind, its major threat, can do so.

Alphaville, Jean-Luc Godard's 1965 *nouvelle vague* film, starring Eddie Constantine and the luscious Anna Karina, posited a future in which people went around assassinating one another for no good reason. It made for exciting, surprise-a-minute cinema, but governments could achieve the same effect—paring of excessive human population—by subsidizing vendettas and blood feuds wherever they exist. Organizations idled by the end of the Cold War, such as the CIA, KGB, RI5, Sureté, and Savak—accomplished provocateurs all—might even trigger a few where none existed before. Idle hands are the devil's workshop. Such a program might even enhance family values. As Mark Twain so ably demonstrated in the feud chapters of *Huckleberry Finn,* nothing brings blood kin together more loyally than a little letting of it by the neighbors.

Set up an opium den on every corner. Nor does anything short of castration dull the sex drive like the fruit of the poppy.

Give Dr. Kevorkian a Nobel prize. As the old song says, suicide is painless. And think of all the good you'll be doing for trees, weeds, birds, bugs, mosses, spores, and fungi, not to mention the porpoises, penguins, and possums now threatened by mankind's inexorable destruction of the planet. The Michigan "suicide doctor" deserves to be as honored as Mother Teresa or Bishop Desmond Tutu.

Back in 1729, that great misanthrope and essayist Jonathan Swift offered "A Modest Proposal" to solve Ireland's overpopulation problems. "It is a melancholy object to those who walk through this great town," he wrote from Dublin, "or travel in the country, when they see the streets, the roads, and cabin doors, crowded with beggars of the female sex, followed by three, four, or six children, all in rags and importuning every passenger for an alms. These mothers, instead of being able to work for their honest livelihood, are forced to employ all their time in strolling to beg sustenance for their helpless infants; who, as they grow up, either turn thieves for want of work, or leave their dear native country to fight for the pretender in Spain, or sell themselves to the Barbadoes."

The good dean's solution was both practical and economical: "I have been assured by a very knowing American of my acquaintance in London, that a young healthy child, well nursed, is at a year old a most delicious, nourishing, and wholesome food, whether stewed, roasted, baked, or boiled; and I make no doubt that it will equally serve in a fricassee or a ragout."

This American proposes nothing so heartless as a boiled baby in every pot, but unless mankind learns to control its runaway population—learns responsible stewardship of what's left of the natural world, recognizes its kinship with all living things, the air, the waters, the very earth itself—the end result will be no less heartless than what Swift so cynically suggested. It is time for humankind the despoiler to become humankind the preserver. After all, extinction is forever.

Or as a great comedian of a bygone era, Mort Sahl, used to say in ending his act: "Is there anyone here I haven't offended?"

A Brooks Range Walk
Thomas J. Lyon

July 16

I IMAGINE THAT LOOKING FOR WILDERNESS IS LIKE LOOKING FOR enlightenment—in essence, paradoxical. Undertaking such a search means that you have a goal—going somewhere that is not where you are—and that you think of life as having two parts, one desirable and one not so good. This mental split goes against the fact that there is only one world, and so today I am in a wry frame of mind. I am flying from Salt Lake City to Anchorage, then on to Fairbanks and Fort Yukon, and tomorrow, if the weather is good, by small plane to our drop-off point on the North Slope in the wilderness area of the Arctic National Wildlife Refuge. With whatever doubts and ambiguity carried along as baggage, I am looking for wilderness.

It seems a bit odd, going somewhere to look for profound experience with absolutely no intention of staying there. It strikes me today as a strange, fragmented way to live. My whole stewardship of the Arctic National Wildlife Refuge has consisted of sending some money to groups that lobby in Washington for its protection. I feel removed, doing everything at a distance. "The reason the world . . . lies broken and in heaps," Ralph Waldo Emerson wrote over a century and a half ago, "is because man is disunited with himself."[1]

I meet Max and Brian at the Fairbanks airport. I haven't seen Brian, who's come from Seattle, since '86, on a San Juan River trip. Max (my oldest son) and I were together in Boulder, just two weeks ago, at his friend Ellen's place, where he made me a power drink consisting of protein powder, yogurt, soy milk, and bananas and told me it would be advisable to eat more for this trip, be a little heftier. We have been thinking about this hike for a long time, planning it, laying out maps on the floor. We're pretty excited, all smiles. We drag our enormous duffles outside and get driven to the air service that will take us to Fort Yukon. The service is an informal outfit after the big airline. The van driver, a young woman, proudly tells us they're the only Fairbanks–Fort Yukon air service that offers sandwiches. The pilot is wearing a checkered shirt and looks like a guy I knew in high school who was deeply into ham radio. "Just so he can fly," I think. The trip is already taking on a glaze of strangeness. The Piper Comanche pulls up steeply off the runway, and as we gain altitude, heading northeast, we can see a dredging operation of some kind below, and then, quite suddenly, nothing but woods and lakes and what look like meadows and meandering streams, everything perfectly unconstrained—no roads, no buildings, no power-line towers marching across the land, nothing but country as far as we can see. I feel buoyant and at the same time disconnected; I have no idea how you would travel in the wet-looking landscape below or what you would do here for a living.

Fort Yukon consists mainly of low log houses scattered amid thick spruce (white spruce, I find out, finally seeing the tree I've read about in Bob Marshall's books). We are dropped off at Roger Dowding's house (he is our pilot tomorrow) and immediately set about lightening our loads. Just dragging all this gear and food onto airplanes has been a job. "How," we ask, "are we ever going to pack it?" Perhaps the light has in some way unhinged us. It is still broad daylight in these parts even at eleven o'clock at night, when, as we will see, small children are still riding their big-wheels in the dirt street. I pull out a small tent, reducing my pack by three pounds. We'll all squeeze into Max's pyramid tent. What else might be left here? We're not thinking now, not in the manner of the sober trip planners we have been for several months. When another traveler shows up (he and his wife will be flown north after us) and tells us he walked to the summit of Mt. Chamberlain in his boots ("piece of cake"), Brian and I jettison our ice axes and crampons. Max thinks awhile, then keeps his. Roger takes off at 9:00 P.M. with another couple, part of a group gathering at the headwaters of the Kongakut. He'll be back about four in the morning, get some sleep, then take us to the Neruokpuk Lakes.

July 17

WE ARE UP LONG before Roger; we're eager. He's a pro; he's been there before—lots of times. Now he's standing by the kitchen sink, tanking up on coffee, staring rather blankly, it seems to me, out the window, as cup after cup of dark high-test-looking stuff goes down. Prompted into conversation, he tells us about another bush pilot who crashed recently and, though covered with fuel from a broken tank, got away and didn't catch fire. The walls of Roger's house have pictures of happy customers, along with a few photos of the crashed planes of other pilots. Max shows Roger our projected hiking route on the big maps pinned to one wall. Roger looks closer and becomes sharply attentive, getting involved as we talk about the food drop. "It's in the gravel; the rocks have been picked off," Roger says, pointing out an area at a bend in the Canning River. This is where our hopefully bear-proof buckets of food will be stashed, if Roger can land his Cessna 185 on what he refers to as the "Cub strip" he points to briefly on the map. It all seems sketchy to me, almost unreal; it might not happen just as easily as it might. I have the feeling of being on another planet or in a dream.

After a fifth or so cup of coffee, Roger is ready, and very soon the little airplane is loaded, crammed I should say, and we are airborne. The air is hazy, full of smoke from a fire somewhere. Some minutes out of Fort Yukon, another pilot's voice comes in on the headphones, and he and Roger exchange brief, workingman information. The country looks a lot like that of yesterday: pond-dotted taiga. The sound of Roger's tapes, a hybrid collection of soft rock and New Age music, floats into our ears with astonishing beauty. Now below us and to the left we see Arctic Village, and then the smoke haze is gone and suddenly the Brooks Range is right there, looming in front of us. Unaccountably, I'd had an image of the range as something like the Uintas; long easy ridges of brownish shale. But here, obviously and undeniably, is a wall of mountains on what seems a Himalayan scale, capped with big, drooping, white glaciers and snowfields, with steep-walled valleys filled with rivers of dirty-looking ice. Peaks upon peaks run to the horizon, east and west. I've never seen anything remotely like it. Brian cuts in on the headset, "It looks like Nepal!" I begin wishing I'd brought along my ice axe and crampons. Max and Roger, with the map open on Max's knees, confer about the food drop again. Taking a plane down into one of these deep canyons doesn't seem at all feasible to me. The Cessna rocks and swings now, and a big, sharp-toothed glaciated peak slides by. Far ahead, a straight shot, is Carnivore Creek, and out at the end of it, the two big Neruokpuk Lakes. We slip down over the straight canyon, dropping swiftly and surely toward those lakes, slowing now in a steeper angle downward, making a tight left turn low over the water of the southernmost lake, then flare lightly onto a ramplike stretch of tundra and run smoothly to a stop. Beautiful.

The ground is covered with dwarf fireweed, and the air, it becomes apparent after about three seconds outside the plane, is full of humming, swarming, landing-on-you mosquitoes. The first impression is of incredible abundance: you can't walk without stepping on a flower, and you can hardly breathe without sucking in a mosquito. We slap on repellent and then dig the head nets out of our packs. From the air we'd seen our fourth member, Craig, a long-time friend who lives in Barrow and who's been flown here from Kaktovik on the Arctic coast, making his way toward the landing strip. In a few minutes we're all together. We talk Roger into accepting our money (we puristically didn't want to be walking around with all that cash, not in the Brooks Range!) and we watch him turn around, power back down toward the lake, and, seemingly at the last possible moment, lift off over the water. Now he's gone, back up Carnivore Creek and over the range, and it begins to be quiet; two hours of engine sound and music and earphone voices start to fade, and a soft, immense quiet becomes more and more apparent. There is the sound of little Chamberlain Creek tumbling down its gully by the strip and the buzz of mosquitoes, but past this you can sense a silence that seems beyond all measure. There is only country as far as you can see. Perhaps the treelessness heightens the effect. Looking to the horizons, you think you've never been anywhere this big. The country is spare, ascetic, silent, seemingly endless.

July 18
THERE ARE HUNDREDS, perhaps thousands, of mosquitoes inside the tent. But strangely enough they do not bite; they just drift upward to the peak and cluster there in dark masses. Max caught a fine lake trout last evening at the inlet, and we poached the fillets. When the wind blows, the mosquitoes hunker down somewhere, making it possible to enjoy the

tundra. The ground is a fabulous carpet of color: tiny flowers, mosses, and lichens take up seemingly every inch. Some of the mosses in Chamberlain Court are bright red; some of the lichens, a neonlike sulfur color. It's dazzling. We're identifying some of the flowers from Craig's book, learning which ones are edible. The pink bistort has a good-tasting root. The totem bird of the area seems to be the Lapland longspur, whose little brief song, "*Tink* illy ink . . . *Tink* illioo," is snatched away on the wind. Somehow the poetic quality of the place, the huge and unbending space combined, paradoxically, with tiny, showy, no-doubt fragile life, seems to be quintessentially represented in this little bird. I follow a pair across the flats where Carnivore Creek comes down to the lake. They rise up into the wind a few feet, bound along, then sink back down onto the colorful turf. "*Tink* illi ink." We've also seen a great many snow buntings, a couple of parasitic jaegers, a glaucous gull; all of these would be outstanding, call-the-hotline rarities in Utah, except perhaps buntings in wintertime, and seeing them makes me feel even more decisively a visitor. This is beautiful country, magnificent country. Just the arctic azalea alone, to name one of the dozens of species making up the tapestry underfoot, would be worthy of lifetime study and appreciation. But we're here for just a few days and then will strike southward into, and hopefully over, the mountains.

The four of us walk up Chamberlain Creek in the rain. Max and Craig will definitely climb Chamberlain, and Brian and I, cramponless and axeless, will look at the allegedly easy ridge. When, at the foot of the glacier, the clouds lift away for a minute, we see that the ridge is deeply hung with new snow. We decide to make better use of our time by observing the lowlands. Max and Craig go up over a moraine and out of sight. Brian and I descend to the creek, and as we start out into the broader valley of Carnivore Creek and the big lakes, a good stiff breeze quite unexpectedly comes up, and the sky opens more and more—the first blue sky we've seen. We sit on a headland a long time, looking up the dramatically rugged drainage of the big creek we'll walk up and have to cross at some point. Beyond the jagged mountains, we can see, there are more—and more.

July 19
MAX AND CRAIG CAME in at 4:30 this morning. They had made the summit in a whiteout, after climbing eight or ten pitches of steep ice to get to the "easy" ridge, and then had descended the next canyon south of camp. They were tired, but this day is a ringing beauty of a blue-sky day, with a good wind blowing all bugs away, and nobody's sleeping. We lay our

damp gear out on the suddenly dry tundra and spend the day in utter lounging, telling stories, pointing out bear-shaped rocks on the hillsides, and eating. I feel a little more like I'm really here today.

July 20

THIS MORNING BRIAN spotted a wolverine as it ran along the shore of the lake north of camp. We watched through binoculars as this rarity eagerly coursed over the ground, twice splashing out into the shallows here and there, quickly, in a flowing canter, turning its head limberly this way and that, astonishingly fast—the very image of wildness and purpose.

At 2:30 we leave Craig. He'll be flown back to Barrow; he's got to get back to work. The three of us have easy walking up Carnivore Creek, making a few miles and cooking supper against a rock face out of the wind. We look down at the several-braided stream, and think about crossing after supper and camping on the opposite side. We saw new birds today: greater yellowlegs, northern wheatear, and long-tailed jaeger.

July 21

THE CROSSING WAS EASY. It rained and blew hard all night, and a caribou trail led water into our tent. It's still raining, but we have a council and decide to move on anyway. We want to make it to the food drop with a little of our present food to spare, just in case. This is a bleak, dark, rainy day. We leave Carnivore and cross a low pass into the Franklin Creek drainage. It's perfectly soggy on the pass, water running everywhere over the ground, and the probably once-small feeder stream, just a short way down from the pass, has become a boulder-rolling, fearsome torrent. We camp on a point between it and the main Franklin and listen to the grinding of boulders in all these mad, swollen streams. To the south, at the head of Franklin Creek, increasingly visible as the clouds lift a bit and the rain diminishes, stands a rampart of glacier-draped peaks that from here looks like very difficult going, if it's passable at all. The map shows the ice mounting smoothly and not too steeply up and over the ridges. But the reality, becoming apparent in our binoculars, is that the ice has somehow shrunk away from the knifelike ridges, leaving climbing too steep for anyone without crampons and ice axe. We will have to "sneak" this range, if we can cross it at all. This is a spooky camp somehow. We find piles of grizzly scat everywhere; the sky is strangely dark; the river, as we call it, is a rolling, opaque impossibility to cross. If we can't get over the ridges and down to the drainage of the Canning River on the other side, we will have to walk the long way around, many more miles and at least three river crossings as ugly as the one we are looking at. We're a bit glum tonight. The river is noisy.

July 22

THE WALKING ALONGSIDE Franklin Creek is very good. The higher we go into the mountains, the fewer lichens there are and thus the less slippery the wet rocks are. Brian has been studying the map and thinks he has found a way, a somewhat convoluted passage, by which we can avoid the unclimbable places. The moraines are huge at the headwaters of Franklin Creek, and we thread a way between, over, and around them. The country is raw and new looking, as if it came out from under the ice only last week. We have gone above the birds and flowers now; the world is rock and ice. At 5,700 feet, we make a platform out of flat rocks and pitch the pyramid tent over it, finishing just before a new rainstorm hits. Now we are sitting in the tent, cooking supper. We have just agreed that we are committed to this mountain route, we've come so far. We can always bail out, go back to Neruokpuk Lakes, but nobody seems to prefer that option.

July 23

THIS WAS A ROUGH DAY. The rain in the night at Platform Camp, as we called it, came violently down on us. It was as if a firehose had somehow been rigged about thirty or forty feet overhead and was foaming back and forth on the tent. I slept only now and then. Max put earplugs in his ears and did a little better. He led the way in the morning at a smart pace. We found, half an hour uphill from the platform, that we were walking on about a foot of loose scree underlaid by iron-hard ice. Tiptoeing, we gingerly made our way up into the clouds. We navigated a good deal by Max's altimeter, by the map, and, when occasionally the clouds thinned, by compass, all of which involved some fairly intense discussion. At one point, having crossed what seemed to be, what must have been, the main ridge, we descended a half mile of scree, still in the clouds, walked out onto a broad, nearly level glacier, and found ourselves groping slowly in pure whiteness. We stopped, having no visibility at all beyond the slush our feet stood in. I've never felt so completely isolated, so foreign feeling. And yet at the same time there were undeniably my wet, cold feet, the heavy pack bearing down on my back—basic animal realities. We waited, standing there. After awhile the light became a little stronger, and we could see a bit farther. Suddenly, we saw the moraine on the far side of the glacier. We walked to it and discovered on its narrow top a most amazingly regular, even sidewalklike, path, probably worn smooth by generation after generation of Dall sheep, we thought. Incredulous, we strolled slowly down this beautiful ramp, down the length of the glacier and into the zone of soil and sod again, into the flowers and the calling of buntings.

July 24

THE CLOUDS ARE LOW down on the mountains this morning, but they must be thin, because there is a wonderful brightness. Within a hundred yards of camp, nine Dall sheep graze over the steep-sided hills or lie on the turf looking down at us. The lambs run back and forth sportively on terrain that would give us pause if not trouble. Suddenly, a white blade of a mountain peak appears high above in a hole in the clouds. The wind picks up, and within a few minutes, we have blue sky, a perfect day to lay over and dry out. We'll take it. The streams will go down, and tomorrow is soon enough to deal with them anyway. (We have two crossings to make before we get to the Cub strip where we hope the food canisters will be waiting.) Max rigs a clothesline. Our gear is scattered over an area about the size of an average suburban lot. It's a great day, a beautiful day, a restoration day. I sit on a rock in the sun in my down jacket, glad to have it, looking at the thick carpet of arctic bell heather and the large-flowered wintergreen (so Craig's book reveals these plants to be). We reseal the seams of the tent. In the afternoon, recharged by two big meals, I have a feeling of animal competence. So what if it rains and blows? Just relax your mind, watch your step (every single one) on the wet lichen, walk within your breath, eat and drink enough. You'll make it. This is beautiful country. Who was it said, "How can I worry, when I am all this?"

July 25

DOWN THE CANNING. Another bright day, and the walking is easy. When we hit a caribou trail, the walking is excellent, just like a pack trail across a meadow in Yellowstone. The country is changing: drier, with more evenly graded, little-scree slopes instead of the big blocks and cliffs and glaciers we have been among. We come over a rise at midday and look down on what we think has to be Roger's Cub strip, perhaps a mile away. Max sits down and steadies his binoculars on his knees, looking for the canisters. In the bright, clean air, Brian and I squint at the huge landscape. "They're there," Max says finally. Full of good thoughts about Roger's skill, we soon arrive at the strip, put the heavy canisters in our packs, and start up the preternaturally clear tributary of the Canning, which will lead us to the Continental Divide.

July 26

LAST EVENING WAS LIKE a camp on a river-rafting trip: wide gravel bar, easy tent setup, chair-size boulders to sit on, everything ready to hand, no scrimping on food, nice breeze coming down the bar. Now we are walking on the cobblestones of a two-hundred-yard-wide streambed in which is flowing a tiny creek no more than six feet across. It's hard going. Brian says, "You've heard of a whiteout? This is a rockout." In the afternoon we turn south on a tributary creek and very soon realize that the map hasn't told us everything. We are confronted by twisty, narrow chasms rather than the bland slopes the map seemed to promise and spend hours reconnoitering, finally finding a steep, mossy chute that takes us onto the broad uplands. Beautiful waterfalls come off the turfed benches here, dropping into dark narrow canyons. We make camp on the high bench, looking up at a dramatic snow-topped peak, and I try to remember if this is a peak we saw on the flight in. If so, we are not far from a crossing of the Divide that looked, from the air, fairly reasonable.

July 27

TODAY WAS OUR all-time low-mileage day. We're tired, or maybe I should say I'm tired. It's evening now and raining off and on. We are camped on a broad saddle, and we leave the tent from time to time, walking the ridges, trying to see across the chasm before us, trying to piece together a route, but clouds keep rolling in, obscuring the view. We go to bed not quite knowing if we can make this crossing. Once in the night I wake up and see Max sitting upright, his legs still in his sleeping bag, studying the map.

July 28

A SUNNY MORNING, thanks be. I dreamed that a British mountaineer came by our camp and told us to descend into the "khud" (Tilman-style), go a short way downstream, take the first left-hand tributary, then climb a buttress to the ridge and the Divide. The buttress is on the map—I must have seen it yesterday—and I attempt to sponsor a naming: "Tom's Dream." Under way, we slip and slide a good 1,500 feet down loose scree to a small creek, make our way down it, then up the first little creek to the left. We eat lunch at the foot of the rocky rib, and it's a good thing we do, for the climb is a nightmare. It's loose footing, and on each eight-inch step upward, a cascade of little shale fragments slides out, and I end up gaining at best three or four inches. The buttress seems to be poised precisely at the angle of repose. Finally at the top, we sit in the cooling breeze, eating dried apricots and drinking water. I'm barely able to chew the fruit, feeling thoroughly burned out, hating the fatigue, the rock, the pack.

July 29

THIS IS BEAUTY CAMP, Paradise Camp, Pleistocene Camp. Yesterday we stumbled down from the divide and lucked onto a beautiful campsite on a level turfy bench above an unnamed tributary of Red Sheep Creek. Where Red Sheep meets the east fork of the Chandalar is our pickup point. It is literally all downhill from here. Tired as we are, the utter wildness, the utter beauty of the valley below our camp, moves us. We half-expect to see a line of woolly mammoths crossing the creek, way out there in the evening shadows. We are back on soil again.

July 30

AS UNMATCHABLE as this camp is, we must move on today. At noon or so we see the first blueberries of the trip, and soon the packs are off and we're grazing. The berries are not quite ripe and don't come off the stem easily, but we eat them anyway. By evening, I'm strangely tired and out of sorts again. My pack, reputedly one of the best designed, feels like a bad fit. We eat supper on a willow-covered gravel bar, and with spoon halfway from bowl to mouth, I have the sudden distinct notion that I can't possibly eat enough to get my strength back. Afterward, walking toward a better place to camp, I fantasize being connected by a flexible straw to a five-gallon container of the power drink Max made in Boulder. I try to imagine a feeling of energy and competence coming back as the nutrients enter into the cells. I look at Max and Brian; they look thinner, Brian decidedly so. His cheekbones are visible. We talk about this. But how could we have carried any more food?

July 31

I FORGOT TO MENTION that yesterday we saw a number of Dall sheep running across a broad steep talus slope—actually not running, *tearing*. What frightened them? We watched for a long time but saw no wolves, no grizzly bears. (Tracks of both are common now in the sand and mud of the gravel bars we mainly walk on.) These sure-footed sheep! How at home they are.

Today we saw *Aufeis* in the streambed, the first since Franklin Creek. This is remnant overflow ice, deep and very white from last winter. Ann Zwinger says of the Colorado tundra that it is never more than six weeks from winter. We wonder what this Red Sheep Creek valley will look like in a month. We will be far away, far to the south. I reach a state pretty near exhaustion, even though it is only midday. This was in a long stretch of tussock walking. You can see the telltale cotton grass a long way away and should be able to find a way around. But sometimes the tussocks are unavoidable, and when you're in them, it's pretty hard to maintain both physical and mental equilibrium. I was saved by the merest accident of place and time, by coming into a bonanza of truly ripe blueberries. The laden bushes occupied a saddle between two little hills, and I saw that an acre or more was absolutely hanging with berries, lending their color to the landscape. I slid out of the torture pack and walked free, a proper animal, a hungry animal. Max and Brian came up and paid similar homage to the suddenly bountiful land.

Tonight in camp we look up and down this beautiful drainage. To the south we can see the first trees—little spindly spruces, but trees nevertheless. I tell mountain man stories from the Old West: great lone journeys made without maps, life-and-death fights with grizzlies, and then, the ironies of history catching up with them—they'd helped to open up the very wilderness they loved. There will never again be a world like that. Us? We're well-equipped visitors. We don't live here, and by law we can't, in any case.

August 1
WE HAVE WALKED MOST of the day in sight of trees. We saw a young peregrine falcon and then, in the evening, a cow moose. We camp on a breezy rise in sight of the Red Sheep–Chandalar landing strip, where we will be picked up tomorrow. Down below, through the binoculars, we see a blue dome tent, some fuel drums lined up, and an unidentifiable, jungle-gymlike structure. We don't feel like going down there. Max fishes Red Sheep Creek, Brian investigates something out in the wide gravel flats that could be a pingo, and I gather more blueberries. We are all tired, and everywhere we go, we go slowly, even without the packs. Uphill steps are hard. When it rains, as it does from time to time this afternoon and evening, the arctic lupine leaves, like the palm of a silver-green hand, hold amazingly large bulbous globules of water, like perfectly round diamonds. Earlier today, we heard and saw the first jets of the trip, high up, leaving trails going from east to west. They were 747s, we discovered through the binoculars, and we speculated that they were on a flight path from Europe to Tokyo. Somewhere in the last mile of the trip, Max picked up a long, thick-walled piece of aluminum pipe.

August 2

IT'S RAINING STEADILY, and where is Roger? This morning when it was clear, we played baseball on the landing strip, using a piece of driftwood for a bat and a climber's hand strengthener for a ball. We've pitched the tent on a wooden platform and sit in it now to be out of the rain. We have enough food for about three smallish meals, but there is no worry in this stock taking. We are on a landing strip where there is jet fuel stored in drums (the Fish and Wildlife Service must come here in helicopters, and this must be their stockpile). We have a schedule and an appointment. If we have gone toward the edge of civilization, and that is about all I would claim, we are decidedly heading back toward the center now. We were looking for wilderness, and I think we saw it and heard it. But were *we* wild too? Will we take care of this place as if it were our flesh and blood, our earned land, our own, ourselves?

A plane has been going up and down the east fork of the Chandalar this afternoon, under the overcast, about a thousand feet up. It is not Roger's 185. Nevertheless, on one of its westbound flights, it suddenly dives with a roar of apparently straining engine and flares out fancily to land on the strip. We walk over as the pilot emerges from the cockpit and comes toward us. "Roger said for me to pick up three guys at Red Sheep Creek. That you?"

1. *Nature* (New York: Modern Library, 1950), 41. Originally published in 1836.

Impotence
Michael Katakis

AS OF LATE I HAVE BEEN FEELING SPIRITUALLY IMPOTENT. I SAY THIS not as an excuse for inaction or to suggest that I have acquiesced to a "what's the use" mentality, but rather to state my thinking at present. Like everyone, I have gone into and out of mild normal depressions before, but this is quite different. I feel like I'm losing faith in humankind and presently seem unable to reinflate my usual optimism, and this is of great concern to me.

I have taken into consideration the possibility that my feelings may be the result of growing older, but after close examination and reflection, I find this not to be the case. Another factor that may be affecting my mental state is that I am not in my beloved Montana. For a time, I am residing in the eastern city of Philadelphia. Philadelphia, like many places of its like, has lost a good deal of its humanity. These kinds of cities with their mindless consumption and lack of civility take on a carnivorous dimension I'm sure is unhealthy for the spirit. While these two elements may have contributed to some of my misgivings, it is neither place nor age that ails me.

What appears to be getting in the way of my recovery are some not-so-simple observations that I can no longer dismiss. It is my fellow citizens I have been observing. The observations are turned inward as well, and I have had to reassess my own actions with a critical, cold eye. These observations have formed some of my present opinions that, while not yet pessimistic, are quite sober. From my experiences it appears that mindlessness and idealistic hyperbole are on the rise, while substantive action and personal responsibility are on the decline. My father used to call people whose actions did not consider the greater good, barbarians. Where my Greek immigrant father picked up that word I do not know. I believe my father was a socialist. I know he was an honorable man.

While growing up in Illinois, I ran across few barbarians, and when I left home to see the world, again I met few people who fit this description. But for the last decade or so I have found it increasingly difficult to avoid them. Barbarians come from all ethnic groups and races. They are liberal and conservative. They are found in fraternities, among the faculty of the finest schools, and in the inner cities. They live in rural areas and in fine brownstones. They wear minks and suits, blue jeans and work shirts. Some have Greenpeace and Trout Unlimited bumper stickers, while others have MontBlanc pens and sign checks to the politically correct cause of the moment. I have encountered these barbarians on trout streams and in movie theaters, in restaurants and on the highway. I've seen them at night, dumping in landfills when they thought no one was watching, and I have confronted them in the field.

The discussion and real practice of stewardship has become increasingly more symbolic and abstract. The people on the supposed left claim that those on the right have ignored or been unconcerned with the consequences of their actions for people and resources. The supposed right says that those on the left are uninformed extremists who are antigrowth, antijobs, and therefore antipeople. Both sides have created a kind of intellectual fundamentalism, a one-way accusatorial debate disguised as discourse that has led to the castration of ideas. Filling the space where ideas could be are opposing dogmas, each with its own agendas and interests. These dogmas do not demand personal responsibility or conscience as much as loyalty. The illusion here is that something is being accomplished. The fact is that no matter how many self-interested discussions take place or how many checks are written to Greenpeace or other organizations, nothing will get better without individuals accepting responsibility for their actions and altering those actions when necessary in regard to the greater good.

Perhaps humankind has romanticized itself too well and, in so doing, removed and elevated itself above nature. We took the idea of dominion over the world and its creatures to mean ownership rather than steward-ship and then raised ourselves to a place we had not earned and were not suited for. We do not do well as gods.

The philosopher William James wished in peacetime for the "moral equivalency of war." This peacetime wish is no less than a call to arms. Even though the enemy now is vague, it is nonetheless discernable: it is our own apathy and indifference. With all of our activity and knowledge, we have failed to understand, or have chosen to ignore, that our actions and their outcomes are not symbolic, that they have potentially serious and far-reaching consequences. I draw no comfort in the realization I am not alone in my spiritual impotence, that many of my fellow citizens are equally paralyzed, infatuated with technology and speed, unable or unwilling to see that these things alone will not save us.

With all of this said, and in spite of evidence to the contrary, I possess some shard of hope. My mind's eye cannot exorcise the acts of courage, compassion, and sacrifice I have witnessed human beings extend to one another. And from the past I am haunted by the words of Roderick Haig-Brown who in 1950 wrote "I want to continue as a man not too remote from the sensations and thoughts of my forebears. I want at least the illusion that I have a place and part in the natural world, some measure of power and freedom to supply my own needs, to protect my own and instruct my own. I want to go on believing it is worthwhile to search for purpose and place and meaning in everything about me."

This small piece of hope survives in spite of myself. It is perhaps the best part of all of us, for it allows us our fatigue, but demands that we move beyond self-importance. For reasons that seem trivial to me now, I have always been a reluctant activist; reluctant because of fear or the weight of my own self-doubts. I am beyond that now. As a citizen I have a duty not only to speak, but to build bridges between the ravines that separate us, and to engage in and introduce, as far as my talents will allow, pieces of ideas that, with other pieces from my fellow citizens, become solutions. I will rest now, then rise to my duties. There is much to be done.

Grandpa's Horse
C. L. Rawlins

IT WAS A GOLD MOUNTAIN. THE GRAY LODGEPOLES OF THE CORRAL sorted it into altitudes: hooves and pasterns, the flaring column of muscle and bone above the knee, the glossy wheatfield of chest, and under a mane of cloud, the great, soft planetary eye.

At four, I learned a trick. I would scoop double handfuls of oats into a rusty pan and carry them out to the corral that held the draft teams, Grandpa's Belgians. The horses would raise their heads and sniff. I knelt and poured oats onto the hoof-chopped ground, just inside the lowest rail.

It seemed to me that it was always the same horse. It moved like a shifting landscape. The eye examined, the nostrils flared, and the head came down, down, down. A gust of breath blew a little crater into the heap of oats. The lips bloomed and the teeth met. I climbed the fence, the rails too thick for a four-year-old's grip. I straddled the top rail, hooked both heels on the inside of the second one, and then—this was the hard part—I jumped. The air parted as I went through it, arms in a half circle, legs half bent, and lit on the horse's back.

Was it the same horse each time? It would stand and raise its head and snort. It wouldn't shy. The hooves, broad and cracked and bound with iron, stayed put. I could see the ears pivot and flatten, then relax. Then the head descended, and I was safe. I crept down the withers to straddle the ribs and lowered myself until my head rested on the swell of the rump, broad and bright as central Asia. I turned my head, pressed my left ear in the center, and closed my eyes.

I could hear it traveling up the massive spine: a ground bass, the oats between the teeth, the great jaw grinding like the edge of a continental plate, the oats becoming horse, gold into gold.

I could hear muscles gather around each swallow, the plucked-cord note of their release, the soft clutch of oats traveling the throat and its arrival at the stomach, which gurgled and popped. When the oats were gone, I could hear the whuffle of breath as the horse sniffed the spot where they had been, and then the settling of the horse's body into the slow alternations of heart and breath.

I could feel heat beneath the glossy hair and thick skin, and smells enclosed me: the neutral scents of stacked hay and binned grain; the tang of pine resin from a new rail; the drift of linseed from freshly painted wood; the brewery smell of oats and piss, rich and sour; the dried sweat and the dust; the green wealth of dung, crushed leaves and flowers, faintly sweet, blended with the strength of horses.

I fell asleep. The horse raised its head and joined the others, moving slowly, so as not to spill the sleeping innocent. Head loose, rolling easily on the broad rump, I slept above the work of lungs and heart, the touch of bone to earth. For a while, we were a single beast. I was the part that slept. The great horse stayed awake, watching the clouds and the changing shadows, drifting slowly with the other horses. I dreamed that some of that larger life was mine, that I absorbed it, like heat, where our bodies touched. At four, life and dreams are one.

A yell woke me. My grandfather charged through the gate and dragged me from the horse's back. He was more scared than angry. I sensed this, even at four, but he held me high by one wrist and spanked me, and the horses shied to the farthest corner and milled uneasily there. "You could get killed . . . those hoofs are bigger than your head . . . dangerous . . . Jesus H. Almighty Christ . . . if you ever try this again . . . "

So I did. I tried it again, and again, and again. It was my first religion.

TRYING TO EXPLAIN what writing means, in the closest terms, I think of this: my insignificance, a mere point of sensation, with the massive body in support. It was my first grasp of how one thing becomes another: trick into ride, oats into horse, gold into gold. I trusted that horse as I never have trusted anything since.

Do we trust the earth? Trying to grasp the notion of stewardship, I think of the horse and how I feared and trusted it. I thought of it as Grandpa's horse, yet the great hooves, the rainbow arch of neck, the watery break of the mane, the secret glossy organs, the powers and movement were all its own. It would serve, drawing the hay-mounded bobsled, but it was also dangerous, huge, self-possessed.

As a man, I would learn to harness that power. It would help me, but only after certain things had been done. I learned also to curry, shoe, doctor, comfort, and reassure. I would drape the reins over my palms and look down from a shifting haysled on those same broad backs, muscles playing like the Gulf Stream under the gleaming skin. There was something of a trick in it, and also something of a marriage. The horses pulled the sled. I had learned not how to force them to do it, but how to make it good for them, bearable, a part of their lives.

I hate the word *steward* if it is applied to how I felt about the horse. A steward is a hired hand, a groom, a gamekeeper, a houseboy, a caretaker for the consequential. Likewise, it sums the earth as something owned. If that's true, our role is one of servitude, of obligation, not to the earth itself, but to the absent owner, the one to whom our labor is owed, whose property values we are to conserve.

In our culture, ownership is the center on which the lives of most people turn. The more ownership—property—one commands, the greater one's right to everything: food, respect, mates, moods, selfhood. Yet the wholly egocentric person has a weakness, for it must be recognized, whether in a chapel or in a thunderstorm, that ownership does not move the earth. Thus, to keep the notion of our rights intact, we will see that larger power as a greater owner, and ourselves, at our most selfless, as stewards.

Horses are dangerous. Middy MacFarland's horse reared and fell on her, splitting her pelvis. Kenny Becker's horse rolled on him and nearly crushed his skull; he spent half a year in hospitals. George Davis, who rode the Pinion Ridge country, shoving cows out of the clear-cuts so the seedlings could grow, was killed last month when a horse fell on him. The earth is dangerous too. It shivers, and the Nimitz Freeway crumbles, like a cement sky, on the drivers under it. The earth is dangerous, beautiful, rich, hungry, incomparable.

WE HAVE TROUBLE when we try to understand the earth in terms of ourselves. Is it property? Does it belong to some absentee father? Perhaps not. But what is it to us? The golden mother in whose lap we buried our earliest faces? The heavy-breasted goddess, dancing with fists full of corpses, rattling a necklace of skulls?

I can't think of the earth as my mother. I have a real mother, a woman I love, who is equally flesh and spirit. She is neither large nor dangerous. I can think of the earth as a grandmother, perhaps, so massive and old and full of life that she's grown into remoteness: one of the oldest, unspeaking, who looks over the country of death and into life again.

But the metaphors clash. Can I be the steward of my grandmother's body? Only if she is weak, incompetent, addled. Or if she is chattel, something owned.

So maybe the earth is too big to love all at once, too great and various to be known by one word or image. I've seen the photograph taken from the moon of our jewelled island in a black sea. Yet at that scale, I can't see faces, can't hear voices, can't discern the landmarks of the place and time in which I live.

Can you love humanity? Can you love women without loving a woman? Can you love men without loving a man? Earth may be too great and various for what we call love, except as intention. There may be no meeting, no enactment, no consummation with the whole of it. When I was four, I knew a horse. All horses, horsekind, the *Horse,* I have yet to know.

We speak more easily of places and things: specific, singular, irreplaceable. This is the scale on which we live. To love the unknown is a ceaseless, bodiless hunger. The trick is to love what you know, what's familiar, what you've endured. To live with it, each day.

I'm not struggling with the earth, which simply *is,* beyond all argument, but with how to see it, think of it, and how to speak. It's a struggle with words and images, and with the deep, shifting strata of mind, the entire history of words and images.

Looking out the east window, now, I see willows and sage fading into heavy snow. If I change the names of things, call the willows *love* and the sage *grace,* the things themselves will not change. But my feelings toward them may. It may be harder to uproot *love* or to bulldoze a thicket of *grace.*

Willow and sage, love and grace. In time, I may be able to say the word *earth* in the same tone, with the same bone-deep knowing, as I say the word *horse.* And we may change our minds, and our hearts, and our ways.

The Tragic Wisdom
of Salamanders
Gerald Vizenor

MOTHER, MOTHER EARTH, THE NAMES HONORED AS TRIBAL VISIONS, could become our nonce words near the sour end of a chemical civilization. These naive and sentimental nicknames, a salutation to a common creation of nature, is the mere mother of manifest manners and tractable consumerism.

The names that mediate natural actions could unbosom the earth from the notions of maternal nonce words. The salamander and the natural mediation of amphibians, for instance, could be an unpretentious signature of the earth, the trace between land, water, and our stories. Consider the stories and memories of salamanders as the natural traces of survivance.

The salamander earth is a wiser name than obtuse tribute to an abused mother. The earth sustains the nonsense romance of the commons and the curses of science, and the earth must crave new narratives to heal the mortal wounds of objectivism and the incoherence of nuclear dominance.

"Scientific knowledge has lost its objective privilege and its epistemology has collapsed into incoherence, and yet our social theorists continue to grant it analytic privilege," wrote Will Wright in *Wild Knowledge*. "I am arguing that the scientific ideas of knowledge and nature are incoherent." Moreover, "nature must be understood reflexively, through a reference to language, not objectively," and "rationality must be criticized in the name of reflexive nature, not accepted in the name of objective nature."

The best tribal stories were never rushed to their extinction in nature or reason. The wise hunters honored the salamanders and endured the winter in the sure memories of their natural survivance. Not even the wicked shamans or predacious hunters in the fur trade could chase the breath of nature out of their own stories. Starvation, disease, and soul death were worries of the heart, but honorable hunters were liberated in the shadows of their natural mediations, memories, visions, and stories. The radioactive ruins and chemical wastes of our time are new worries and without the narratives of regeneration. The winter memories of survivance are denied in the ruins of a chemical civilization.

The earth must bear, as no mother would, the abuses, banes, and miseries of manifest manners. To name the wounded earth our mother, the insinuation of a wanton nurturance, is to avoid our own burdens in a nuclear nation.

Mother earth, the earth as our abused mother, is a misogynous metaphor; once more, the narratives of our parents have been abandoned in the ruins of sentimental representations. We are the heirs, to be sure; at the same time we are the orphans of our own dead tropes and narratives. We are the earth mutants, the lonesome survivors, who convene at night on the borders of tribal memories, creation, and treacherous observance.

"It is an indisputable fact that the concept of the earth goddess has grown strongest among the cultivating peoples," wrote Åke Hultkrantz in *The Religions of the American Indians*. "Many hunting tribes in North America manifest the same primitive belief in 'our mother,' 'mother earth.' The more recent peyote religion has accommodated Mother Earth to some extent under the influence of the Catholic cult of the Virgin Mary." The manifest notion of "primitive belief" is due no doubt to his patent on objective nature.

"Mother Earth will retaliate, the whole environment will retaliate, and the abusers will be eliminated," Russell Means maintained in *Mother Jones*.

"Things will come full circle, back to where they started." He announced that "it is the role of American Indian peoples, the role of all natural beings, to survive."

Åke Hultkrantz and Russell Means seem to accede to the tribal creation notions of mother earth. Means avouches a natural order in the language of functional religion and resistance. Hultkrantz inscribes the notion of mother earth as a universal representation of tribal favors and succors. He wrote in *Belief and Worship in Native North America* that "Mother Earth is a common idea among Indians over large parts of North America."

Sam Gill, however, wrote in *Mother Earth* that the "origins of Mother Earth as a Native American goddess were in some measure encouraged by the exigencies of the emergence of an 'Indian' identity that has complemented and often supplanted tribal identities." He pointed out that until "after the middle of this century, there is scant evidence that any Native American spoke of the earth as mother in any manner that could be understood as attesting to a major figure or a great goddess."

The earth as our mother would never endure the nuclear silence of the seasons in our stories, or the death count of natural reason in the common abuses of the earth in our name. We must be remembered as the earth with names that mediate natural actions, and new creations must be heard in our narratives.

Laban Roborant, the salamander man, and other characters in these stories, are the tribal tricksters of the mundane, the traces of the marvelous, and the solace of an escape distance. These trickster stories are aired to creation, natural reason, human unities, and the earth in the wild literature of survivance.

Roborant was born in the lonesome winter on a woodland reservation; he studied philosophies, established his own school of amphibian meditation, and ruled a boat dock at the tribal marina.

The salamander is a man of natural reason, and he holds attributive names and culture at an escape distance. The stories heard in his nickname are the trickster shadows of creation, the stories of mythic creatures. He would misuse the obvious over and over to hear common ecstasies in winter stories at the tree lines.

Roborant is a trickster healer who overturns the sentiments of mother earth to embrace the traces of the moist snails on cold concrete. Early every morning he copies the snail trails at the marina and traces them on fish location maps for the tourists.

"We cast our hearts to the cold water, and the snails smear the same stories on the concrete overnight," he said on the boat dock. "Here we are at the end of the dock, domestic animals who prey to be lonesome humans so we can name the earth our culture, and then we poison our natural relatives, poison the memories of our own creation in the literature of dominance, and that literature is no more original than the traces of snails."

"The traces of silence?"

"Survivance meditation," he whispered on the cold wind.

"Sounds like a lonesome literary theory."

"Meditation is not theoretical," said the salamander.

"Snails were never my signature."

"Their traces end in our memories," said the salamander. He watched my hands and mocked my signature moves. Then he laughed, and the wind carried the sound of his amphibian stories back over the water.

I was touched by this man with the amphibian nickname, this salamander of the tribal marina. He told elusive trickster stories, traced the terrestrial snails, and menaced the black flies on the dock. No one has ever demanded more of my emotions and reason at the same time than this salamander. No wild children, no sure advocates of the heart, no wicked shamans have reached into the silence of my memories, shadows, and creation with such worrisome stories as the salamander man. I learned in time that he was more treacherous than nature, more elusive than winter bears, more obscure than spiders at the seams of civilization, more audacious than crows in the birch, and more memorable than the salamanders in his meditation. He was the natural reason and ironies of the earth in his own stories.

Mother earth is the nickname of a tribal man who once lived in a paradise of black flies on a woodland reservation. The lake near his cabin was decorated with rich ribbons of natural light that summer. The rush of dawn touched the stones on the natural shore at the tribal marina and landed later in weakened shadows behind the medicine poles. Hundreds of black flies waited on the boat dock for the first glance of the sunrise, the sudden beams that would warm their wings into graceless flight.

"Black flies remember our creation," said the mother earth man.

"Not on this dock," said the salamander of the marina. He beat the sun to bash the black flies on the rails of the wooden dock, and then he brushed their remains into the water. The bodies of the flies floated near shore without honor, even the fish seemed to wait for the wings to move as a lure. The sun bounced on the water and roused the bodies of the wounded flies; their wings buzzed and turned in wild circles.

"There, listen to the flies, the signatures of creation even at their death," said the mother earth man. He leaned over the water and handed the cold bodies to the warm stones. The flies buzzed in the sun on the stones.

"Flies are bait not stories," said the salamander.

"Black flies are the earth mothers," said the mother earth man.

"Must be your cousins," said the salamander of the marina. He crushed more flies on the dock with his wide hand. "There, more relatives to mourn over on the stones." He raised three flies to the sun and then pulled out their wings.

"Black flies are my stories," said the mother earth man.

"Now you tell me," said the salamander.

"Thousands of black flies live on my name."

"You must mean *live* on your body," said the salamander. He covered his nose with his hands. Mother earth never washed, and he wore the same stained shirt for more than a year. The fetor of the mother earth man raised hundreds of generations of grateful black flies. When he moved into the light, the flies circled his head and crotch in great black orbits.

"They land on my middle name."

"Do the flies have nicknames?"

"More than one," said the mother earth man.

"Then you are the man of this house of mother flies?"

"You boast, but the earth hears the flies."

"Mother, my stories are about salamanders."

"Black flies are the same."

"Wash you body once and your relatives are gone."

"Once, many years ago, there were four flies caught in a bottle right on my desk," said the mother earth man. "We heard them buzz and watched them weaken day after day, and near the end, one after the other, they marched in circles close to the rim and then died upside down."

"Mother, are you ready to fly?"

"Almost every morning, summer and winter, for months and months after their death, the wings of the flies would buzz when the first blaze of sunlight bounced in the bottle," said the mother earth man.

"Weird suckers," said the salamander.

"Those black flies were the sound of creation."

"What kind of bottle was it?"

"Something in clear glass," said the mother earth man.

"Black flies sound much better in aluminum."

"To the ordinary person, the body of humanity seems vast," wrote Brian Walker in *Hua Hu Ching,* the teachings of Lao Tzu. "In truth, it is neither bigger nor smaller than anything else. To the ordinary person, there are others whose awareness needs raising. In truth, there is no self, and no other. To the ordinary person, the temple is sacred and the field is not. This, too, is a dualism which runs counter to the truth."

The salamander and the mother earth man were never the other in their stories of black flies, snails, ants, and crows; never the outsiders on the uncommon fields of tribal consciousness. The mother earth man returned to the reservation in silence; no one heard his stories but the black flies and the salamander; no one else could chase him out of his human silence. The mother earth man teased the salamander that there is no reason for silence in nature.

The stories of the salamander were worrisome to be sure, but he countered the names of dominance over natural reason, and he teased the mother earth man right back that the earth could become an absolute human silence, a nuclear silence.

The salamander boat man was the crossblood mandarin of the tribal marina. The solace of his natural memories was burdened with the remains of the causal philosophies that he had studied at more than seven universities; lonesome and morose, he dreamed his creation out on the ocean, founded the new school of amphibian meditation, and returned to the reservation. He envisioned natural reason over tribal silence and worried that the stories of amphibian creation had landed in mean translations. He teased the mother earth man that "some of our best stories died over and over again in romantic confessions to blond anthropologists."

"The earth mothers," he announced on his return to the reservation, "were much too intricate and bewildered to hear their own creation and regeneration as salamanders." So he became the tribal master of amphibian meditation moves. The salamander lived alone in the boat house over the water at the marina; he ate alone once a day, either baked walleye or venison stew with boiled potatoes. His thick white hair bounced with each move as he roamed the shores with the seasons, and the reservation mongrels were close at hand.

The salamander creates and remembers descriptive names, but nothing more since the time he flushed out philosophies and the cruelties of the mind at the universities. No one ever heard his sacred name, and he never responded to his birth name since he returned to the reservation as the salamander.

He is awakened by the natural rise of water and tours the dock at dawn. He hears the motion of the waves, that certain amphibian rush with the sunrise, and senses the natural hour even over wind and storms. That salamander bashes flies to feed his favorite fish near the dock. Later in the morning he rents boats and motors to the tourists.

"You must be the boat man," said the number woman.

"I am the salamander," declared the boat man.

"Greek surname, to be sure," said the number woman. Even on vacation she wore a badge that indicated she was a corporate real estate sales executive. Numbers became her nickname that second season at the marina because she would announce the time on clocks, dates, numbers on menus, road signs, and every number she noticed in the world. She mounted an electronic muskie sounder on the rented tribal boat and then read the numbers out. She turned the codes and sounded the numbers.

The salamander provided her with a snail map of the best fishing sites, one of the original snail trails he had traced earlier. He insisted that the snails knew more than machines, and the traces of snails to point to the best locations to catch muskies had at least the same chance as the usual fish stories. So he asked the mother earth man, "What does it matter that the snails are my original source of the best locations?"

"Then the snails deserve the credit," said mother earth man.

"The trace is not the catch," said the salamander.

"But the catch is in the name," said the mother earth man. "Salamander the Greek Indian, seven meters, now that's an unusual combination, there's a writer who makes such a claim, nine, thirteen, now what was his real name?"

"THOMAS KING," said the salamander.

"Right, he wrote *Medicine Creek*," said the numbers.

"No, *Medicine River* is the name of his novel."

"Right, damn good stories about softball."

"No, basketball," said the salamander.

"Right, natural players," said the numbers.

"Salamander is not a surname."

"First name, seventeen?"

"No, salamander is a meditation move."

"Right, what's the word on the catch?" asked the numbers.

"Try your sounder," said the salamander.

"Right, this mother sounder can locate a minnow in a rainstorm," said the numbers. She turned toward the marina and waved to the mother earth man who had paused between two medicine poles. Two wide belts of black flies shrouded the blue poles. "Now that is a strange man, so many flies follow him around he must be the best shit trick of the season."

"Black flies are his relatives," said the salamander.

"Right, think of all those mouths to feed," said the numbers.

"He does, and they eat together."

"Spare the flies and spoil the meal," said the numbers.

"The marina restaurant refused to let him through the door at first, because his families were sure to follow," said the salamander. "The tourists were sick when he was in the restaurant, but the owners soon changed the rule and turned him into the best fly catcher on the reservation."

"Right, he ate his relatives."

"No, mother earth was rushed through the back door without his relatives, and then when the inside flies circled the table in his honor he wiped his mouth with his hand and marched them right out the front of the restaurant," said the salamander. "He led those flies away without poisons, swatters, or tanglefoot paper."

"Give me some numbers," said the numbers.

"Ten thousand black flies waited outside the restaurant, and a hundred or so were at the table inside," said the salamander. "Mother earth is related to every black fly on the reservation, so the ones in the restaurant were distant cousins and ever so pleased to be back in the circle of his stench."

"Mother earth could make a fortune on fleas, ants, and crows, not to mention rats and cockroaches," said the numbers. "The ants would march by the thousands to his odor, and the crows would circle mother earth right out of the corn fields."

I FIRED AT THOSE crows over and over on the wing, and nothing died but natural reason and the stories of the earth in me. The crows were the enemies of the farmers not the corn, but the crows outwitted me that autumn and became my enemies. I was slow to learn that we heard the same seasons and survivance on the earth. My shotgun was cold, the crows were wiser, and that was a truer measure of the incoherence in the causal rush to science.

The corn honored the crows in some stories. The corn cursed the farmers and shouted to be liberated from science and human machines.

The corn teased the crows to be taken into their wise paradise. Otherwise, the corn would be dried and stored for the pigs to eat.

I tried to shoot those crows to save the corn, to land my honor as a hunter, and the corn tried to save the crows. The farmers hated the crows, poisoned the corn, and braced the hunters to terminate his enemies. The earth was poisoned, songbirds died in silence, and investors dickered over the corn futures; the futures that no other creatures could endure.

I shot at those crows over and over on the wing. I roamed the corn fields and cursed the wind that carried the crows out of my range of fire. The crows outwitted me with such ease, and tormented the farmers. The crows were in my sights, but the crows could see me much better and turned on the wind, a natural survivance, when the shots exploded.

The corn teased the crows to the bitter end of that season in my memories. The crows raided the machines over winter, the farmer lost his land to the bankers, not the crows, and the crows in me were wise not to aim and shot at the real enemies of this salamander earth.

"Children stationed in the fields or on the platforms of watch houses among the corn rows drove away blackbirds, crows, and chipmunks from the seed and young plants," wrote Carolyn Merchant in *Ecological Revolutions*. "Seed soaked previously in hellebore caused drunkenness in the marauding birds."

"Indian poke harrowed the settlers," said the salamander.

"That mother earth man would be a natural monarch of the cockroaches and the crows," said the numbers. "Can you imagine, the tribal marina and the dock secured by thousands of wise crows?"

"They talk too much," said the salamander.

"Imagine hordes of cockroaches marching out of their seams in the concrete, out of their cracks in bathrooms, out of ceilings, out of the woodwork everywhere to be in the wicked scent of this strange man," said the numbers.

"Indian poke enticed the anthropologists," said the salamander.

"Right, we could borrow his clothes and do the same."

"Some tourists were out here drinking one night, and they stole his shirt because they could not understand why any woman, much less an attractive blonde, would touch the mother earth man," said the salamander.

"Right, clothes are not the man," said the numbers.

"Anyway, mother earth was under the dock with a woman and the tourists stole his shirt," said the salamander. "The shirt was not his power, but it did have the wicked stench of power, and in the morning his abandoned shirt was covered with brown ants, millions of ants marched to touch his shirt and then returned to the earth."

I CAME BACK FROM a visit with relatives on the reservation and was horrified to discover that two armies of brown ants had invaded my house. The armies marched in two columns, one marched through the house to the pantry, and the second column turned around and marched out under the front door.

I crushed the armies under my shoes. I walked on the ants in both directions of their march, but there were millions of ants in two wide brown columns. My house was occupied by two cruel armies of brown ants. I worried that the ants would cover my shoes and climb up my legs. I needed a new weapon to kill the ants.

The armies were no match for a straw broom. I beat the ants with the side of the broom and then swept their crushed bodies into brown piles on the dining room floor. I was a warrior and beat the armies from one end of the house to the other. These ants would claim no rations in my pantry.

I had wounded hundreds of brown ants and hundreds more were dead on the hardwood floor. Brown bodies blocked the columns that moved near the baseboards to the pantry. I was furious that my house had been invaded, and tormented, at first, by the comeback of the ants. Their certain moves were not separation or panic in the face of the enemy; rather, the ants carried their dead and wounded from the battlefield. The enemy had attacked their columns with superior weapons and the ants carried their dead away. This was a body count, not a coup de main with the earth.

I moved closer to the armies and watched the soldiers honor their dead in battle. Their disaster was mine. I became the lonesome witness in the literature of solace and domination. The distance of my violence haunted the earth in my memories. I cried over the miseries my violence had caused in the lines of the ants. They might have carried me away if the earth had been turned in other stories.

The ants were in search of nothing more than a meal that summer. I discovered at last the most obvious conditions of their invasion. My superior weapons held the line between humans and the ants, otherwise the ants might have driven me out of my own house. At the turnaround in the pantry the armies were nourished by the remains of cola in several overturned bottles. These ants wanted nothing more from me than a taste of cola that summer and they landed in these stories. I had terminated hundreds of ants, and then, struck by the obvious, moved the cola bottles outside near the front door. The ants were spared the dangerous march through the house of their enemies.

Later that summer, I convinced a friend, who was about to spray ant killer on the kitchen counter, to give me two days to solve the problem without poison. Not only the ants, but humans would be poisoned with the spray. I placed a bottle cap filled with strawberry jam near the crack in the brick wall over the counter where the ants had entered. The next morning we discovered that the ants had gathered around the jelly and not the crumbs on the counter.

That night, over dinner, my friend told the story about my war and peace with the ants. Later we poured a few drops of liqueur into the bottle cap with the preserve. The next morning the ants were gone. Not one could be found in the kitchen. My friends reasoned that several scouts came home drunk and the ant families decided it was time to leave that decadent house forever. There was much laughter over my stories.

"MOTHER EARTH MAN'S shirt in a bottle cap," said the numbers.

"New meaning to ants in one's pants," said salamander.

"Mother earth man is my happy camper," said the numbers.

"Why do you say that?" asked the salamander.

"Well, because the earth loves him without a bath."

"This earth is a wounded man," said the salamander. "He is the mother cant of misused memories, the unwashed mother of trickster humor and romantic amusement, the wise hunter of liberation stories."

"Right, mother earth the transvestite," said the numbers.

"Never, mother earth is a holosexual trickster."

"Right, mother earth with the lonesome nickname."

"The earth has no name or reason," said the salamander.

"Whatever, but mother earth is my man."

"You and that horde of relatives."

"Never mind, the black flies are unmanned at night."

"Remember to hold your breath over his shirt," said the salamander as he traced an original snail trail on a new fish locator map. The map was plastic covered and embossed with a corporate real estate seal. "Not even the reservation mongrels can stand to be near his clothes for more than a few minutes at a time, so when do you plan to leave?"

"Does mother earth like to fish?"

"He would rather fly than catch a fish," said the salamander.

"Right, fly is his number," said the numbers.

"Mother earth landed once in Santa Cruz, California."

"Were the flies there?"

"No, he was at the university."

"The paradise of acute humdrum," said the numbers.

"That's where he earned his clever nickname," said the salamander. He turned and watched the mother earth man rush through the backdoor of the marina restaurant. "Who would believe that he was once a professor of literature and provost of a college at the university there?"

"Fantastic, the provost mother earth," said the numbers.

"Mother earth owned a townhouse in a faculty community on university land, and that is the reason he is here with the flies," said the salamander. "He lost his humor and returned to the reservation in silence when his learned colleagues and neighbors voted to use toxic chemicals on the common areas."

THE EARTH AS OUR mother has been wounded, and the rivers, birds, animals, and insects have been poisoned near the universities. We are the salamander earth, and no other names mean as much as the mediation of our names in stories. We bear the wounds of the earth, and that must be an obscure suicide. We are the mutants of chemical civilization.

I lived in a new faculty housing area on the campus and discovered on a casual evening walk that the university had been dumping toxic chemicals from the science laboratories within several hundred feet of family residences.

I called the campus fire department and was told that no one there knew anything about a toxic dump or how dangerous a mixture of the chemicals might be in a fire or earthquake. No one knew what had been dumped there, and no one seemed worried about the families who lived nearby. The faculty homeowners would not support a demand to remove the toxic dump from a housing area. These were the same faculty members who would subscribe to various ideologies and manifest manners, but they would not act in their ultimate identities as the earth. They were orphans who had lost their stories of survivance.

Ordinary citizens were able to understand the risks and use their common sense and communal interests to correct these hazardous conditions, but the most learned faculty homeowners would not confront the university administration over the toxic dump, not even in the interests of their own families.

Clearly, in this instance and many others that year in the glorious redwoods of the University of California, Santa Cruz, a higher education was not in the best interests of families or the earth. The faculty was burdened with careerism, the humdrum of elitism, and an unwise contract with objectivism. The earth cries to be heard, and the faculty critiques radical environmentalism. Not even the radical feminists, who ruled a separatist house on campus close to the toxic dump, would support the petition to remove the chemicals from a residential area. Other recourse identities, such as race, class, and gender, were much more significant in their considerations.

Several months later, the earth around the trees in the faculty housing area were removed by the landscape company, and then the holes were filled a few weeks later with a special chemical mixture of earth—so special, and so toxic, that when rain flooded the circles around the trees, the chemical mixture killed the grass. The lawn was marked with dead trails of grass from the trees to the drains.

Animals, birds, cultured pets, and children were drawn to the fresh earth around the trees. How would the children and other creatures know that the earth of our creation had become an attractive nuisance at a university?

Dare we breathe?

Dare we eat?

Dare we drink the water?

Dare we touch the poisoned earth?

Dare we touch ourselves?

Dare we listen to the sycophants of science?

I was closer to silence when the faculty homeowners once more voted down my proposal not to use toxic chemicals to maintain the common areas. The faculty seemed to have no other sources of wisdom than the minimal realities of objectivism. The president of the homeowners' association, an anthropologist and former marine, told me that lawn chemicals are not dangerous in the least. "Listen up," he shouted, "water is a chemical, do you want us to stop drinking water?"

"Indian poke is the best medicine for anthropologists."

"As a formal structure, language mediates between actions and the world, between social life and natural processes, and if this structure is to sustain its own possibility, then it must generate and legitimate actions that will successfully sustain this mediation," wrote Will Wright in *Wild*

Knowledge. "In order to sustain itself, language must generate practices that are ecologically coherent, which means that if knowledge is referred to language then the formal criteria for knowledge must include a reference to ecological coherence, to sustainability."

The University of California has established environmental policies that provide for "applicable health and safety standards." The regulations assure that "continuous attention shall be paid to the identification, monitoring, and control of potentially harmful substances and physical agents in the campus environment. The scope of this program shall include but not be limited to toxic materials, air quality in controlled environments, and elements of physical exposure such as lighting, noise, and temperature."

The Santa Cruz campus is a scene of entranced duplicities over the environment. The university administration there has failed in certain considerations to "maintain a reasonably safe environment for its students, academic appointees, staff, and visitors." The recourse of environmentalism on this campus is unusual because of these delusions; at the same time, there are chastened sermons on separatism; a withered inheritance of the last hurrah of elitism in the redwoods.

Michael Tanner, the academic vice chancellor, told me not to be concerned about the hazardous electrical transformers located on the campus. Hundreds of students could be exposed to polychlorinated biphenyls and many other toxic compounds from an electrical equipment fire. The provosts of the eight colleges on the campus reported to the academic vice chancellor, and we reported that the recent earthquake in the area was a reminder that the risks of chemical and electrical fires could never be underestimated.

"Professor Vizenor," announced the vice chancellor in a tense, avuncular tone of voice. "May I ask, are you a man who is afraid of snakes?" He leaned back from the conference table, pleased with the interrogative and the advantage he assumed as a senior administrator.

"No, not really, why would you ask me that?"

"Well, let me put it this way," he continued with no obvious sense of the ironic turn of his representation. "If you were afraid of snakes, surely you would not want us to kill all the snakes on the campus because of your fear, would you?" At last his provincial arrogance overcame his obtuse and unreasonable consideration of the issue.

"Would you be serious?"

"We cannot act on your fear of snakes," he assured me.

"These are electrical transformers, not snakes, and they use toxic compounds that may be carcinogenic if burned, and many industrial accidents have shown that polychlorinated biphenyls are dangerous and can cause birth defects in humans."

Michael Tanner listened, but he would not respond to my formal recommendation to remove the transformers that used polychlorinated biphenyls. He must have reasoned that his snake ruse would resolve my concern as a provost to "maintain a reasonably safe environment" for students on the campus.

Two years later, and much to my surprise, the San Francisco Chronicle reported that the United States Environmental Protection Agency had reached an agreement with the University of California that resolved "violations of federal regulations that govern the proper management of polychlorinated biphenyls" and that the "university agreed to pay a civil penalty of $150,000." Moreover, the university agreed to remove the hazardous electrical transformers from several campus, including Santa Cruz.

The federal regulators, to be sure, would not have been touched by the simulated snake stories that slithered in the office of the academic vice chancellor. Michael Tanner misused and abused natural reason as a method of institutional management; he might have used the weather as an execration of environmental issues. There are, of course, many dubious stories about the mutations of other creatures in academic administration.

"WE HAVE CHANGED the atmosphere, and thus we are changing the weather," wrote Bill McKibben in The End of Nature. "By changing the weather, we make every spot on earth man-made and artificial. We deprive nature of its independence, and that is fatal to its meaning. Nature's independence is its meaning; without it there is nothing but us."

We have misused the narratives of natural reason as we have the environment; we have abused the names of the seasons, the weather, salamanders, bears, crows, and ants in our creation stories, and that has weakened our survivance. The earth is burdened with our memories. We are the anomalous orphans who would ruin the narratives of natural reason and our own survivance.

The salamander is the new signature of the earth because we must learn to hear once more the tragic wisdom of natural reason and survivance. That humans turn to silence does not menace the earth, but the silence of the salamander could be the end of our nature and evolution.

Over and over "scientists say amphibians represent the global equivalent of the proverbial canary in the coal mine," wrote Emily Yoffe in "Silence of the Frogs," in *The New York Times Magazine*. The reasons for the silence of the salamander and the sudden decline of frogs are not understood by scientists.

Yoffe pointed out that herpetologists, those who study reptiles and amphibians, or frogs, toads, and salamanders, "with perhaps not the greatest objectivity, say frogs are the ideal creature to reflect the health of the environment. In their view, frogs are living environmental assayers, moving over their life cycles from water to land, from plant-eater to insect-eater, covered only by a permeable skin that offers little shield from the outside world."

The outside world has misused natural habitats and the narratives of amphibian survivance. We are the heinous other in the outside world of the salamander, the other in habitat destruction, the other in the ruins of our own stories about the atmosphere, the weather, the oceans, and our stories have turned to ultraviolet burns, pesticides, acid rain, sour snow, deforestation, soil erosion, radioactive waste, the dubious management of the environment, and the introduction of nonnative species of fish into rivers and pristine mountain lakes. "No pristine place can protect a species," wrote Yoffe. "At the top of the list is an increase in ultraviolet radiation. Among the hardest-hit amphibians are those that live at high altitudes." Many highland species of frogs "lay black eggs and have a black peritoneum and, in the male, black testes," a survival strategy "to protect themselves from harmful radiation."

The salamander earth must hear many great stories to regenerate our survivance in a chemical civilization. The silence of our nature is heeded by the salamanders. The lost creatures and mutations are phantom memories that may be too much even for the giants of amphibian meditation to endure.

The salamander hears the water rise to the sun over the tribal marina. He crushes the slow black flies, but never to extinction, and teases the mother earth man who liberates the same number of flies from the restaurant every morning. We do this over and over again because the stories hold us to natural reason and our mortality. The salamander earth is a story of liberation.

"For unless you own the whale, you are but a provincial and sentimentalist in Truth," wrote Herman Melville in *Moby Dick*. "But clear Truth is a thing for salamander giants only to encounter; how small the chances for the provincial then?"

Montana Return:
A Story about Stewardship
Alston Chase

THE ROAD WAS EVEN WORSE THAN I REMEMBERED IT, WHICH WAS A
good sign. Ignoring my steering efforts the pickup lurched from one set
of ruts to another, as though it had a will of its own. Keith Lowrie sat
beside me, eyes focused straight ahead. Our route followed Rock Creek,
as this tiny serpentine stream ducked through thickets of still-green willow and past hillside stands of aspen, glowing gold in the late fall sun.

We passed an abandoned house, nearly invisible in deep shadow. On a
bare knoll above the house we could see the shell of a one-room school.
Its white paint had turned lead gray; its windows were broken and the
cupola was missing. A sign in front of the house said, "No Hunting. No
Fishing. Don't Ask."

"This was Lingshire," I said, anticipating Keith's question. "Our old
ranch is just nine miles farther. Used to be quite a community here—

dances in the schoolhouse every Saturday night, everything. Then Wellington Rankin—who was already the biggest landowner in Montana—bought everybody out and hired ex-convicts as ranch hands. Lingshire got a reputation as a tough place, and the town died. When we came, Rankin's foreman, who everyone called 'Pap,' was the only one left. I used to visit Pap and talk about the old days. But he died fifteen years ago."

"It must feel funny coming back," Keith said. "Are you afraid what you'll find?"

"Terrified," I answered.

I was showing Keith, a friend from Australia, where I once lived. And as Keith intuited, I had misgivings about the whole idea.

This was known as Millegan country, a remote expanse of land lying alongside Montana's Smith River. The nearest town was sixty miles away and closest neighbors thirty, along a road that was closed in winter and a bottomless mud trench when it rained in summer. When I and my wife, Diana, came here more than twenty years ago, we swore we would never leave. We had found where we wanted to live until we died. That thought sustained us, like morphine for the psyche, dulling the pain of money worries. But eventually money, or rather the lack of it, prevailed. We were forced to sell our ranch.

After leaving Millegan country, I wrote a book revealing how inept rangers in Yellowstone turned that magnificent park into a black hole for wildlife. I went on to study land management in other preserves as well. I hiked thousands of miles through many national parks, and I never encountered the diversity of life I found on the ranches by the Smith River.

We amputated the deep roots that we had sunk into this land, and they never ceased to bleed. Something died inside us—as though our vision of ourselves, our future, of what is good and valuable in the world, became illusion. We did not come back to visit. We loved Millegan too much to see it again. Returning would only revive the pain of loss.

I also wanted to keep my memories intact, and was afraid I would find this land changed beyond recognition. That is the American Way: paradise found and paradise destroyed by commercial excrescence, greed, and plain stupidity.

But driving through Lingshire with Keith was reassuring. The cycle of nature continued. Twenty years ago beaver had consumed the aspen and willow along Rock Creek, leaving the stream barren as a ditch. Now this vegetation once more grew in profusion, and beaver were back. These changes signified some things endured. I wondered what our old ranch would be like.

LOOKING BACK, THE escape to Montana was a matter of necessity, not choice. The idea to come struck like lightning as I attended a special meeting of the board of trustees of Macalester College. The chairman of the board was describing me as "irresponsible" for suggesting that academic programs be given highest priority in the college budget. And this public condemnation pleased the mob of students who packed the hall calling for my head.

I was chairman of the philosophy department and Diana had a good job writing curricula in environmental studies for the Minneapolis public schools. But Macalester was self-destructing. Deeply in debt, the college had gone through five presidents in three years. Students ruled the campus. Hostile to learning, they displayed an uncanny genius for wreaking havoc, once even locking professors in the hall during a faculty meeting and refusing to let them out until they voted as the students decreed. Another time, students occupied Old Main, staying until the board fired the president.

Barbarians had breached the gates, and I and our oldest son, David, headed west during spring break, looking for a place to hide. In Cascade, Montana, a real estate agent named Warren Hastings drove us to Millegan country. We traveled over bare hills that looked down on the Missouri plain, then past rolling slopes where pine forests framed snow-covered meadows. We plowed through deep drifts until we came to collapsing log buildings hidden in a declivity next to a spring.

We peered into the hole in the roof of the log barn and through the glassless windows of the bunkhouse and blacksmith's shed. We drove across an open field that seemed to go on forever, until suddenly Hastings braked hard. Getting out, we stood at the lip of a magnificent canyon. Later we would call this precipice "the point." In the distance, the Little Belt Mountains crowded the sky. At our feet, one thousand feet below, the Smith River snaked between vertical red and orange limestone cliffs. A prairie falcon circled overhead.

"This is it," David said.

WE BOUGHT THIS dream we could not afford: a three-thousand-acre homestead stretching from the Smith River canyon through pine forests to the high open fields that straddled Gaddis Hill. We had no telephone, running water, or electricity. The ranch was fifty-five miles from Great Falls and twenty-five from the nearest maintained road.

But this was not a wilderness experience. Millegan country, we discovered, had its own history, and we became part of it.

Locals called our ranch the Ben Dunn place after the first white owner who moved there in 1916. But Blackfoot Indians came before Dunn. Teepee rings signifying their occupation were visible in the pasture, and the steep trail they built, known as "the packdown," was still the best way to the river. In the 1920s, Millegan was bootlegging country, where cowboys made whiskey in high-country caves, beyond the reach of federal agents. A bootlegger's widow named Bessie Vineyard went to work for Dunn, and eventually bought the place from him. She was a tough cowgal who could shoe a horse better than any man, and in 1948 she married her neighbor, Jerrold Cope. Bessie and Jerrold lived at the Dunn place until, as all Milleganers eventually discover, this uncompromising country became too hard for them. They moved to Townsend, and Diana and I took their place.

We arrived in June 1972 with our three sons, Sidney, 11, Lawrance, 13, and David, 15. It was the beginning of a magic summer, a crystalline interlude that remains shimmering in memory.

We hired a carpenter named Charley Reissing, who pitched a tent in our front yard and took meals with us. Together with Charley, our three boys and I, armed with nail-pullers and crowbars, tore down the blacksmith's shed and built a log cabin we dubbed "the kitchen house."

Charley spent three summers with us. Gray-haired and rosy-cheeked, he talked about himself in the third person, beginning sentences with "Old Charley boy was darned mad when . . ." In evenings, as coyotes howled in the distance, we sat by the kitchen house and listened to Charley tell stories about Charles M. Russell, the famous western artist he had known as a boy.

Together with Charley, we tapped another spring and built a bath house, putting in running water. We also built a bunkhouse, but Diana and I stayed in Jerrold's and Bessy's cabin, sixteen feet square, lined with beaverboard inside and plywood outside. We called it "the manse."

An elderly ranch couple, Bud and Annie Laurie Dawson, summered cattle across the Smith. About twice a month they drove their red stock truck with two brown geldings to the packdown, unloaded the horses, and rode to a little cabin on Tenderfoot Creek. Annie Laurie was a former schoolteacher and a flaming liberal who loved to complain that the *New*

Republic magazine had become too conservative. Bud was fiercely loyal to his place and had a reputation for cantankerous territoriality. But they adopted us. When we went to Great Falls we stayed at their house, drinking beer and arguing about fence lines and socialism until the sun came up and our mouths turned dry.

Shopping for riding horses, we visited a rancher named Art Watson who lived in a spring-filled valley known as Benton Gulch thirty miles south. In his eighties, Art had lived there all his life and knew more about Millegan than any man alive. His ranch was the most beautiful we ever saw. His father homesteaded the place in 1865, and in the 1920s Art turned down a $2 million offer for it from a New York stockbroker.

We bought a wonderful horse named Dandy from Art and visited the rancher often to hear stories about the old days. Many ranchers once lived in this country, Art told us. Lingshire and Millegan were bustling communities. But one by one ranchers died, got too old or went broke, and the land emptied.

Three times a week I drove ten miles to Millegan to pick up mail and talk about the weather with our nearest neighbors, Carl and Betty Anderson. Carl loved a good joke. He glued a nickel to the floor of the kitchen and collapsed with laughter every time someone tried to pick it up.

One evening in July, a small man walked by the kitchen house, not stopping until we hailed him. About five feet tall, he wore rubber hip boots folded down to his knees and a tattered army fatigue jacket. His name was Scott Allen. A veteran of the Spanish-American War, he had been a trapper in this country ever since. His wife, a Blackfoot Indian, was in a nursing home, but Scott still lived in his grass-roofed log cabin by the river. That day, this ninety-year-old man had hiked three miles and climbed a thousand feet from the Smith to visit his favorite rhubarb patch.

Our children visited Scott's tiny cabin regularly. He cooked them griddlecakes on a woodstove made from a fifty-five-gallon oil drum and told them stories about meeting mountain lions and trapping beaver.

In fall we packed our cars and returned to Minnesota. But having tasted Millegan, we could not stay away. Three years later, when David and Lawrance were in college and Sidney at boarding school, we returned, determined to stay forever. We moved into the manse. We made friends with the land, and the seasons defined our days.

In summer, we hiked or rode to the river, where the boys hung a rope from a tree over-hanging a cliff and used it to make bungee dives. I flyfished, catching and releasing the big brown and rainbow trout. We watched herds of antelope canter across our pasture like wildebeest on the Serengeti. Diana took day rides, and I long hikes. In fall, when short-ening days provoked a sense of urgency, we cut and split logs for our wood stove. I hiked alone into the dark shadows of the canyon, stalking spawning browns as ice formed on the guides of my rod and as deer watched black bears hungrily devour chokecherries.

In winter, we sat next to the woodstove reading by Coleman lantern and watched as elk, their breath visible in the frigid dry air, silently careened down the hill, a herd without thunder, sending up clouds of snow carried by the wind. We sometimes snowshoed to the top of Gad-dis Hill in forty-below cold to check on our horses, which each fall we turned loose to forage for themselves. Three times a week I rode the snowmobile to Millegan, to drink coffee with Andersons and pick up the mail. In spring, we sat in our pasture, watching a pair of bobcats catch ground squirrels for their young. And each day, every season, Diana and I walked to the point, where we stood in silence.

Throughout the seasons we felt like privileged visitors enjoying the company of animals—mountain lions, lynx, bobcats, elk, whitetail and mule deer, antelope, big horn sheep, mountain goats, porcupines, skunks, coyotes, black bears, badgers, hawks, and falcons—that called Millegan home and that always seemed surprised to find us among them.

But our idyll did not last long. We ran out of money and had to sell the ranch. In July 1981 we left, not looking back.

AND NOW, THIS late October of 1992, I was returning after all. I found the land had changed little, but all the people we knew were gone.

At the ranch, we encountered carpenters building a new bunkhouse where the old one had stood. Charley Reissing, the workmen told us, died in 1986. Hiking to the point, we found the scene exactly as it had been more than twenty years before.

We walked down the packdown. Every pebble under my feet seemed exactly as it was in 1972, when our family scampered down this trail for the first time. At the river we found Scott Allen's cabin half buried in silt by a flood. The earth was slowly reclaiming his legacy. Scott had died sev-eral years before, but his pots and pans stood by the stove, as though he had just stepped outside for a minute.

Floods had changed the river bottom, filling in my favorite pools with gravel and creating new holes. The pool where our boys had bungied was dry land, and the fishing was now much poorer, no doubt impoverished by the thousands of floaters who take rafts and canoes down the Smith each summer.

PEOPLE DIE, BUT the earth endures. Nearly everyone we had known in Millegan was dead: Warren Hastings, Charley Reissing, Jerrold and Bessie Cope, Scott Allen, Art Watson, Annie Laurie Dawson, and Carl Anderson. They were the stewards of Millegan. The land we found and loved was as they kept it. They preserved it and they are gone. Seriously depleted even when we lived there, Millegan was now empty.

To qualify as a caretaker of a place, one must first vow to remain ten thousand years, poet Gary Snyder observed. Stewardship requires faithfulness. But while Snyder may believe in commitment, he was married four times. And as we found, pledges are hard to keep. The people of Millegan—the Blackfoot and early ranchers—intended to stay forever. Their resolve made them good stewards of the land. But eventually they, like our family, had to leave. They were casualties of the slow death of rural America, of an economy that has no use for people who live on the land. I wonder who will replace them.

Today, ranchers are under attack from environmentalists and animal rights advocates. It has become fashionable to view stockmen as ecological sinners, guilty of overgrazing, killing predators, misusing water, and generally laying waste to the landscape.

Activists, most of whom live in or near great cities, would take the land from these people. They would end grazing and build more national parks and wildernesses. Others want to evict ranchers and transform the West into a "great open" or a "buffalo commons." Some, promising to go "beyond beef," would kill ranching altogether. By these steps they would sever America's last thin threads to the land, and rural culture, already sick, would die.

Ranchers would be replaced by rangers who grew up in places like Cincinnati and Los Angeles, who move to a new post every four years, and who serve only Washington. The diversity of wildlife I found in Millegan would vanish as it has already in many national parks, and the scandals of mismanagement and declining biodiversity of public lands, such as I uncovered in Yellowstone, would multiply.

I shudder. Some ranchers do indeed abuse the land, and we should not tolerate their transgressions. But only rural folk can save nature. The abundance of wildlife we found in Millegan was the product of the stewardship of people who were born and buried there. But economic reality, demographic forces, and even, more recently, environmental activism, are killing this way of life. Meanwhile, rootless urban values are ascendent, even in Montana. Eighty percent of those who moved to Bozeman in the 1980s, sociologists tell us, have already left.

So the culture that preserves is dying and the values that destroy are ascendent. Even environmentalists forget that stewardship requires the survival of rural communities. Unless we can save them, nothing else we do will matter.

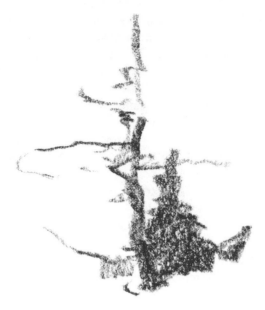

A Quiet Revolution
Jack Hemingway

WE WERE ENJOYING THE GREATEST STEELHEAD SEASON IN TERMS OF numbers of fish into the Snake River system since records were first kept. We were also experiencing far and away the greatest number of steelhead fly-fishermen ever assembled in the general area of the Clearwater, Snake, Grande Ronde, and Salmon rivers. There was a time when this would have delighted me. That so many of the good runs should be occupied by fly anglers would have been a joy. But that time was long ago. No longer are the odds better than even that a fly-fisherman met on the stream will be a "good guy" who has at least a fundamental understanding of stream-side etiquette and a modicum of manners. And what was particularly disturbing was that a substantial proportion of the fly-rod wielders were guides from other areas. The guiding seasons were over for them, and they were on a busman's holiday. Nothing wrong with that if they had set the sort of example for others one would have expected. Instead, they were consistently the worst pool hogs—scarcely the sort of behavior one would expect from those who introduce beginners to our sport.

I parked off the road near a long broad run on the Snake River after finding most of my favorite runs already in use by one or more anglers. I proceeded to put on waders, lace my boots. As I started to put my rod together, a four-wheel-drive vehicle pulled in right beside mine, and the occupant, a youngster in his early twenties, by the look of him, got out and, waders already on, started for the tailgate of his car to fetch his already-set-up rod. I asked him rather pointedly, "Are you actually planning to fish this run?"

"Of course," he replied, as he started for the best part of the run.

"In that case I'll go somewhere else."

"You don't have to do that. There's plenty of room for two."

"Only if you fish for companionship," I replied somewhat ungraciously. I left him with the pool to himself and a puzzled look on his face. He hadn't a clue, and therein lies the problem.

WHEN MANY OF US now "old-timers" first became involved with the fledgling Federation of Fly Fisherman in the mid to late sixties, most of us already had years of fly-fishing experience under our collective belts. We had suffered through the spinning-gear revolution that followed World War II, which populated our rivers, lakes, and streams with an explosion of newcomers attracted to fishing by the ease with which the use of the new spinning tackle could be mastered by even the most uncoordinated beginner. We hoped that we would be able to start a meaningful move to convert many of these newcomers to the ancient art of the fly rod. The reasons were many, but certainly among the most important, in our view, were the gentler aspect of the sport and the fact that, by its very nature, it lent itself more easily to such conservation measures as catch-and-release. While it formed no formal part of our logic, there was an unspoken feeling among us that fly-fishermen were somehow a superior breed and more likely to be gentlemen than would other anglers. Initially this attitude created some serious difficulties in our relations with other groups and opened us to the valid criticism that we were "elitists." Nevertheless, the federation made enormous strides in the years that followed and, along with the less method-oriented Trout Unlimited, was instrumental in changing attitudes about the value of our freshwater fishing resources. What it also accomplished was totally unlooked for: an unprecedented explosion in fly-fishing that was augmented by the booming economy of the Reagan era and the consequent rise of the yuppies.

What was also exploding during this era was the fly-fishing industry. This proliferation had positive aspects, including marvelous technological innovations in tackle, a rebirth of fly-fishing literature, new learning tools such as video, and the ubiquitous fly-fishing school. The tackle industry suddenly recognized the importance of the fly-fishing sector, and fly-fisherman mailing lists grew almost overnight from around twenty thousand to between five and ten times that number, and continue growing. New and wonderful specialty magazines were born, and most have made it.

Fly-tying became not just a serious hobby but, in many cases, a profitable enterprise that spawned fly-tying conglomerates based in low labor-cost countries. The best ones created a self-policed system for awarding royalties to the innovative American tyers whose patterns were changing much of fly-fishing and being reproduced en masse in South America, India, Sri Lanka, and East Africa.

Old fishing lodges were refurbished, and hundreds of new ones were created in unlikely locations. Entire communities previously devoted to logging suddenly spewed forth fly-fishing guides as their principal product. While some states, such as Idaho, sought to control guide numbers by limiting outfitter licenses, others viewed the trend as an income producer, and anyone willing to pay for a guide license became a guide. Even limiting the number of outfitters in any particular area failed to solve the problem in its entirety, as the outfitters could employ an unlimited number of guides. Outfitters, however, by having to post bonds, did impose a measure of responsibility on their guides.

Perhaps the biggest single development of the new age of fly-fishing was the research done in Montana by Richard Vincent in the late sixties and early seventies on the Madison River and O'Dell Creek. While there was already a growing interest in special regulations such as catch-and-release, fly-only, and single-hook-artificial-only, the solidly entrenched fish hatchery bureaucrats in the state fisheries agencies were loathe to cede any ground to plans that would inevitably lead to the diminution of their role in coldwater fisheries. They had the support of a constituency nurtured by years of easy handouts, which, however, were becoming increasingly expensive in view of higher feed costs and the poor rate of return-to-creel in all but heavily fished urban waters. Vincent's research, done in stages over a number of years, proved beyond a doubt that:

- The hatchery catchables that survived the fishing season had a poor chance of survival in the wild through a severe winter
- The cost of providing these fish was substantially greater than the revenue from fishing licenses
- In those sections of river where catchables were introduced, the populations of larger wild trout were almost entirely eliminated
- The virtual elimination of larger wild trout was caused by the social behavior of the catchable hatchery trout whose schooling patterns, learned in the confines of crowded concrete rearing ponds, totally disregarded the territorial behavior of the larger wild fish, who were used to defending their favored lines against the attempted forays of a few competitors but were unable to do so against the continuous crowding of the congenital idiots from the concrete pens

These conclusions, and a growing interest in fishing for wild fish as well as an expressed preference for stream and river fishing, finally led fish and game agencies to modify their views and advocate wild trout management in those places where it was deemed appropriate.

Research on such endangered late-maturing species as the West Slope cutthroat led to the adoption by Idaho of catch-and-release regulations in much of its habitat and a consequent resurgence of this completely wild native species. This was a biological decision. Later moves toward catch-and-release were made in response to public pressure exerted by the growing forces of the fly-fishermen. The hatchery bureaucracy was able to perform yeoman service in the stocking of fingerlings in reservoirs and lakes, where nature could grow them to suitable size, and to assume a leading role in the new steelhead and salmon recovery programs that were then just coming on line. The byword of this time of change was *quality*. Strangely, the word became an adjective, and suddenly everyone was seeking a "quality experience."

For a while it appeared that nirvana was fast approaching. Each new area designated for special regulations brought joy to all fly-fishermen and especially to those of us who had struggled for years to help bring all this about. Unfortunately, we hadn't anticipated the sheeplike herd instinct of the new wave of fly-fishermen. None of them wanted to fish anywhere but where there were special regulations. Within a ten-year span, such former paradises as the Railroad Ranch stretch of Henry's Fork of the Snake and the Sun Valley Ranch stretch of Silver Creek in my part of the West became overcrowded hells.

The plus side was that above and below these stretches one could fish in unregulated waters in more or less complete solitude, with only an occasional immobile bait fisherman to add flair to the landscape. Unfortunately, the explosion in guides soon brought even these places into their fold as their clients hungered continually for new secret places. Waters heretofore fished only by a few cognoscenti and locals sported all-day, guided, nonstop float traffic. The new generation of guides came to consider these fisheries as a private domain owed to them so they could a earn a living. It has even reached a point where a guide who doesn't spend his winters in the tropics or the antipodes hasn't got it all together.

The far corners of the world are currently being invaded by a horde as devastating to the art of contemplative angling as the barbarians to Rome or the sod busters to the Old West.

Fortunes are being spent in the feverish pursuit of Atlantic salmon throughout their range, proving that a fat wallet can indeed bring a measure of happiness to those who know how best to spend it. Similarly, the pursuit of steelhead has created crowded fly-fishing conditions throughout their range, with the possible exception of a few fly-in locations and the newly opened areas of Kamchatka.

While hatchery stocks of steelhead seem to be holding their own in many areas, there are already signs that drastic measures must be taken to rejuvenate the genetic strains being used and to protect the genetic variety of the wild strains. Furthermore, the success of some salmon programs in British Columbia has imperiled wild steelhead races because of the taking of huge salmon quotas by "commercials" in nonselective fisheries at the mouths of such key steelhead rivers as the Dean and the Skeena. The ratio of steelhead to salmon is now so small that those segments of the steelhead runs entering the river during the salmon netting season are being virtually wiped out. This has served to diminish the early fly-fishing available in many Skeena tributaries and in the Dean River and to concentrate the best fishing into the latter part of the season when the vagaries of equinoxal weather and possible early freeze-up can hamper already crowded conditions.

The search for the Holy Grail—large, relatively easy fish in uncrowded conditions—has become the new fetish of our sport, and few of us can plead "not guilty" of this pursuit. When the promised rewards of a costly and lengthy journey fail to materialize, it can be a serious blow, not only to our pocketbooks, but also to our egos.

What many newcomers to the sport may not realize is that something very important has almost disappeared from fly-fishing, though it can still be found in a few backwaters that have been passed by in the frantic search for new, more productive waters. This "something important" can best be expressed by such words as *peace, calm, tranquility, gentleness, quiet, modesty, solitude, appreciation, consideration,* and *contemplation.*

Rare indeed is the angler who has acquired his skills or his ethics entirely on his own. Most of us who are old-timers learned by the example of those who preceded us, either by watching and emulating or because of the generosity of those willing to give us some of their precious time astream. While the angling literature helped to guide our progress, most of it was sufficiently vague to require our experimenting on our own and consequently evolving our own techniques to solve the myriad problems a stream and its trout can pose. Social problems posed by the necessary crowding resulting from steelhead and salmon runs on waters close to urban areas were solved by practical working rules adapted to the predominant method of angling. Where wet fly-fishing was the accepted norm, for example, it rapidly became understood that a rotation system, with no breaking into the middle of the run being fished, was the accepted rule. Anyone seeking to break into the pattern anywhere but at the top was severely chastised by all present.

Under more normal, less crowded conditions on public waters, a strict code of ethics prevailed. It was unheard of for anyone to enter any pool or reach of water being fished by another angler unless invited. It was also considered extremely poor form to hog a pool by staying indefinitely in one spot. If you found an angler fishing one of your favorite spots, it was unthinkable to position yourself obtrusively while awaiting his departure. The proper procedure was either to go elsewhere, leaving the angler to enjoy his fishing undisturbed, or to hide in such a manner as to remain totally undetected. The latter was one of the best ways to learn, whether by detecting errors in the angler's approach to fishing the pool or by noting something innovative and successful.

In relatively featureless waters, such as long freestone flows without obvious riffle-pool sequence or on meadow waters, the drill consisted of ascertaining whether an angler was fishing up or downstream and then only to fish the water behind him and at a distance sufficiently removed that he could in no way ever feel that he was being hurried; in other words, to fish at the same or a slower pace than the angler with precedence. To tell the truth, some of the finest stretches of stream I've ever fished I discovered as a result of seeking out new places because the old,

popular, obvious spots were already occupied. In years with goodly numbers of summer steelhead showing in the sparkling pools of the North
Umpqua, Dan Callaghan and I fished the river together; one of us would
fish the principal runs while the other concentrated on water above and
below, nameless and outwardly featureless but often providing exciting
surprises. Several of these waters have since acquired name status and
have proved reliable even in fish-scarce years.

Unfortunately, it is becoming more and more difficult to find waters to
fish without the company of others. Such strategems as avoiding the
major hatches of green drake, brown drake, salmon fly, willow fly, and
tricos can prove helpful. For instance, if a particular hatch attracts all the
anglers for its emergence at nine A.M. every morning, these fellows tend
to leave when it is over at eleven thirty. The rest of the day can be quite
pleasing with much of the stream to yourself.

Opening-day circuses and the major large fly hatches, such as the
salmon fly hatch in the West, should be avoided at all costs unless you do
indeed fish for the pleasure of the company of other fishermen. My preference is for "dog day" fishing, when no one wants to be astream and the
fish are not interested in anything. Any fish caught on these days is a true
achievement, and solitude is indeed possible.

Still, these strategems are only escapes from the real problems: the
commercialization, the newcomers' general ignorance of the manners
and morals of fly-fishing, and the elevation of technical knowledge and
result-oriented success to greater importance than the appreciation of the
real values of this sport.

I have recently chosen no longer to respond to language that I once
espoused fervently. At one time I took pride in knowing the Latin or scientific name of every fish and every insect with which I was ever likely to
come into contact anywhere I might fish. In an effort to take some of the
wind out of the sails of those new experts who know everything and
nothing about fly-fishing for trout, who are totally and expensively
equipped and have been inappropriately educated by hero figure guides
and fly-fishing school gurus, I have joined the "little gray fucker" school
of fly-fishing, size and color being adjustable. I continue to encourage
honesty and lament such responses to the question of "Where did you
catch him?" as "in the mouth" or some fictitious location. My friend
Adrian Dufflocq, who sees many anglers fish at his Cumilahue Lodge in
Chile, rates them according to their "slime factor." This is an exponential
number indicating the extent to which an angler will lie about the results

of his fishing in order to appear to be a better or at least a more successful fisherman than he really is.

I remember a crowded August on the North Umpqua when, the water
skeleton low, no fish were being caught—no fish, that is, except for those
one particular angler reported having released each of these otherwise
fishless days. Six turned out to be his slime factor. I sacrificed one shameful day to spying on the poor fellow with my ten-power field glasses, and
nary a fish did he touch. However, at kiss-and-tell time over iced Bombay
gin, six fish had again been released. I decided thereafter to believe all fish
reports. I'm convinced that a doubted tale-teller may be prodded into
exerting superhuman efforts to justify his claims and may kill fish he
would otherwise have released because he thinks he will not be believed
if he doesn't produce the cold corpus delicti.

A certain portion of the South Fork of the Boise River here in Idaho
remained the almost exclusive province of a small group of serious fly-
fishermen during the fifties and sixties. Their secret lay in some profes-
sionally prepared signs that they posted throughout the area proclaiming
it a dangerous rattlesnake area. Such simple strategies no longer have
much effect. Today's fly-fishermen are too competitive to be put off so
easily. The rattlesnakes have long since been crowded out of that canyon.

Four hundred years ago, on the ninth of August 1592, the patron saint
of fly-fishermen, Izaak Walton, was born into what was essentially still a
pastoral society. Until the heavy water demands of the past decade caused
damaging abstractions of ground water from the chalk downs of Dorset,
Hampshire, and Wiltshire, trout fishing was able to survive in Walton's
bailiwick despite its closeness to London and despite the Industrial Revolution. While the fly-fishing explosion had an impact in England, it was
mostly in the field of reservoir fishing, which became available on a daily
ticket basis at fairly reasonable prices to the general public but with fly-
fishing restrictions. Stream fishing remained, as it had for generations,
the purview of the landed and wealthy. Riparian rights include the water,
its fish, and the right to fish. Good manners tend to be a characteristic of
the British. Fishing there is still a pleasure, if you can afford it.

We are the legatees of a wonderful tradition of hunting and fishing
being available to one and all. Public hunting is, sadly, already becoming
increasingly expensive except on the National Forest and Bureau of Land
Management lands. As to fishing, recent court decisions have guaranteed
public access to navigable rivers, but the restriction to remain below the
high-water mark has eliminated the nonboating fisherman in many

instances. Pressure is building quickly on public waters countrywide. It is not inconceivable that fish and game agencies may be forced to limit access in premium areas, providing access maps as is now done for special game management units. Thorough planning would be required to accommodate both local and vacationing fishermen. In response to a request for public opinion on this matter, regarding the Nature Conservancy waters of Silver Creek in Idaho, a surprising number of anglers felt that the increasing numbers of anglers didn't adversely affect the fishing results and that any attempt to limit access would be an imposition. My own position is that results are not what's at stake but rather the sort of experience the angler will enjoy. And since that poll was taken, there are indications that the increasing angler numbers are stressing the fish.

A historical view of the advent of manners in Western civilization points up the fact that politeness was first and most often practiced by those who were unarmed in the presence of those with weapons and by armed men in each other's presence. In other words, what most inspired politeness was respect and fear. I hope that to inspire respect it won't become necessary to carry weapons into the fly-fishing fray. What we badly need is a strong educational program which can give a different slant to the values that so many of today's fly-fishermen have espoused. A behavioral code should be established and taught with the same vehemence as is catch-and-release and be given as high a priority by those organizations that promote fly-fishing. Furthermore, the competitiveness that is taking over the sport must give way to a greater appreciation for the quieter aspects of the sport. The "in-your-face" angler so often encountered these days who typically, when confronted with his trespasses, retorts, with, "Do ya think you own the fucking stream?" must somehow be shamed into modifying this behavior.

A whole generation of fishermen has missed an integral part of their education. In addition to an educational program to emphasize a behavioral code, it should be the objective of every old-timer to teach these values to new anglers, and if necessary even to bring the error of their ways to their attention. The question to a fellow angler should no longer be, "How'd you do?" but rather, "Enjoying your fishing?" We should begin to focus on enjoyment, not achievement.

We can keep the gains we've made and learn to share our enjoyment of the sport. I came to realize that I had demonstrated an ungenerous spirit when I left that young fellow to fish the run alone. My remark, though meant to illuminate, may well have further entrenched him in a bad habit. I should have stayed and taken the time to enlighten him by setting a good example and giving a little of myself. Only by analyzing our own errors and correcting them can we set the right example and help lead others into a "quiet revolution"—one in which peace, calm, tranquility, gentleness, quiet, modesty, solitude, appreciation, consideration, and a contemplative nature comprise the standard of perfection.

Landscape with Figures
Ted Kooser

He that bites on every weed must needs light on poison.
                                                    —Old proverb

IT'S A HOT JULY AFTERNOON IN NEBRASKA, AND ALONG THE GRAVEL
road past our acreage comes what could be a parade float for this year's
Poison Queen that somehow wandered away from last week's Independence Day festivities. It's a red-and-white '78 Ford pickup, creeping along
at maybe five miles an hour, its rusted-through fenders rattling and its
muffler popping. One of the rearview mirrors swings from its bolt like a
saucepan. There's an air compressor and a big white plastic tank in the
back, sloshing with a milky fluid. All this is followed by a rising plume of
yellow dust, the sweet perfume of leaking brake fluid, and the peculiar

metallic odor of herbicide. The conveyances in which death comes riding arrive in all manner of guises.

That's Arnie Perkins standing in the back, next to the tank, and that's his cousin, Earl Walters, in the cab, one raw elbow out in the wind like the snout of a torpedo. Strips of duct tape hold the windshield together, and Earl peers out between them. There's a cooler full of iced-down beer on the passenger's seat, and the crotch of Earl's overalls is soaked from holding a can of Lite between his thighs. Earl has been drinking beer since noon, and his eyes and his cigarette butt are sinking into the hot red quicksand of his face.

Arnie is doing the spraying just now, but the two of them will change jobs after a while so that Arnie can sit for a spell and take advantage of the beer. To keep his sizable belly counterbalanced, Arnie presses his big hams back against the chemical tank while he swivels back and forth and bathes the ditch with herbicide. Below the sleeves of his T-shirt, his fat arms glisten with sweat and poison. There's a gleam in his eyes as he peers out from under the bill of his cap, cigar clenched in his teeth: Rambo wielding a flamethrower.

Behind the rolling truck, the herbicide beads up on the grasses, trickles down the troughs of the blades, and runs into cracks in the soil. Crickets gleam under the wet lacquer of the poison, and field mice huddled in nests in old beer cans lick the moisture from the fur of their little ones. In a week to ten days, the leaves on all of these plants will turn a dried-blood brown, a color like nothing else in summer.

And a good part of the spray lifts and drifts, wafted along on the breeze. You can smell it for a quarter mile. There's a state regulation against spraying when the wind is over six miles an hour, but in Nebraska the wind never blows that softly. Throw your hat up in the air anywhere on these prairies, and you have to run fast to get to the place where it comes down again.

Not only do Arnie and Earl do the spraying, they also mix the chemicals, stirring the concentrated powder into water in the tank. While they're stirring, you can see the powder in the creases in their necks and at the corners of their mouths.

Arnie and Earl farm little patches and do odd jobs all year round. They're known to be steady, reliable workers as long as you keep a six-pack of cold beer within reach. Their first cutting of hay is in, their few acres of corn are more than knee-high, and their garden plots of potatoes are covered with pale violet flowers. They're just filling in for a week or so with a little low-speed weed killing at $5.75 an hour. The air compressor and the chemical tank belong to the county, and the poison is the county's too, but the pickup is Earl's. One of the doors—the yellow one on the passenger's side—is Arnie's, but that's another story.

Not being official county employees, Arnie and Earl are hired out by the hour to spray weeds. They report to the county superintendent, who serves "at the pleasure of the county commissioners." The superintendent has an office in the county courthouse, and from his own round table there he sends out these very unlikely knights to quest after the dragons of weeds.

If Arnie and Earl were employees of the county, they'd be required to wear protective clothing and chemical masks and they'd have some health insurance and disability benefits for when their lungs go bad or when their leukocyte count goes off the chart. But they don't. "Don't need it yet," they'd likely say.

The county superintendent knows he has a pretty good thing going in Arnie and Earl. He's got them doing work the regular county employees are too intelligent to do. He's paying these men to take risks he's afraid to ask his regular employees to take. The county couldn't afford to include risks like Arnie and Earl on the regular group health insurance. Why, the premiums for everybody would go up!

And if Arnie and Earl get sick, they aren't the kind of folks to sue the county. Farm boys, they grew up victims of the whims of weather and markets. Like so many farmers on the Great Plains, they'll go to their graves as victims, humble and holding their own hats, believing that fate has ordained that they will draw all the short straws. None of the Perkinses or Walters has ever hired a lawyer to prosecute a lawsuit. They and their neighbors settle things themselves, and if it comes down to shooting somebody's dog that's become a nuisance by chasing calves— well, everybody understands that it was inevitable.

The county's policy is to kill all the wild plum bushes and sumac and all the miscellaneous volunteer saplings in the ditch by the road. Tradition holds that these thickets can cause snow to drift across the road in winter, endangering traffic or just slowing down the school bus. There's very little traffic in the winter (or in the summer, for that matter), but it's the *principle* of the thing, you see: you can't let plum bushes just take over your right-of-way.

They also spray the branches of full-grown trees if those trees hang a little way over the road. One of those branches might knock the rearview mirror off the school bus. The weed spray just kills the leaves and the branches still hang there over the road, but that's the way we do it in Mason County. Kill or be killed.

But while Arnie is killing the things he's supposed to be killing, he's spraying nearly everything else as well: the tall compass plants with their yellow, daisylike flowers, the wild roses with their delicate pink blossoms, the wild grapevines, the chokecherries. Why the hell not? If they're living in the ditch, or maybe just over the fence, they're all fair game. The weeds set back from the road are the most fun, anyway, because Arnie gets to screw down the nozzle and spray a lot farther. He likes that white arc reaching out and out and the fine mist blowing off its crest.

Ten minutes back they soaked the ditch, the driveway, and the mailbox in front of Rex Butler's place. Lena Butler lives alone, and right now she's probably out in the garden assessing the damage to her roses. Her children are all grown and gone. Her husband died two years back. He was sixty-two years old and one of that first generation of farmers to use chemicals all of their productive lives. Rex didn't worry about the dangers of herbicides and insecticides. When the nozzles on his spraying equipment got plugged up, he put them in his mouth and blew them out. If he got chemicals on his hands, he just wiped them off on his overalls. If he had some spray left after making the rounds with his tractor, he dumped it in the corner of a field.

About three years ago, Rex was out in his soybean field when the spray plane came over. He'd paid for it to make a run from Mill Springs, and he wanted to be sure he got his money's worth. Rather than go up to the house to wash off afterward, he just worked on through the day and let the spray dry on his skin. A couple of weeks later he came down with a high fever, and they rushed him into Lincoln, where the doctors diagnosed acute leukemia. He was dead in a matter of weeks. Nearly all of the people in our little community agree it was that last spraying that finally opened the little cancer valves in Rex's bone marrow. Like Arnie and Earl, Rex would have accepted this without a word of complaint. People in our part of the world have a long tradition of bowing to destiny.

But most young farmers are more careful these days. They've learned from the stories of people like Rex. Those air-conditioned glassed-in cabs on the tractors may look like an expensive luxury, but they keep the deadly chemicals off the driver. Most of them read and follow the instructions on the labels, though at the tavern recently I overheard Junior Newman answer a neighbor's question about his spraying practices by saying that he just mixes different kinds of chemicals together, a little of this and a little of that. He says it doesn't seem to make much difference; they all work, sooner or later. Junior never was screwed down too tight, as they say around here.

The chemigators—those high-production farmers who mix herbicides and insecticides with the water pumping through their big center-pivot irrigation systems—generally follow the chemical companies' instructions, but there are notable exceptions. A couple of years ago a farmer out in western Nebraska thought that mixing the chemicals above ground took up too much time. So he poured a barrel of herbicide down the shaft of his irrigation well where it would get all mixed in proper (and mixed into the water table too).

Most of the eight thousand people in our county have the good sense to come in out of the rain. Oh, the people in our county-seat town may stuff a few empty chemical bottles or half-full cans of paint into the bottoms of their garbage bags, thinking the people who run the landfill won't notice, and most of the farmers still change their oil in the side yard and let the used oil soak into the earth, but most of us are relatively responsible when it comes to handling and disposing of hazardous chemicals. Let's say that 99 percent of us aren't dangerous. But it only takes two or three people like Earl or Arnie and Junior to poison an entire ecosystem. How can the rest of us defend ourselves against a couple of bachelor cousins riding around in a pickup with two hundred gallons of poison?

I once tried to frighten the county commissioners. I wrote a series of letters to the weekly newspaper warning readers that county officials ought to be worrying about the degree of liability they'll have when people like Earl and Arnie eventually get sick. But, somehow, you can't frighten a county. A county is like a shadow. You can poke a stick through it anywhere and never leave so much as a little hole to let the light in. Besides, the fellow who runs the aerial crop-spraying service wrote a series of letters saying that I didn't know what I was talking about. I suspect I was the only person who thought he had a conflict of interest.

I also had the audacity to suggest that the county could hire people to do the work with loppers and saws but was told that most county workers are too old and stiff to be climbing around in the ditches.

If I could start a rumor that Arnie and Earl are running around after dark barking after calves, I could get local support for shooting them. But I don't really wish these two men any harm. In fact, I worry for their health. They likely will suffer the effects of the county's weed policy long before the rest of us do. Once they're gone, someone else will eagerly take up the hose and nozzle where Arnie and Earl dropped it. There are dozens of people around here ready, willing, and able to spray weeds for $5.75 an hour.

Can Fly-fishing Survive the Twenty-first Century?
George Anderson

THE PASSAGE OF FLY-FISHING THROUGH THE TWENTY-FIRST CENTURY will not be as simple a matter as tacking a new calendar up on the wall each year. Fly-fishing as we know it today may well be ancient history by the coming century. But by then, the changes probably won't seem dramatic, since the passage of time tends to dissolve vivid memories of the past. I can remember often having a favorite stretch of stream to myself, fishing water that had been untouched that day by other anglers. The trout were larger then too. A three-pound rainbow from the Madison or Yellowstone was considered a nice fish, but four- and five-pound fish were not uncommon either. But the increase in fishing pressure, combined with the lack of quality regulations, hurt the population of larger trout, and the average size of the larger fish dropped by several inches. The discouraging aspect is we're not talking about an evolutionary period of time, just a couple of decades! Multiply this change by a factor of ten, and you will quickly see the dangerous direction the future of fly-fishing is taking.

Some might ask why we should even be concerned about the future of fly-fishing. Such global problems as overpopulation, starvation, the desta-bilization that has taken place in Europe and Russia, and AIDS would seem to take precedence over enticing some silly little trout to bite a hook wrapped with fur and feathers. Fly-fishing, however, is like the legendary canary in the mine shaft. Fly-fishing is a litmus test, if you will, for our environment. If we cannot protect our rivers and fisheries, or strive to make fly-fishing a quality experience, our commitment to stewardship has failed.

Increased fishing pressure is one of the major threats to the future of fly-fishing. The recent explosion in popularity of fly-fishing has resulted in a dramatic increase in fishing pressure, especially on the most popular public waters. There are frighteningly few premier fly-fishing waters in the world left, and this finite number is decreasing daily due to natural and man-made disasters as well as the systematic destruction of the surround-ing environment by those more concerned about jobs and wealth than the protection of our trout streams or the surrounding environment.

Along with the dramatic increase in numbers of anglers has come an overall degradation of the fly-fishing experience. Ironically, much of the fishing pressure results from regulations, like slot limits or catch-and-release, designed to protect fisheries. Because these regulations have dra-matically improved the fishing on many rivers, scores of fly-fishermen seek out these more highly regulated streams and rivers.

Certainly, this has been the case in Montana on famous rivers like the Madison and Bighorn. Thirty years ago, when I started floating the Madi-son, fishing the famous salmon fly hatch, you might have seen twenty boats floating a given stretch of water on any day. Now it is common to count eighty boats a day on this same stretch. If you are the first boat down the river that morning you'll find some cooperative trout and uncongested water to fish, but if you are the seventy-fifth boat, the trout are getting shellshocked and not nearly as anxious to take a fly. Fishermen floating ahead of you have pulled their boats out and are wade fishing the best water, so you won't be able to jump out of the boat anywhere you like and fish your favorite pool.

The Bighorn in recent years is a good example of fishing pressure run-ning rampant. The river has experienced some extremely heavy fishing pressure, especially during the late summer months when the river is low, insect hatches are prolific, and dry fly-fishing is at its peak. The Bighorn's reputation as perhaps the finest trout stream in the country with good public access adds to the frenzy. Fishing pressure from wade and float fishermen can be so heavy in prime time that I've floated 3 to 4 miles at a time without finding a single place to pull over to do some wade fishing, without encroaching on other anglers. Times like these make you feel like throwing in the towel and saying, "To hell with it. This kind of fly-fishing just isn't worth the trouble."

Fly-fishermen are drawn to the sport largely because of the solitude it can offer. Difficulty in finding a decent piece of water to fish or having problems with other fishermen can quickly ruin your day. On congested rivers like the Bighorn, proper fishing etiquette often takes a backseat to obnoxious tactics fishermen and guides use to tie up their favorite water. Unpleasant confrontations occur, with anglers and sometimes even guides yelling at one another. Inattentive boat fishermen will drift toward you, putting down your school of rising fish. Often other fly-fishermen are just ignorant, or have perhaps dismissed some of the most basic rules of fishing etiquette. Even fly-fishing neophytes know that it's not proper to walk right into a pool and fish the water in front of a fellow angler, but today on these crowded streams anglers and guides are pulling sophisticated stunts that tread squarely in the gray area—or beyond the fringe of acceptable fishing etiquette.

On the spring creeks, with fish everywhere and plenty of good water to fish, an angler often will sit in one spot all day so that he won't have to give up his favorite pool to another fisherman. On the Bighorn, guides are getting their clients on the water at 6 A.M., rowing downriver to stake out their favorite piece of water, then waiting hours for the good hatches to start, and the fish to start rising. Some of these guides work the very same water every day, making it nearly impossible for anyone else to fish these prime pools.

On waters where other anglers are often only a stone's throw away, one needs to be especially conscious of fishing etiquette, and how his actions will affect or offend fellow anglers. If, at the end of the day, you can say that you haven't encroached on other anglers, put their fish down, or somehow fouled up their fishing, it's been a good day of fly-fishing.

In the future, fly-fishing on many well-known public waters will become less of a quality experience unless unprecedented changes take place. Fly-fishermen seeking less congested angling will have to revert to fishing private water, often paying a fee to fish. Others will have to exchange solitude for larger fish. Many experienced fly-fishermen seek out lesser-known waters, content to scale down their tackle and catch smaller fish if it means that they will have the stream to themselves. The measure of a good day of fly-fishing isn't just the catch, it's also the enjoyment of the outdoors in a beautiful, uncrowded setting, and the camaraderie of friends.

Without any regulation on fishing pressure, future public waters will become a zoo of inconsiderate, intolerant fly-fishers threatening the very existence of the fly-fishing values we hold so sacred. Even in the near future, the only waters where one will still be able to find larger fish and pursue that "quality experience" may be on private water, where the angler must pay a fee but where the numbers of fly-fishermen are carefully matched to each stretch of water. Such is the case today in England and across most of Europe. Free public fishing is a thing of the past unless you are after "rough" fish like chubs and carp.

It's sad to think that in the future, high-quality fly-fishing will only be found on private water, available only for the wealthy. But it doesn't have to be this way if people are willing to accept some level of control that would protect the fishing environment and also enhance everyone's fishing experience. The federal government and state agencies are currently attempting to regulate access and fishing pressure on some rivers, such as the Colorado River through the Grand Canyon and the Smith River in Montana, where the sole access is on state or national forest land. By limiting daily launches, these agencies closely control boating and fishing pressure on these rivers, which results in a quality experience for everyone.

State fish and game departments need to find ways to limit fishing access on the most crowded streams and rivers. Management plans can be designed for overly crowded rivers with operational costs funded by anglers paying a fee for daily rod rights. Fly-fishermen would make reservations in advance, much as they do on the privately owned Montana spring creeks like Armstrong's, Nelson's, and DePuy's. The remaining available space could be set aside on a first-come-first-served basis.

I dream of a plan like this, but of course it's about as likely to happen as Atlantic salmon running up the Yellowstone. I've seen it all before. Greed enters the equation and decimates the best-laid plans. At the Fish and Game hearings, everyone would be screaming at the commissioners, wanting their little piece of the pie. No one would be willing to compromise. Outfitters and guides wouldn't want any limitations on the numbers and makeup of outfitters on the river or how many guides they could run each day. Nonfishing pleasure boaters just out to float and drink beer or paddle their kayak would scream bloody murder. Private land owners along the river wouldn't stand for being told they could fish only certain days. Threats of lawsuits would unfold and the state agencies would drop the whole issue like a hot potato!

But without some kind of limitation on the number of fishermen on these crowded waters, conflicts arise. Fly-fishermen seeking more than catching a lot of big fish leave these streams. Ironically, the people that are left to fish these waters are often the most obnoxious and have the least regard for fishing etiquette.

Waters where a quality fly-fishing experience is likely to survive are in our national parks. The National Park Service is well aware of the effects of population pressures on our environment and has taken steps to limit the number of campers, hikers, and fishermen when specific natural resources are being overused. For instance, limits are imposed on the number of daily visitors to parks like Yosemite. In Yellowstone Park, the number of campsites has been reduced in many areas, and strict limitations have been imposed on back country use by both outfitters and private individuals. Unfortunately, the park service has not regulated the number of anglers on any given stream and at times the fishing pressure has increased to objectionable levels on some streams such as the Firehole, Madison, and the Yellowstone above the falls. Even back country streams open to daily use like upper Slough Creek have experienced a noticeable increase in fishing pressure just in the past ten years. Overnight camping on many back country streams like Slough Creek is limited to a few existing campsites and these are tightly controlled by the Park Service, which in turn effectively moderates fishing pressure.

Most fly-fishermen are reluctant to hike more than a mile or so to get to their fishing, so most of these back country streams in Yellowstone and other parks will not face the more immediate problems of heavy fishing pressure.

Unlike rivers such as the Madison or Bighorn, which run through both public and private lands, waters inside national parks can be regulated with relative ease. However, one threat to fly-fishing in national parks is posed by environmental extremists who want nothing but pristine wilderness in the parks. These people consider even catch-and-release fishing to be unacceptable. Fishermen are seen as upsetting a fragile environment by wading in the streams, stressing trout or spooking wild animals such as elk and moose that graze along the waterways. Fishermen also present potential conflicts with endangered species such as the grizzly bear, and for this reason some of Yellowstone Park's waters are currently closed to any fishing. Perhaps these national park waters will remain a model for the preservation of large wild trout and a unique fly-fishing experience.

The destruction of fish habitat and reduced water quality also pose major hurdles for the survival of fly-fishing. Organizations like Trout Unlimited and the Federation of Fly Fishermen have been instrumental in launching projects to improve trout streams, with the goal of perpetuating quality fly-fishing as well as protecting the environment. Nevertheless, many of our finest waters are feeling the long-term effects of pollution or dewatering that could spell the death knell for these great streams.

Pollution has many ugly faces. It's not only the obvious pollution from chemical spills or industrial waste that gets into our trout streams, but also more subtle types of pollution like silt pollution or the leeching of drain fields into our river systems. In many resort areas, there is unregulated building close to rivers and steams, and the resultant long-term pollution problems are just now becoming evident. Summer homes, which are often built close to the floodplain, depend on septic systems and drain fields. Homeowners and builders often don't consider the ramifications of the failure of these systems or the cumulative long-term effects of discharges into aquifers and groundwater table. Nutrients and phosphates added to these systems affect pH levels and can be just as devastating as acidic or metallic discharge from mining activities. As a result, aquatic vegetation can change rapidly, often threatening insect populations. Insects like stoneflies and mayflies, primary trout food, are often the first to be affected.

Indiscriminate use of fertilizers, insecticides, and weed killers have tragic results, degrading overall water quality and, in some instances, causing severe fish mortality. In the West, little attention has been paid to the long-term effects of these farming practices on our rivers and streams.

Years ago I found a beautiful little spring creek that held a lot of large fish—big browns which ran up into the creek from one of our major rivers and found the perfect balance of superior habitat, abundant food, and ideal spawning conditions. We often found these three- to five-pound browns in the deeper bends the spring creek had created as it meandered through a meadow on its course to join the larger river. Where there was deeper holding water and good cover we would find big fish. There was enough gradient and current speed between some pools to find a good gravel bottom that provided ideal spawning habitat and a nursery for the younger trout. We became friends with the rancher and he gave us permission to fish. Of course, my friend and I vowed to keep our little stream a secret, and since it was off the beaten track, few other fishermen discovered it.

Things changed sooner than we would have ever thought. The cattle market was down and our rancher friend was looking to supplement his income by raising some wheat up on a big bench of land overlooking the meadow and spring creek. Early that spring he plowed the land and put in a pumping station on the spring creek, which would push water up a half mile to a big pivot sprinkler on the bench. The wheat crop flourished, but this was the beginning of the end for the fishery. The fertilizers the rancher used were carried back into the spring creek with the irrigation water, and within a couple of months, the weed growth in the spring creek had increased tenfold. Even the deep pools and undercut banks in the stream bends were soon choked with algae growth we had never seen before. It became impossible to find open water to fish, much less find any of the big brown trout. With the algae choking the water flow and spreading it out, the deeper channels and bends filled in with silt. By the late fall none of the big fish were able to run into the creek to spawn as they had in the past. With all the weed growth they simply couldn't navigate the stream to get to the headwaters where they had spawned in past years. Even if they could have somehow gotten through, silt now covered the gravel beds where these big browns spawned in the past. It was over. Our wonderful little stream had changed so dramatically that the following spring we could hardly recognize the pools we used to fish. Five years after the farmer developed the bench and planted his wheat, he was bankrupt and sold the ranch. The damage had been done and today, nearly ten years later, the stream is still badly silted but slowly returning to its natural state. The browns haven't yet returned, but without the wheat, fertilizer, and pesticides at least there is hope.

Silt pollution in our streams and rivers has more recently been recognized as one of the primary reasons for the destruction of trout habitat. Silt washed into streams can build up over time, threatening insect populations that depend on clean gravels for their existence. Excessive silt can decrease water depth and eliminate deeper channels in smaller streams, severely limiting the habitat for larger fish. Silt pollution that occurs during the time when trout are spawning can cut off the flow of clean water over the eggs, substantially reducing the number of fry that will survive.

Silt pollution is often the result of mismanaged logging operations. Clear-cutting vast tracts of timber without regard for the headwaters of rivers is one obvious source. There will be many battles fought in the future to protect our old growth forests of the west and northwest, and the outcome will have a direct bearing on the future of high-quality trout fishing in these river systems. While our national forest systems do have some control over logging operations on federal lands, a great deal of logging is done on private land, where there are few limitations on timber harvest or regulations for erosion control. Other major sources of silt pollution include commercial and residential building, and highway construction.

Fortunately, environmental impact statements are now required for many large development projects. Water quality is of primary concern to everyone today, and various state agencies, as well as environmentally conscious organizations like Trout Unlimited, are making developers aware of the legal consequences of degrading water quality.

Overgrazing or bad grazing practices also have come into focus as a primary source of silt pollution. Cattle and other livestock have traditionally been given unlimited access to the land, and the resultant damage caused to streams and rivers is dramatic, especially over time. The damage is particularly noticeable on smaller streams, where livestock eat down the vegetation along the banks and cause an enormous amount of silt pollution by breaking down the banks and wading through the middle of the streams. Projects by private landowners to fence off most of the streambanks and allow access for livestock only at certain points have been very successful in improving the stream environment and fishery. Fishing clubs and other organizations have undertaken many of these projects, providing the manpower and funds to help landowners improve streams. This is expensive work and it makes sense for us to find new ways to help farmers and ranchers participate in these programs. Funding on a federal level or some form of tax relief could provide the needed incentive.

Another significant factor in the survival of fly-fishing for trout is the amount of water itself. In the past there was plenty of water for everyone—farming and ranching interests as well as cities and commercial development. Today there is a critical shortage of water. Larger rivers have felt the ill effects of a reduction in flow, and many reservoirs and smaller streams are drained dry to satisfy demands for water. Growth of larger cities has placed further demands on the availability of water, often from headwaters of rivers hundreds of miles away.

The future of trout fishing depends on our ability to formulate a plan that will protect minimum stream flows in all of our rivers and streams. Such a plan would allow state agencies like fish and game departments as well as environmentally conscious organizations to buy water rights from landowners and then to keep water flowing on a constant, year-round basis to protect streams and rivers. Water rights are the key to the equation, and have been the source of bitter battles in the past. As incredible as it may seem, until recently fishing was not even considered a beneficial use of water in Montana. Ranching, farming, and other commercial interests, as well as cities and towns, had the right to every drop of water. Many smaller streams that could be wonderful fishing are sucked bone dry in the summer months when all the available water is rerouted off into fields to flood irrigate water-intensive crops.

Recently, state fish and game departments have been able to get some minimal reservations for instream flows on larger streams and rivers. Next, we must somehow devise a means of promoting and protecting minimal flows in our smaller streams. Farmers and ranchers are utilizing more efficient methods of watering crops today than in the past, when they relied almost entirely on gravity-flow flood irrigation. Large pivot and wheelline irrigation systems are proving to be more cost-efficient but more importantly, use a lot less water than was needed in the past. As a result, excess water is available to remain in streams for the protection of trout and the aquatic environment.

I believe fly-fishing will survive its passage through the twenty-first century. Complex variables will force changes, but all is not gloomy on the horizon. In my view, fly-fishing will be seen as an integral part of a greater plan to save our environment for future generations. Many people today have a greater concern than ever before about protecting the environment, even if they are not fishermen. And there is a growing realization that our environment is already in trouble and must be protected in order for us to survive.

For a Handful of Feathers
Guy de la Valdéne

I LIVE ON THE OUTSKIRTS OF TALLAHASSEE, FLORIDA, ON A FARM IN Gadsten county, nine miles west of Coon Bottom and thirteen miles south of Booger Bay, Georgia. The region is referred to as the red hills of Florida for its abundance of clay and the rolling nature of its topography. All and all, this is a fine place to live, particularly if one has the means to travel, every so often, to where people speak the king's English and where chewing tobacco is thought of in the same vein as messing one's pants; a small price to pay, I might add, for an otherwise wild and as yet untainted piece of geography.

My land lies between the sandy coastal soil south of Tallahassee and the flat piney forests of Georgia. The barrel-like hills, hardwood bottoms, and deep chasms that cut into the earth for no apparent reason exist, I am told, because this is where the southernmost tip of the Appalachian mountain chain falls to the sea, a romantic theory that explains some of the tortured gullies my turkeys strut in.

The farm was once part of a much larger plantation, and since early in its existence, the land has produced cotton and the slaves to pick it, cattle, shade tobacco, peanuts, corn, and throughout its existence, a large, rambunctious southern family. In 1990, I bought eight hundred acres of what remained of the homestead, changed its name and status to Dogwood farm, and to the utter delight of my hunting dogs, proceeded to grow birds: wild eastern bobwhite quail, *Colinus virginianus* for those interested in the specifics of what things are and where they come from.

I am a good bird hunter, a novice bird watcher, an amateur naturalist, and a practicing ecologist. My formal training in the two latter sciences is nonexistent, as I never finished my second year in college, so what general knowledge I have of the natural world has been obtained by reading, avoiding humans, and spending as much of my life as possible on the water or in the woods. Our species' interaction with the natural world revolts me, but it is what it is, and as I cannot change humankind's inherent venality, what I will do is care for what is mine. So, along with providing *Colinus virginianus* with a comfortable place to live, I am shaping this small corner of nature into the vision of what I believe will best glorify its intrinsic qualities.

I think of this sculpturing of the land—heresy to many who would leave nature to its own devices—as gardening on a grand scale, subjective landscaping for beauty's sake. And, as I like to see as far as my eyes will allow me, I remove what is diseased, repetitious, and ugly: cat-faced, topless, rachitic, stunted, and otherwise suppressed trees that compete for food with specimens that would otherwise grow strong and straight. To offset this inclination to prune, I plant five times as many trees as I remove, so that one day, unless I go broke in the process, no matter where I stand, I will see only what pleases me and makes the right picture. When I want ugly, I'll ride into town.

In conjuncture with this bit of gardening insanity, I do everything, short of killing predators (I feel, as I grow older, a kinship with animals that kill to survive), to grow bobwhite quail, feed visiting turkeys, and improve the local deer herd. I offer a free meal, and any animal or bird that migrates over or takes up residence on this land will find food and shelter.

In the fall and winter I kill a small percentage of my tenants and eat them. Those I don't eat, I give to others who do. Nothing is wasted except

the money and time it takes to run the operation, and it might be argued
that neither is wasted. In my lifetime, I have polluted, destroyed, and
abused nature and thousands of her tenants, but despite this, nature has
granted me what I cherish most in life: beauty. Now that I have the where-
withal to manage and tend this land and the species that live on it, it
would be a moral waste not to do so. The more food and cover I plant,
the more game and nongame species will live here; the more water there
is, the more fish; the more wildlife, the more predators. Small as it may
be, I will make this sequestered world revolve with the assurance of time.

I stop hunting around the middle of February, when instead of finding
quail in coveys, my dogs point singles and pairs. No matter what anyone
says, our quail hunting season is too long (three and a half months) for
the good of the species. The joys of hunting I experience in September
erode over the months, and by February I am loath to pull the trigger on
anything that breathes. Each season has its priorities, and by the end of
winter, mine turn to growing things. The irony is that if I want to grow
strong trees and provide a plenitude of food and safe habitat for my
boarders, I have to promote an interaction between organisms, both veg-
etal and biological, and their environment (specifically, the science of
ecology), and in the Southeast, that means setting fire to the land.

The practice of burning the pine woods of the South predates the
arrival of the white man by thousands of years, so that by the time the
explorers, Cabeza de Vaca in 1528 and de Soto a decade later, brutalized
their way up to north Florida and south Georgia, they reported large
parklike meadows with widely separated trees, tremendous herds of deer,
and rafters of turkey. Those forests had been burned by the natives as far
back as 1000 B.C. by Indians of the woodland tradition and probably by the
archaic Indians (8000 B.C.) before them. Fire was used as a means of opening the woods for travel, of herding and concentrating deer by creating
grazing land, and of exposing food in the form of acorns and chestnuts to
turkeys. Fire was also instrumental in preparing fields for the annual sow-
ing of corn, squash, beans, gourds, and melons.

The application of a hot summer sun on a pine forest floor provokes a
growth reaction unique to the Southeast. No other forest in the country
is blessed with such a rich, diversified, and permanent undergrowth, perfectly located and adapted to overwinter migratory birds. The down side
to this lush evolution of vegetation is that, left unchecked, in five years the
understory becomes so dense and constricting that few if any ground animals use it. Pine straw and grass turn into solid mats of dead vegetation,
unsuitable to most birds, including quail, a bird that likes to feel dirt

under its feet, hates heavy cover, and is not equipped to scratch through litter for food. The slow progression from fields, to pine trees, to an eventual climax of hardwood forests promotes a steady ground-floor progression from grass and weeds to an impenetrable deciduous jungle.

From a wildlife management point of view, the application of fire serves to clean the ground litter and retard a prolific sapling growth that chokes the pine forests' availability to species that otherwise thrive in this climate. From a forestry point of view, the argument for controlled burns is to restrain the undergrowth, so that when lightning strikes, it doesn't ignite a dry, overgrown source of fuel that could rage out of control over tens of thousands of acres. The practice of burning was common at the beginning of the century to promote grazing land in the South; then it was banned when the demand for timber overshadowed the cattlemen's needs. However, without fire, the grazing land grew back into nondesirable hardwoods, and it wasn't until the silviculture industry recognized the benefits of burning the nutrient-stealing undergrowth that fire was reinstated; to this day fire remains a controversial tool.

Those who do not want to modify nature in any way, particularly not for the benefit of specific species, feel that the biological development of the planet is a continuous mutation of life, encouraged by natural occurrences as tedious as the advance and retreat of glaciers and as rapid as the eruption of a volcano. Species that do not adapt to one ecosystem adapt to another or disappear. The questions are: What do you want? and What are you willing to give up? No management program can serve all needs, much less all species.

We have altered the face of the world by moving hundreds of millions of our own species into the natural ecosystems. It seems only fair that we manage what we have altered and clean up what we have soiled. This specific ecosystem was historically groomed through the propagation of wildfires. In this day and age, wildfires represent unacceptable dangers to human and animal life and, more pragmatically, unacceptable losses to the timber industry. We cannot buy plywood without cutting trees any more than we can delight in nature without working at it.

The controversy that surrounds the use of fire to benefit certain animal and vegetable species usually grows out of a lack of information, greed, or radicalism. What appears to upset most people is the fact that a civilized culture is using a primeval tool to do its work. It doesn't fit with our experience of science, where everything is invisible and seems clean. Smoke is a pollutant, and this raises the hackles of city dwellers, regardless of the fact that smoke is a natural phenomenon and, compared with what cars and factories spew out, a nonissue. On the other side, there is mounting concern that extensive pine management will affect the lives of millions of new tropical birds (song birds) that migrate up from the rain forests of Central America and need the junglelike habitat we work so hard to clear. All these issues warrant a great deal of thought by both interested and uninterested parties. This century's historical volatility, population growth, and the shift from rural to city life excludes absolute solutions to the interaction between humans and nature. Those whose livelihoods depend on timber are going to side with those who own the timber. Those who love nature for its own sake are not swayed by scientific rhetoric. That leaves the majority of mankind, which doesn't give a damn one way or another, a handful of professionals who care, and a minority of amateurs like me.

WHEN THE YELLOW jessamine flowers swell the rural fence rows of northern Florida and the hardwood bottoms are laced with pink honeysuckle vines, everyone knows that it is only a matter of time before the fires begin. The moment the quail season is over (the first week in March), white smoke rises and drifts over tens of thousands of acres of south Georgia and north Florida's forests.

The wind moves the smoke that rises from the burning earth in great white sheets across the countryside, and one cannot help thinking of the Civil War and of Sherman's army and of the thousands of small critters incapable of getting out of the way. For them, it is war; for the rest of the natural world, relief is at hand for hundreds of species that otherwise would strangle under the suffocating accumulation of southern vegetation. Simply put, the number of dead box turtles I see after burning my woods is minute compared with the numbers of turtles that without fire would starve.

Bill Poppell, who works for me, plows firebreaks around the perimeters of those sections of woods left unburned the year before. (I burn 50 percent of the farm every second year, in increments of five to twenty acres.) A master tractor operator, Bill is at his best dancing on the brake pedal and clutch. I set the fires while he pushes over trees, logs, and stumps; crowds the flames; and spins the harrow blades over potential problems. During it all, he furiously works over a huge plug of chew. This bit of legal speed, coupled with coffee chasers, keeps him wired until he gets home to his double-wide, where he spoons a quart of vanilla ice cream into his mouth to ease his weakened stomach, his own personal approach to checks and balances.

Firing a section of woods, particularly if it's your responsibility or ownership, awakens something old and fearful in man, like great storms and near accidents. I have been mixing fuel for a decade now, at a ratio of four parts of diesel to one part gasoline, into four-gallon firepots and have set thousands of acres on fire, but every spring, particularly the first morning, I do so with the innate feeling that I am disobeying a fundamental rule, a rule repeated over and over to me by my mother as far back as I can remember: "Do not play with fire!" And, therein lies part of the fascination, because putting aside the scientific benefits of controlled fires, there is something visceral and unknown about cracking a match that gathers a man's testicles like only a glance at death or the promise of sex ever does.

Fire licks the disease off the trunks of my pine trees and, if properly applied, kills enough of the lower limbs for the trees to grow tall and without rickets. The heat rids the woods of pests such as ticks, chiggers, and other parasites, as well as bark-boring pine beetles, beetles that hone in on a scent emanated by weak or wounded trees and kill the tree in a matter of days. The resin flows out of a crippled pine tree, acting like a salve, and if the bugs don't find it, the fire usually does, and the hot resin carves black catfaces into the thick multilayered bark. The cat faces grow every year, burying deeper and deeper into the pine, slowly breaking its resilience until one day the tree falls over and rots and grows mushrooms and the process of life begins all over.

On this March morning, I burned the bottoms on the northern boundaries of the farm. It was clear and cool, and the wind was out of the north at ten miles an hour. I'd hoped to burn two hundred acres, but the wind direction kept changing. The first time, it came up behind me, swirling the pine tops and fueling the fire into an unwanted rage, the heat shriveling the undergrowth ahead of the flames. The smoke turned black.

When the fire reached the breaks it stopped, just as suddenly as it had started, leaving in its path tall pine trees with trunks blackened fifteen feet up, dead hardwood trees whose thinner bark had collapsed under the heat, and, where the fire had moved at its fastest, perfectly shaped white-tipped blades of black grass.

The smell of pine heart burning is distinct and addictive, a stickiness that coats the air for weeks and, along with gas and diesel fuel, releases an odor one shouldn't forget from one year to the next, but for reasons I don't understand, I do. The first day I cracked a match on my woods, my brain shrieked and revolted. Now, a week later, I don't want the smell of pine sap to ever go away.

That afternoon we backfired a block of young pine trees. The fire skulked away from the wind like an ebbing tide, a tiny red wave scorching the earth six inches high, weaving in and out of debris, leaving in its wake a uniform blanket of soot. Backfires are as fascinating to me as their counterparts, the rolling headfires that suck the air out of gopher holes and hurl flames beyond the smoke to where the sky is blue. The first fire cleans; the latter, kills. Both have a place in woodland management, but unless the burn is meant to kill overly dense hardwood saplings, or for reasons of time versus acreage, I prefer backburning because it's a gentle burn.

Afternoon clouds pushed long shadows over the blackened earth. The fire had barely singed the meager litter of leaves under the live oak trees and had halted at the strips of annual rye and winter wheat I'd sowed back in November; there, green ribbons of grass undulated in the breeze, undaunted by my devices. Meanwhile, because spring was on the way, the live oak leaves that survived winter had turned yellow and brown from the fire.

When the fires were out, the stumps on the side of the shadowed slopes smoldered into a gray world of bats and owls. I saw a woodcock rise out of a burned creek bottom, outlined against a silver sky; the bird looked fake, a freeze-frame picture of nature projected onto a canvas, traced by an impersonator. Diesel fuel lingered on my skin, oily, determined, and unaffected by soap. Soot clung to my boots,and smoke had parched my eyes. At the house, I built myself a drink. My daughter called it a killer drink. She was right.

I had been reminded again how quickly a fickle wind can turn a creeping backfire into a maelstrom, and how heat races up hills and creeps down hollows, but mostly I learned about the lay of my land, about its vulnerability to judgmental errors, and most of all about its finiteness.

The strange irregularities and texture of the earth are apparent when a rain follows a fire. The earth is hard, strewn with mortified limbs and treetops, logs, smoking stumps that refuse to rot, shriveled leaves in a motif of black on black. Rain sinks potash and minerals into the ground and drags the surplus to the creek bottoms. It washes color back into the face of darkness and exposes the red clay domes of thousands upon thousands of ant hills, on the slopes, in the woods, the hollows, everywhere.

Nature is at its most naked after a burn, and like a molting bird, it's both vulnerable and risible, if one feels like laughing.

Two weeks later, sometimes sooner, depending on the rain and the nighttime temperatures, the land greens up. Miniature fingers of chlorophyll stipple the earth, and these first revelations of color, pinned on shadowy backgrounds, deepen the landscape.

Six weeks beyond that, the minerals that have sifted into the earth, the scarification of dormant seeds, the rains, and the hot sun combine to accelerate a vegetable explosion. Lupines and coral beans, violets, azaleas, redbud, and wild green onions are everywhere. Insects multiply uncontrollably in the lush evolution of legumes. These insects contribute, more than any other food, to the growth of turkey poults and young quail during the summer months, and the whitetail does and their fawns eat the beans of the legumes for their high protein content.

I alter the circle of life and death on my land every year. I believe it is for the better of one ecosystem, as opposed to another. Perhaps I am wrong, perhaps I am right. In the long end it makes no difference; short of nuclear holocaust, the earth will outlive this present set of species. Regardless, my heart goes out to the creatures that aren't nimble enough to avoid death on those days when I walk the woods with a dripping fire-pot in my hand. I look at the empty shells of box turtles and armadillos, the ashes of skinks, hooked-shaped and white against the pitch-black earth, and I feel remorse for them and the thousands of crawling creatures that blew away in the updraft of my tempest. But it is a short sorrow; death came and went quickly over my land, and unlike most modern disasters, this ending is as old as the planet and leaves behind, if not solace for the sentient ones that perished, at least faith and a future for those that survived.

When all is said and done, it boils down to this: the farmer in me grows an annual crop of wild flying delicacies, and the hunter in me harvests a percentage of this fruitage; the businessman in me recognizes a losing proposition, and the child in me doesn't give a damn. Any other lingering doubts as to the simplistic nature of my endeavors need only be addressed to my dogs.

Hanging Out the Dirty Laundry
Gary Paul Nabhan

> Once upon a time, taking out the garbage was an event in our lives. . . . We were part of the rituals connecting us to the earth, from the places food grew, through the house and our bodies, and then back to the earth. Garbage was real, part of creation, not an objective invasion of cans and cartons. . . . We are the garbage, the waste, we make it and dump it.
>
> —Gerald Vizenor, *Landfill Meditation*

I CONFESS TO A BAD HABIT. WHENEVER I GO SOUTH INTO SONORA, between the waning of summer monsoons and the closing-in of winter solstice, I indiscriminately choose campsites long after the light has faded. By that time of night, the cues to comfortable locales are already long gone, and serendipity has come out to play. My excuses for such god-awful arrival times have varied over the years, but whatever the reason, I have been forced to sleep in places I would not necessarily choose were my eyes wide open, my pockets not empty, and my head on straight. And, as all us proclaim after surviving a rotten time or place, I am a richer man for it.

I remember a particular evening in Magdalena, Sonora, after departing from an all-night dance. My sidekick and I wanted to sleep well beyond the lights and horns and grinding gears of semis, but not so far out as to limit our crawling back into town in the morning for the obligatory cowboy coffee and *menudo* breakfast. To make things simple, I merely drove another two hundred yards beyond the last lights on the edge of town. As I hit the shadows, I banked my truck off one set of ruts, into the sandy wash that trailed off to the north of us. There, I dug in for the night, unfurling my tarp and cloth bag, kicking off my boots, crawling into the flannel-lined warmth, and closing my eyes. I would postpone the worry over how to get out of the sand until the next morning, when I might have all my wits back together again.

My wits remained scattered through the night, and into the following morning. The cocks at the nearest ranch began crowing around four in the morning; at five, a braying burro wandered through camp and nudged me awake. When I finally dared to open my eyes to meet the *madrugada*, twilight, I was instantly unsure that I was ready for the day.

All around me, in the muted light of the predawn hours, I could make out patches of color hanging from bushes and lower branches of trees. Botanist that I am, I first thought, "Flowers!" but no; late fall was the wrong time of year for a peak in blooming. So I glanced around once more, trying to get a sense of the textures and shapes as well as the colors. I noticed glitter, dazzle, ruffle, and lace. "Christmas tree decorations?" I wondered. Yet I could not for the life of me figure out why the locals would bedeck hackberry bushes and cholla cactus with such gaudy ornaments; the winter holidays were almost two months away.

Then, as my eyes began to focus, the flamboyant forms turned into fire-engine red panties, pink fishnet stockings, leopard-spotted bras, baby-blue boxer shorts, and tinsel-glittered pantyhose. I rolled over and looked up the wash: still-turgid plastic blooms, Fruit-of-the-Loom jockey shorts, red-flannel long johns, and cologne decanters were strewn hither and yon, tossed down from a low hill above the arroyo where we were camped. I took a harder look at the adobe buildings up on the hill, and they appeared a bit peculiar for a Sonoran ranchstead; there were red lights running around the windows and the doors.

We were camped in the dump heap of the local house of ill repute, the *zona,* on the edge of civilization. Now the inventory of items in the wash made more sense to me. That was the first time I had come to read trash. And now I know that I am a richer man for it.

OVER THE YEARS of camping in and around dumps, I have come to make fine distinctions between the different kinds of "sign" I can find in a Mexican *basurero.* In the typical debris of any locality, I see the script acted out by the *pueblo,* a collective signature as legible as a carcass left by wolves.

To learn if it is a heap used by families that farm, I search to see how much of their food comes from nearby fields and gardens. Among the usual battery of food scraps, I search for the inedible debris that indicates local harvests: spent bean pods, sunflower stalks, corn husks too small for wrapping tamales and ears half chewed by raccoons.

If it is a dumping ground for the local butcher shop, I know by scanning the sky for resident caracaras and turkey vultures, who circle over and then land to debone the remaining meat.

If it serves a borderland shantytown, the *chamacos* will be out there scavenging all burnable wood and all wearable clothes. Not a single stale tortilla will be found, for they all go into soups and chilaquiles before the trash is tossed.

I have made it a custom to enter into my field journal all the various forms of cultural remains I find within reach of my campsite, recording both the perishable and persistent cast-offs that catch my eye. My journals read something like this:

> At a remote train stop in the Gran Desierto—the continent's largest sea of dunes—I walked along the railroad tracks to find out what human industry the sands had not already buried. Monstrosities: oversized iron rack and pinion gears from caterpillars or cranes. Rarities: lumps of salt quarried from nearby flats. Routine debris: motor oil vats, drive shafts, burnt adobes, and rubber boots. Curiosities: coconuts, broomsticks broken by sweeping too much drifted sand, and abandoned but unrusted mattress springs (left where so little rain comes that even rust must either sleep or die of thirst).
>
> From the mess around the railroad yard, we wandered out onto the Bahia Adair mudflats, still a ways from the Sea of Cortez. How far we were from low-tide levels we could not tell, for we were surrounded by mirages and other illusions. The refraction of light near the horizon made some distant trees and boats appear to float in the air above water and shoreline. In fact, we had lost our ability to estimate dis-

tance or size, and every item stranded on those thousands of nearly flat acres seemed to be larger and more pronounced than the same object would be anywhere else. After hours of walking against the wind with nothing in the way of our feet, we came on a single pole with a wooden perch on it, stained white with bird droppings. Below it were three owl pellets and the tail of a fish. From there, we followed the tracks of two coyotes past a lone piece of stranded driftwood and an intact heron skeleton. The coyote paws were engraved in the mud as clearly as the heelprints of stars left in concrete at Hollywood and Vine. When we arrived again at the sand dunes, I could not believe the increased density of debris. We had stumbled on a shell midden that extended for hundreds of yards, where prehistoric peoples had eaten clams and discarded millions of bivalve shells. After realizing that the mudflats were barren because so much was buried underfoot, the blatant litter of the sand dunes signaled a welcome home.

Unfortunately, I've found that my penchant for rural Sonoran trash piles disgusts many of my fellow travelers, especially those accustomed to the neatness of upper-class suburbs. Consider this complaint from Albert, a high-strung photographer from Westchester County, New York: "The goddamn stuff is blowing all over the place. Don't these people care about the quality of scenery around here?" Or listen to the disappointment in these words from Jacques, a semiotic archaeologist from Gland, Switzerland, who apparently arrived in the Americas six centuries too late to gain proof for his theories: "I can't find a single potsherd beneath all this plastic! It all went downhill after the Indians adopted zip-lock bags and tupperware. Before that, the storage of food in pottery vessels was so womblike and nurturing."

Of course, modern-day North Americans and Western Europeans consume 80 percent of the world's wealth and leave behind 75 percent of its waste and pollution. Still, we pride ourselves on how neatly we do it. We construct the planet's most concentrated sanitary landfills to hide from the eye how many resources we have let drop in our careless fashion. The toxics in our disposal sites seep down into the groundwater in such heavy doses that they poison anyone—usually poverty-level minority populations that cannot escape to more pristine conditions—who drink out of wells in the vicinity. These toxics cause cancer, birth defects, and myriad other health problems. Nonetheless, our society remains haughty about its superior capacity to contain and conceal all our chemically loaded cultural residue.

This point was powerfully made by a Native American doctor I heard

one Sunday morning on the radio while I was driving across the San Car-
los Apache reservation. His topic was alcoholism among Native Americans. "Sure," he said, "you find us in the gutter, in front of the liquor
store, wasted out in the open where everyone can see that we're drunk.
But is that any worse than the white man, who hides a bottle in his office
desk or leaves work early to sneak out to a dimly lit lounge? Is it any more
tragic than what happens to that businessman's wife, who pops pills all
day within the confines of their suburban home? Ours is just more out in
the open, but we've all got the same problem—we're wasting ourselves."

IF I COULD BE granted three wishes for change in our society, they would
be these. First, we would have to confront how much we squander by
having all our "refuse" pass before our eyes and noses. The garbage col-
lectors would no longer buffer us from what is rotten with our lives, the
way butchers do the dirty work for wimpy meat-eaters who can't kill animals themselves. We would accept what goes out of our lives as being as
sacred as what goes into our mouths, guts, and homes.

Second, I would hope that such a confrontation would move us to
waste less. We would no longer promote the conspicuous proliferation of
rubbish as the indicator of an individual's freedom and wealth.

Third, we would graciously return whatever we only half waste—or at
least that which remains half-valuable—to those resourceful microbes
and carrion feeders who will make good use of it. We are a society that
vacuum-packs day-old foodstuffs in stories-deep landfills rather than letting those scraps nourish other animals. We burn crop remains rather
than letting them ferment in compost heaps to replenish the depleted fertility of our soils. We have become stingy in what we are willing to pass
on through the food chain.

So why not hang our entrails out where everyone can see and smell
them? Why not take all the cow entrails not eaten in *menudo* and *tripas de
leche* and set them out for vultures, ravens, caracaras, and other scavengers? At a historical moment when captive-bred condors are being
released into the overpopulated and contaminated stretches of southern
California, why not open up some scavengers' restaurants, where fresh,
organically grown viscera would be readily available daily? It's time to set
up a restaurant chain, reaching from Baja California, to the Grand
Canyon and Big Bend, where condors and vultures might feast on all the
carnage that we produce but cannot stomach as a result of its high cho-
lesterol and our low moral fiber.

If you haven't already guessed, I am protesting the cleaned-up version of nature promoted by the media—the one that spotlights fuzzy herbivores and a few charismatic predators, while leaving little room for detritivores, saprophytes, and scavengers. Our society has so sanitized the wild world that we barely allow for the existence of death and decay.

This is not true of all cultures. Some desert people savor the rotting fragrance of flood-washed detritus, which they incorporate into their fields and sing of in their songs for crop fertility. They know that the desert is too dry during most months to allow for much decomposition of organic matter and release of nutrients. It is only when the first summer storms come to windrow piles of water-logged leaf litter, cowpies, and silt in floodplain fields that enough moisture and nitrogen become available for desert crops to thrive. Some of their songs celebrate the arrival of decaying flotsam as an omen that bountiful harvests will result in coming months. Yet when urban Anglo anthropologists have tried to translate such songs from native dialects, the words indicating the earth's renewal have been reduced to one term: "rubbish." Something deeply fecund has been lost in translation.

I ponder this problem as I wander down a desert wash below my November campsite. There, I see the last windrows left by the monsoons, stuck in the stems of streamside shrubbery, still decaying. Above them, in the highest branches, hang a few coyote gourds, their vines already withered but the fruit itself plump and ripe.

They remind me that gourds were among the first plants to become botanical "camp followers" of our ancestors. Civilization was founded on the fertility of campside dump heaps, where early sedentary human populations came to thrive on the abundant food resources engendered by organic waste and offal. The first plants domesticated by humankind were gourds and amaranths and cannabis that adapted to the nutrient-rich debris and disturbed soils left on the edge of hunter-gatherer campsites. Once humans realized that they could sow the seeds of these disturbance-adapted plants into other dump heaps and clearings, they produced so much food close to home that they stopped foraging so widely and could be more sedentary. Our civilization was spawned on the riches resulting from disturbances, decomposition, and fast-paced nutrient dynamics.

For years, I yearned for a way to immortalize our putrid beginnings. Then one fall, on a plant-collecting trip near Tepic, Mexico, I found my opportunity. There, in a garbage dump, I gathered a museum specimen I now cherish as my most prized botanical specimen. It came from a feral gourd plant that grew luxuriantly atop a ten-foot-high heap of spoiled vegetables and house scraps. Its delicate tendrils, drenched in slops, had wrapped around potsherds, broken glass fragments, and bottle caps. Rather than wresting them from these embraces, I pressed the vine, with all its trashy attachments.

When I returned to the border crossing, I declared the whole as a valuable addition to American museum collections. The plant inspector at the border scrutinized my botanical composition trapped between two stained sheets of absorbent paper. He then gave me a long, hard look, and asked, "I'll be damned. . . . You mean you're going to put some putrefying trash on exhibit?"

"I hope I can," I sighed. "It's time to celebrate what is rotten in this world."

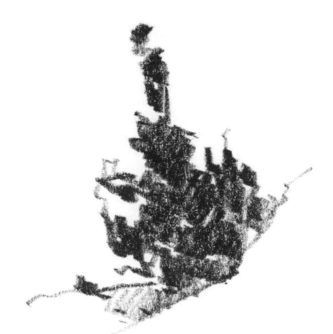

The Quality of Restraint
John Gierach

I USED TO THINK I WAS A FAIRLY RADICAL, NOT TO MENTION UP-TO-DATE, environmentalist, but when I read the newer literature of the movement, I realize that I'm not exactly an antihumanist anarchist, a primitivist, a humanist ecoanarchist, a green Marxist, or an ecofeminist. I probably *am* a bioregionalist (a pretty tame stance these days). More to the point, I'm a fly-fisherman, and that comes with its own political agenda.

My position is: we should have a clean, healthy, diverse natural environment so I can go fishing—because fishing makes me happy.

Granted, that kind of happiness seems like a simple-minded goal in these grim times, but there it is nonetheless: without becoming overly romantic, without ignoring reality, given the normal limitations, from now until hell freezes over, I would like to be reasonably happy.

And yes, maybe that is too much to ask. Then again, I haven't had the dreaded middle-age crisis, and I don't detect one brewing. Of course I have an advantage. Half the men and a few of the women I know who've wigged out in their forties wanted to run off and do what I do now, which is fish a lot and write books about it for a living. (The other half wanted sports cars and younger lovers, but that's a whole other story.) These people, after a life of working and striving, wanted to chuck it all and become one with nature in some kind of particularly human way, which is the only way available to us. (After twenty-some years of listening to New Age sanctimony, I cringe a little at the mention of becoming "one with" anything, but I guess it's like wanting happiness: corny but undeniable.) They saw this as a route to truth and salvation and, for some of them at least, it was just that.

What is it about fly-fishing? Well, it's difficult, complicated, expensive, and fashionable in a nonconformist sort of way (Ernest Hemingway fly-fished; so did Richard Brautigan), but I think it's actually because fly-fishers occupy a kind of middle ground between the two real poles of environmental thought—that is, observation versus participation. You can draw the line where you like, but to my mind, observation ranges from watching wildlife shows on television to, perhaps, birdwatching in the field, while participation includes, say, wild mushroom gathering on up to the killing and eating of large game animals. Land and wildlife managers like to characterize this polarity as consumptive versus non-consumptive use, with the dividing line falling between those who have to buy licenses and those who don't.

The line between politically correct and incorrect seems to fall somewhere else, although exactly where depends on how much of a jerk you are. I've already left instructions that if I ever become politically correct I'm to be shot. However you look at it (and there's a big gray area in the middle), it's probably fair to say that if you don't at least own a pair of hiking boots, your love of nature can be considered somewhat theoretical.

There's nothing theoretical about fly-fishing, though. The angler strings up a rod, ties on a fly, wades into the stream, and participates in the natural process by capturing fish—or at least trying to. The catch (no pun intended) is that these days fly-fishers probably release what they land, even on waters where the regulations don't require them to do that. They have recreated successfully and contributed to management efforts through their license fees and the taxes on some of their gear, but they've left the fish in the river. In a way, it's like they were never there.

Once catch-and-release fishing was only practiced by a bunch of fly-fishers releasing their trout and spouting slogans like Lee Wulff's, "A wild trout is too valuable to be caught just once." We felt we were on the cutting edge of something: a way to end the depredations of the frontier mentality without walking away from the old ways entirely. We had a lot of fun then because most fishermen thought we were nuts and, after all, the seething pride that comes from being wrongly misunderstood is one of the great kicks of belonging to a counterculture.

But catch-and-release has finally taken hold. Many great wild fisheries now have regulations requiring anglers to release some, if not all, of the fish they catch. Professional bass tournaments have reached the point where a dead fish costs you points, and even some remote, fly-in wilderness fisheries have a limit of one trophy fish per fisherman. I was at a camp in the Northwest Territories several years ago where the fisherman who released the largest lake trout of the year got a free trip the next season. It was a great gimmick, and guys were dumping wall-hangers back into the lake at the same rate they'd been taking them out for the past twenty years.

Things could be better, of course. Crowds of fishermen do have an impact on the environment, even when they're not killing fish. But catch-and-release does seem to be working fairly well. It's not clear how many people are fly-fishing now, but Jim Butler of *Fly Tackle Dealer* magazine, a man who pays attention to such things, estimates that there may now be as many as two million fly-fishers in the United States. It's clear to most fisheries managers that if all those people were keeping a limit every time they could, there probably wouldn't be any fish left, especially when you consider that there are fewer good trout streams now than there once were and, as I once overheard someone say, "God ain't makin' no new ones."

Angling has always been viewed as an essentially harmless business, institutionalized laziness at the worst, but now it's become almost pacifistic, and there really are some fly-fishers around who think that killing a trout amounts to murder. (This is a hard position to defend in a blood sport, and I've noticed that many of these guys lighten up over time.) Some others never keep a fish because, they say, they just don't feel like it or never get around to it, while most of the rest limit their kill in one way or another.

Like many of my friends who also spend a lot of time with a fly rod, there are times when I have no fish at all in the freezer. At the moment (I just looked) I have five foot-long brook trout. That seems about right, since I could legally have a possession limit of sixteen. I make a point of killing fish now and then because I like wild food and also because I don't want the sport to become completely sanitized. The matter gets complicated, and there are lots of ways to determine if you're going to feel right about keeping a couple of fish to eat. But the important thing is you have to feel right about it. The end result is always the same: you end up taking a lot less than you're legally entitled to. There was a time when you bragged about killing your limit. Now you brag about stopping short. Things have definitely changed.

Meanwhile, the debate goes on in the angling community. The newest idea I've heard is that of actually limiting the number of fish you catch and release to reduce the cumulative stress on the fish population. The number I hear most often is eight, which is coincidentally the number of trout in a legal daily bag limit here in Colorado. Not everyone has bought into this, but it has introduced an interesting question: Since you're not keeping them anyway, how many fish constitutes "enough"?

That reminds me of a story. I was in a fly shop once when a guy came in, bought some flies and a nonresident fishing license, and asked, "What's the limit on trout in this state?" There were two clerks, a guide, and several fishermen standing around. No one knew. They had to dig out a copy of the regulations and look it up.

Over the years, for one reason or another, I've asked a lot of fly-fishers why they like what they do or what they think they get out of it. Discounting replies like "It's none of your business" or "You're not gonna write about this, are you?" most answers indicate that it's either so simple it should be obvious or it's too complicated to go into.

That answers the question perfectly. Fly-fishing does have its social aspects—on some of our crowded trout streams it can get too social—but essentially it's a solitary, contemplative sport. People are left alone with themselves in beautiful surroundings to try to accomplish something that seems to have genuine value. They like that, and I don't think a lot of them go around asking themselves why—which is really better, because coming to understand your own motivation is overrated. Such analysis usually amounts to surgically removing any trace of poetry from your life; things get easier, but they're no fun.

Speaking of poetry, before *A River Runs Through It* opened, some people in the tackle industry were saying the movie was going to do a lot to further popularize fly-fishing. At the time I thought this was just the usual hopeful bullshit businessmen try to perpetrate on each other, but it may actually be happening in a small way. Aside from being a great, poignant story about life, love, death, and such, the film showed fly-fishing in all its prettiness but otherwise largely without comment. And, sure enough, I know of at least two people who saw the light, walked out of the theater, and drove to the nearest fly shop as if in a trance. (I can be a little superior about this because I'm an old-timer now, if only because I remember when *A River Runs Through It* was "just a book.")

I can't tell you why *I* like fly-fishing either. I've tried a few times, and I always get tangled up in sentiment or politics. I've read books on the subject by fine writers who've tried to explain it. Many failed, and the best only gave tantalizing hints. Robert Traver said he fishes not because it's so important, but because everything else is equally unimportant. Jim Harrison said, "Few of us shoot ourselves during an evening hatch." Tom McGuane said, "If the trout are lost, smash the state." Harry Middleton said he's addicted "not so much to fly-fishing but to what it sinks me in."

All I know is that it has to do with *doing* something: closing the instruction book, putting on a pair of waders, and going out there where things are as they are because they couldn't possibly be otherwise. You need waders because you'll be in the water, and the water is cold.

It's participation—the opposite of wilderness behind a velvet cord, to be looked at but not touched; the opposite of nature as theme park. It's hard to explain what it does for you, but you know that without it your life would become pale and hopeless.

From a theoretical distance, wild rivers are a nice idea, and it's hard to find anyone these days who doesn't at least claim to be an environmentalist. (Remember George Bush?) As for me, if I couldn't fish those rivers, I don't know how interested I'd be in them—possibly not very. But as it is now, precious few things interest me more.

Fly-fishers are tenacious conservationists if only because they benefit more than most from wild rivers with fish in them, and this allows them to draw logical, uncluttered conclusions. If the fisheries we have are getting crowded, it just means we have to save all the ones we have left and restore some that have been lost. It's simple.

Compromise? Those who understand wildness—which, after all, is the true nature of reality—understand that nine times out of ten, compromise means you lost, only you might not be smart enough to realize it.

A philosophy professor of mine used to say you can tell more about someone by examining his assumptions than by analyzing his logic. The assumption behind catch-and-release fly-fishing is that we should be responsible; if we err, it should be on the side of low-impact, but *we should go on fishing*. The quality we're looking for is not detachment but restraint.

The Man of Vines
Frederick Turner

I WONDER IF THERE CAN BE A MORE REVEALING CULTURAL PHENOMENON in America than the common wine tasting? Half a century ago when I was a kid in Chicago there wasn't any such thing, nor was wine part of the adult scene I observed. I have to think my experience in this regard wasn't singular. In America in the forties and fifties, it was Cuba Libra, si, bordeaux, non, and I'll bet you could page through issues of *LIFE, Look, Collier's,* and the *Saturday Evening Post* from those decades and not come across a dozen ads for nonfortified wines.

But from that point, the national culture leaped directly to a significant per capita consumption of wine by the eighties, without having passed through the steeping stages that produce authentic appreciation. For whatever reasons—including, of course, the historic American inferiority complex in the face of Old World polish—we have been in a furious haste in this matter of wine. We have longed to be at ease with a glass of wine, to be able to casually order a decent bottle for the restaurant dinner table, to be able to talk about fine wines and one's collection of them. Yet if popular wine tasting has become our symbol of cultural arrival, then we seem to have come to this century's end, in this regard anyway, in about the state of Fitzgerald's bootlegger Gatsby when he bought his fake Norman castle with its "thin beard of raw ivy" and essayed entrance to the high society of West Egg. That is to say, we have the money to talk wine and certainly to buy and consume it, but we don't have much behind this. We now have the wealthy wine collector, the wine speculator, the wine snob, and the phenomenon of the wine tasting, generally a shallow and silly affair. We also have now the wine souse, what the French might call the *soiffard*, along with whom I have myself sometimes uncharitably been placed. The poet and radical ecologist Gary Snyder is said once to have observed that Americans don't know much about the flora and fauna of their native places because we are descendants of conquerors, and historically conquerors are not much interested in the natural order or the discrete facts of the places they have overrun. That might well bear on our ignorant, broad-gauge attitude toward wine, for wine is in truth and not just in trope, the "fruit of the vine."

I might not have understood even so much about wine in America had I not blundered into a man whose words and presence put this aspect of our national behavior into what was for me a new light. This happened at a wine tasting in my adopted hometown of Santa Fe. Stepping aside for a moment from the throng of those avid for their first hit, I loitered near the domestic whites, waiting for the line to shorten. But the shop was small, and my strategic positioning put me nearly in the lap of a man sitting quietly in the corner, a glass of red held firmly yet with a delicacy in a broad hand that had surely known manual labor. I judged him to be a very vigorous fifty. He had a full head of dark hair, and there was a sparkle of amused interest in his eye as he observed the wine habits of these thirsty celebrants. Shortly I learned that it was in fact his wines that were providing the afternoon's occasion. Alain Querre was modest enough in giving this information, but the modesty was personal rather than professional: he clearly took pride in his St. Emilion, his Pomerol, his St.-Estèphe. These were, he now told me, produced on eight chateaus in the Bordeaux region under the aegis of Maison Daniel Querre. The Querre family had been in the wine trade since the latter decades of the nineteenth century, but he wished to remind me that the land on which these grapes grew had been nurturing vines since at least the fourth century A.D., when the poet and Roman consul Ausonius had planted extensive vineyards at what is now the village of St. Emilion. So, he said, although it was true enough that he was here in America representing Maison Daniel Querre, in a much more important way he was representing an ancient tradition that had its roots deep in the soil of a particular place. The wines being featured here today were to him not only a product of that place but also a portrait of it and of all those who had ever worked that small surface of the globe. His wines were, he felt, a fitting portrait of the place and the people, but, he added, "I do not even mind tasting a bad country wine, as long as it is that: an authentic portrait of the people and the soil. Then it is all right. It is another page in the book, and after all, what is life if you are not interested in all the pages?"

Some weeks after Alain Querre had returned to his Libourne home, I was prompted by our conversation to send him a copy of *Beyond Geography,* a book I had written about Western civilization's historic rootlessness and the consequences of this for the New World. Querre wrote back a long and generous response that included these words: "You make me realize how privileged I am to live on the same spot my caveman ancestors were hunting over more than ten thousand years ago, and to be able to enjoy a landscape which has been slowly and respectfully sculpted throughout the centuries by careful and loving hands." Perhaps, he suggested, sometime I might make a visit and see for myself what he was trying to put into words.

That was how my wife and I found ourselves in the Libourne/St. Emilion area on some rainy March days in 1988. Querre met us at the Libourne train station, and then we drove the few kilometers to Chateau Monbousquet, which had been established around 1540 and which Daniel Querre, Alain's father, had restored to splendor just after World War II. Under a sky like dripping sheet metal, the great house sat behind a wall heavily veined with ivy. A gravel drive took you through the gate and to the edge of a large pond on the far side of which a majestic chestnut spread out its arms in enduring benediction. Querre let us take all this in without saying anything more than that the chestnut had for many years been the site of family gatherings. On all sides of the house were the vineyards; the individual vines stood against the faint green of the spring earth in naked black twists, looking so vulnerable in this season and light that I was moved to say so.

"Oh, yes, they are," Querre responded. "The vine is a fragile and mysterious plant, almost supernatural. It can no longer live without the help of man. There are five thousand of them in each hectare you are looking at, and each one of them must be constantly tended. They must be

pruned and protected. They must be trained. We must restrain their natural tendency to sprawl by means of those wires you see strung between
them." Before my remark he had seemed to be leading us up the steps
and into the house, but now he turned and went out again through the
gate to the vineyards that flanked the drive, oblivious to the rain that had
now turned from a mizzle into a downpour. Yet Querre entered the vineyard and, walking a short distance between the rows, paused before a
thick, bent trunk. "Grape juice," he said, "is natural. Wine is not. The
smell and taste of a good wine is something God did not make. He gave
us the materials to make it, but it is we who must do it, and it is an art. It
is the fruit of the union of man and soil.

"The man must have the knowledge of how to produce wine from
grapes, and for that he must above all know and love his soil." He knelt
and cupped a handful of brown earth that glinted dully in the rain. "He
must know which part of his land is best for young and fruity wines, and
which part contains in its subsoil the makings of great bottles for aging.
He must submit himself to his soil like a musician to his score. And all
this is to reach his goal, which is to extract the very soul of the land from
its soil. When you drink a glass of good wine, you drink the soul of the
land. And that is why here we say, 'Il faut boire avec esprit!'

"Yes, the vine is very vulnerable, as you say, and it needs our assistance.
But at the same time it is a great teacher. It has been the great teacher of
my family from my grandfather on. It is my great teacher. If I make a bad
wine, it is because I have not listened to it, because I have not paid the
proper attention." He stood up and regarded the rows that marched back
along the drive to the road by which we'd come, the trees at the road's
edge dark and streaming. Suddenly he laughed, dropped his handful of
soil, and rubbed his hands together. "But I am not listening to you, and
you are getting very wet out here!" And then we retraced our steps and
went into the house where Querre's brother and sister-in-law waited with
a bottle of Chateau Monbousquet Grand Cru and hot hors d'oeuvres.

That evening at the Hotel Loubat in Libourne, Maison Daniel Querre
hosted a wine tasting in honor of the visit of Edmund Penning-Rowsell,
author of the definitive *The Wines of Bordeaux*. (San Francisco: The Wine
Appreciation Guild, 1985). I wish I could honestly write that Alain
Querre's poetic, rain-pelted words had sufficiently reformed me so that I
behaved better than characteristically. Mr. Penning-Rowsell inhaled the
bouquets of the vintages of Maison Daniel Querre, he chewed the wines,
he rolled them back on his tongue, and spat them into the silver decanter
provided for this purpose. The others in attendance did the same,

conversing quietly about the wines' properties, of the weather in the
years the wines were made. My wife was too honest and self-conscious to
do any of these things and so contented herself with a few small swallows
of the various vintages. Old Turner, however, unsteadily upheld the
national escutcheon, drinking deeply of the Canon Fronsac, the Pomerol,
St. Emilion, St.-Estèphe, and so forth, quite incapable of letting loose of a
single delicious mouthful. After a dinner of oysters, stewed *lamproie* (eels
from the nearby Gironde), duck, cake (it was Penning-Rowsell's birth-
day), cheese, Barsac, and brandy, I had reason to be grateful that our hotel
room was only one flight up.

Alain Querre chose to overlook this performance and the next afternoon took us on a tour of some of the vineyards of the Querre cooperative and then the village of St. Emilion. He seemed to feel that if you
wanted to understand something about fine wine, it was best to start at
the source itself, the fields. Everybody, he said, knows what a glass of
wine is, or thinks he knows. But what was generally known of the mysterious vine that produced the grapes and that had so much to teach?
Actually, he told us, the man who worked long enough with the vine and
with proper respect came to understand that men and vines were much
alike: "For a grower, the vine is just like him—his feet in the mud, his
body working vertically, his head in the sky. The vinelike man is a bridge
between earth and heaven above." Thus the tending of the vines had
something of the sacred about it and was here traditionally surrounded
by rituals like the annual blessing of the fields by the village priest and by
the call to harvest, the *ban des vendanges,* in which the spirits of the ancestors were invoked and asked for assistance. Nor were these rituals, he
wanted us to understand, mere romantic vestiges, gestures toward a past
that was honored and superseded. They were, instead, meant and profoundly felt. Once, he said, as his father was preparing to issue the *ban des
vendanges,* he had told his young son that he would be calling to his own
father, now dead. "'And someday, you will do the same. You will call to
me.' And I have done so."

As for the village itself, I found something compellingly appropriate in
the fact that the cavernous, ochre-colored Eglise Monolithe underlay and
supported the village's old square. Benedictine monks had begun to hack
its outlines from the great limestone crag during the eighth century, and
after Alain Querre had taken us through its vaults and we stood again on
the flagging of the square with its border of shops and restaurants, I could
indeed see what Querre had been putting into the words of his letter to
me months before: here in physical fact the present stood on the massive

hunched shoulders of the past. Here even the dullard tourist could feel a tug greater than gravity.

We broke for lunch at Chateau Puy-Razac, one of the chateaus in the Querre cooperative. Its owner, Guy Thoilliez, Alain Querre told us, was a master grower to whom agricultural students from all parts of Europe came for advice and example. Thoilliez was a short, spare man in his sixties with a weather-roughened face and a reserved manner with these two Americans whose French was so clumsy. Simone Thoilliez, his wife, was as open as her husband was reserved, immediately enfolding my wife in a big hug and smilingly waiting out my attempts at conversational politeness. Neither Thoilliez spoke English, but their teenage daughter was studying it in school, and I told her in English that when my wife and I put our French together we were almost the equivalent of a half-wit. When she translated that for her father, it broke the ice.

During a long lunch of steak, *pommes frites,* and freshly baked bread, Guy Thoilliez kept producing bottles of Chateau Puy-Razac Grand Cru, their only visible identifications the dates chalked on their dark smooth sides—1976, 1983, 1986, 1987. Here there was no need to spit anything out, though we did move pretty smartly from one bottle to another without finishing any of them. But Alain Querre used the occasion to continue his gentle tutelage of this American man whose appetite so evidently exceeded his understanding. At one point after Guy Thoilliez had poured from yet another vintage, Querre held his glass up to the gray afternoon light and said to me that rightly understood, the drinking of wine was not a means of escaping reality into stupefaction but rather a means of entering more deeply into the true nature of existence. "Grapes," he continued, "can produce vinegar. They can produce grape juice, which is nice but boring. And they can produce a wine like this one. Fine wines appeal to man's intelligence; they improve it. They contribute to the enlargement of man's consciousness. But, of course, this depends partly on the man!" He laughed. I felt no barb here and laughed along with him.

Later, I would think back on this—on all he had been showing us during our wet, muddy tramps through the vineyards, during the hour we spent in the cold stone vaults his grandfather had built for his vats at Monbousquet, the great oak barrels surrounding us and their sides gleaming faintly under coats of varnish. It was a matter of understanding, in the moment of holding your glass, the whole complex process, of sensing then what had gone into the making of that glassful: the microclimate of the soil that grew the grapes, the varietals planted there, the sort of care these required, the attitudes of the men and women who harvested them, the whole ancient tradition of producing fine wines—wines that truly were loved by those who made them—all the way back to Ausonius at his villa Lucaniacus at the foot of St. Emilion's limestone crag. It made the drinking of a glass of fine wine a sort of sacrament, as indeed it was to these men at the laden table at Chateau Puy-Razac, and to the wives of these men as well, who had spent their own backbreaking hours in the vineyards, grafting and pruning. For just as the production of these wines was a matter of quality versus mere quantity, so should the drinking of them be a matter of quality, of a mindfulness that was yet not the pompous sobriety of the wine snob.

Earlier that day Querre had referred to the matter of quality versus quantity, remarking that when a wine grower chose to produce in quantity at the expense of quality, turning out what Querre called a "standard, boring, destructive alcoholic beverage," then he was "acting like a bad angel. And for what? For money, of course. But then he is working against himself. He is using black magic. Only black magic is operated for money. White magic, which is only transference, which is in communion with nature's objectives, is acted for happiness. Nature is our mother. If some people are mad enough to prostitute their mother, you will not find them in St. Emilion!" Similarly, you might find in St. Emilion those who drank for quantity—*soiffards*—probably could, given the fact that France has more than its share of alcoholics. But you probably would not find them among the men and women who have so lovingly and mindfully worked with the vines.

On our last day in the Libourne/St. Emilion area, we took another, smaller, tour with Alain Querre, this time to see Les Grottes, a connected series of caves that lay in a limestone hillside outside St. Emilion. We drove along a woods-bowered country road to get as close as we could in the car, for it was now raining harder than ever. The streams were brimful, and the ditches along the roads had taken all they could and had begun to well out, sending small meanders of water along the dirt and gravel of the road beds.

Where Querre parked there was a stone sepulcher lying exposed by the roadside and partly overgrown with weeds, the sides falling away and its original contents long since gone back into the surrounding earth. As we went down through an old wood of oaks, we passed a charnel house with its western end open to the weather, and inside it you could see the unassorted heaps of fibias, ribs, and skulls. Past this the trail swung up against the limestone cliff, and presently we were at the caves. Most of them, we discovered, were pretty small, about big enough for a group to hunker about a fire. Alain Querre said that as far as he knew, their age hadn't been certainly established, but it was evident from the markings on their friable walls that they went back several centuries at least. In the center of the series was a cave somewhat larger than the others, and into its western wall had been carved a rude throne. Above it in the roof and facing east was a sizable hole. Querre said that if you were seated on the throne on a particular day in spring, the sun would shine full in your face.

It was dank in the throne room, and it smelled of limestone that probably never thoroughly dried out, of charred wood, leaf mold, and at last of earth. And with the rain, the dimness, and the vacant throne that kept its secrets, my wife and I felt suddenly subdued, as if here the past was bearing us to earth with its ponderous weight. To be sure, we had come happily to this Old World, eager to encounter again its very historicity, its masterpieces of painting and sculpture and architecture, its immemorially domesticated landscape. But it is one thing to gaze in awe at the Obelisk of Luxor in the Place de la Concorde and another to confront the past standing where we now were. We seemed at this moment descending ever deeper into this Old World, ever deeper into that well of the past that Thomas Mann had said was bottomless. Our breaths hung in the air, tiny, evanescent clouds of mortality, momentarily suspended against an unfathomed gloom and the streaming light of the present.

Here, I Am the Deer:
A Meandering Meditation
on Grizzly Wilderness
David Petersen

ON A POSTCARD-PERFECT COLORADO EVENING IN JUNE 1991, IN A wooded back corner of a private ranch near the bustling tourist village of Pagosa Springs, a stout, scruffy man in his late forties addresses an equally scruffy audience lazing around a campfire. The speaker is Douglas Arapahoe Peacock—writer, filmmaker, and arguably the world's leading authority on the behavior of grizzly bears in the wild and up close. Peacock's dozen and more listeners include a couple of wildlife biologists, a conservation ecologist, an environmental attorney, a few ranchers, a pair of writers, and various others . . . your proverbial motley crew.

After self-introductions around the fire circle, Peacock opens by explaining why he called this informal conference just now, here in the midst of the wraparound San Juan Mountains. Speaking quietly, he tells us that information gathered with his own eyes during recent treks into the remotest backcountry of the south San Juans, strengthened by a muscular body of "external" evidence, has convinced him that a remnant population of native grizzly bears still exists hereabouts.

While I would never second-guess my pal Peacock's sixth sense for grizzlies, what he is proposing strikes me initially as—well, maybe just a little too good to be true.

After all, as recently as the early 1980s, the Colorado Division of Wildlife's leading bear biologist, Tom Beck, had spent two years searching for grizzlies in the south San Juans. Beck's search had been politically necessitated when a healthy, mature grizzly sow was killed by (and had almost killed) a local hunting guide named Ed Wiseman up along the headwaters of the Navajo. The official pronouncement following the Beck search was: "No." The Wiseman bear, the DOW announced, had quite probably been the last grizzly in Colorado.

But then, "no" had also been the official pronouncement back in 1952, when grizzlies were declared extinct statewide following a century-long campaign against predatory megafauna waged by ranchers and—on private ranchers' behalf and largely at public expense—government trappers.

Wrong about the 1950s extirpation, the DOW could be just as wrong about the Wiseman grizzly being the last. Suggesting this probability was the size and coloration of the Wiseman sow's teats, which indicated she'd likely given birth to at least one more generation of ultimate wildness. And, of course, a papa griz was implied.

Citing grizzly evidence he's seen himself, Peacock tells us that he and two hiking companions, in late September of 1990, found a huge track they all felt certain was made by a grizzly. Then, perhaps more than coincidentally, only a couple of weeks later a respected local rancher with extensive wilderness experience watched for more than half an hour what he was positive was a grizzly sow with three half-grown cubs playing at the edge of an alpine meadow. A week later, the local game warden returned with the foreman and, sure enough, found the snow tracked with huge, grizzlylike bear prints.

Considering these things, it takes no great leap of logic, Peacock feels, to conclude that at least a handful of native grizzlies are miraculously still hanging on, still holding out "up there"—he points to the jagged mountains looming like a ruined castle wall in the near south.

Taking into account all this evidence and more, it's easy to believe that both the Colorado DOW and the U.S. Fish and Wildlife Service know more than they're publicly letting on. At the least, it's apparent that neither outfit is eager to confirm the continued presence of this controversial endangered species in Colorado. Their reluctance is not hard to understand: Why, they must be thinking, should they invite the political headaches and financial burden attendant to enforcing Endangered Species Act protections for, and trying to recover, the grizzly bear in yet another western state? Even if it is their moral and legal responsibility?

But headaches come in many flavors. Enter Doug Peacock and friends, who decide and vow at the Pagosa meeting to do what the DOW and FWS should have been doing all along but haven't. The time has come, they conclude, for a grizzly hunt. Thus, the Colorado Grizzly Project is born.

IN THE MONTHS following the organization of CGP, Doug Peacock—a man with many irons in many fires—opted to back off to a position jokingly described as "spiritual leader" of the project, with active control passing to Round River Conservation Studies of Salt Lake City, a non-profit environmental research and education foundation headed by bear biologist Dennis Sizemore, on whose board of directors Peacock sits.

While not a card-carrying member of either Round River or CGP, I have been an intensely interested observer from the beginning. Along the way, I've learned that it's far more than a desire to prove that grizzlies still roam the San Juans that drives the project, entering its third year at this writing. It is more even than a desire to protect the ghostly bears Peacock and the others believe are there. It is, bottom line, a commitment to preserve the rich ecosystem that has allowed a species as feared, misunderstood, and ultimately delicate as the grizzly to survive into the ravenous teeth of the twenty-first century.

The way CGP proposes to attack this mountain-sized task is by winning both grass-roots and governmental support, the latter comprising the Big Three of Colorado wildlands and wildlife management: the DOW, the FWS, and the U.S. Forest Service. Round River believes that documenting irrefutable proof of a remnant native grizzly population will help win that wide-spectrum support.

As for me . . . well, I've been forced into semicynicism by nearly five decades of living, grown doubtful that anything will ever be more important to at least a narrow majority of rural and small-town westerners than a new 4x4 every few years, a dish antenna in the front yard, and a vacation to someplace warm and sunny each winter. My fellow westerners, many of them, see the national forests, even designated wilderness, not as delicate preserves of biological diversity and national pride, but merely as a resource from which to chain-saw, blast, and graze a living. To this common species of indigenous grass roots, the Forest Service motto "Land of many uses" translates—exactly as Earth First! bumper stickers have long proclaimed—to "Land of many *abuses.*"

Grizzly bears are anathema to this sagebrush-scented, so-called wise-use worldview. Already, suspicious locals are whispering that should there in fact be a few grizzlies roaming the San Juans today, they were "planted" here recently by the DOW or FWS. A strikingly ignorant contention, this, yet eagerly accepted by many old-line westerners, traditionally suspicious of government. Besides, truth has never been a prerequisite for true-believerism anywhere, anytime—witness the world's mutually contradictory religions; witness our perpetual gullibility to the predictable lies of politicians. If only these blissfully uninformed gossips knew how very little the management agencies want grizzlies in Colorado, their necks would go yet a darker shade of red. Fact is, at least at the higher levels of agency management, grizzlies are about as welcome here as a budget slash.

Thus, while Round River's avowed goal of winning grass-roots and agency support for a more conservation-minded management of the San Juans is both noble and necessary, it won't come easily—at either end.

Nor am I totally convinced that identifying and revealing the precise turf of Colorado's ghost grizzlies, which CGP will be obliged to do in order to prove their fundamental point, will necessarily help the bears.

One worry in that direction is that if and when the agencies finally acknowledge a grizzly presence hereabouts, among their first acts will be to send in platoons of Nazi Dr. Doolittle biologists to trap, radio collar, and electronically hound-dog any and every grizzly they can find—exactly as the DOW hoped to do during its hit-and-miss search a decade ago. While such hands-on monitoring may be necessary to keep the peace in places such as Yellowstone, where large numbers of people and more than a few grizzlies are concentrated on the same turf, such drastically intrusive measures hardly seem called for here in the San Juans. Experience shows that handled bears are disadvantaged bears. After being trapped, tranquilized, pricked, probed, ear-tagged, lip-tattooed, radio-collared, and released, those animals that survive the ordeal—and some may not—will no longer be the ultimately wild, supremely secretive creatures they now are. They will have been technologically raped, their anonymity destroyed, their very grizzlyness diminished. There is a significant difference between agency biologists, who—a few sterling exceptions noted—are career-driven to generate data, to handle and dissect their subjects both physically and statistically, and old-school naturalists like Doug Peacock, who are satisfied to observe wildlife from an unobtrusive distance, exerting patience rather than control, wishing to learn rather than to prove.

Still, I feel no choice but to hope for the Colorado Grizzly Project's rapid success in proving the existence of a relict population of native grizzlies here, keeping my fingers crossed that the agencies will go easy when that happens. We can't afford to love even one Colorado grizzly to death.

Wasting no time, Round River launched its first grizzly search as soon as the mountain snows would allow in the summer of 1991, employing a crew of enthusiastic, if somewhat uncoordinated, volunteers to comb promising bits of the 127,000-acre South San Juan Wilderness. It was a start.

This summer, the volunteers have been replaced with an equally enthusiastic but much better organized team, working under the leadership of an experienced professional. For a week in late June, I was a drop-in member of that team.

SCRIBBLING THESE NOTES, I'M sprawled prostrate beneath a late-afternoon cobalt sun in a field of wildflowers near the headwaters of a river I shall disguise, out of respect for the privacy of the place and its wild inhabitants, as the White, enjoying the pure solitude and unmolested scenery only true wilderness can provide. Appropriate to such a heaven on earth, getting here was not easy.

On the topographical maps, the hike into this subalpine redoubt looked like a cakewalk: a short stroll along an almost-level forest service trail, a ford of the narrow White, a gently undulating side-hill bushwhack a few miles upstream to the confluence of a feeder creek near the White's headwaters, ford again, hump the far slope . . . home.

So very easy appeared the hike on paper, in fact, and so swollen was my ex-marine, local-mountain-man machismo, that I was mildly miffed to learn that search leader Jim Tolisano would be hiking down from his mobile base camp to guide my little group of visitors back up.

I'd spoken with Tolisano briefly at Peacock's Pagosa congress, sizing him up then as a likable fellow with credentials aplenty for the job: master's in forest and watershed management; contract forest ecology researcher for the U.S. Forest Service; consulting naturalist and ecologist for the U.S. Park Service, United Nations, USAID, Peace Corps, World Wildlife Fund; and more.

But all that's beside the point, I thought; the San Juans are my home turf (notwithstanding I'd never been into the White headwaters before); I don't need no stinkin' guide. (Ironically, while Tolisano was on station on time, I and my three companions—a fellow scrivener, a National Public Radio reporter, and a veteran of the previous summer's search—were a tad late; some local Hayduke type had chain-sawed down the trailhead sign.)

A dark, compact dynamo of a man, hardened by a life lived actively in nature, Tolisano led out briskly—loping upstream along a gravely riverbank, winging over a foaming whitewater race on a spray-slicked blow-down log, scrambling up a near-vertical scree slope where each of his steps sent an avalanche of sharp-edged shale slabs bombing down to slash and bruise the bare bony legs of the hiker below him (me), striding down and huffing back up no less than five steep lateral drainages. A final plummeting switch-back descent down a muddy, (black) bear-tracked elk trail into the rocky bowels of what had become a Grand Canyon of a river gorge; a numbing barefoot ford of the swift, blue-cold, knee-deep headwaters; a rope-assisted two-hundred-foot ascent of the facing cliff wall—and we'd arrived.

Some cakewalk.

In painful point of fact, it was a long, sweat-soaked day of double-time scrambling over terrain that held no resemblance whatsoever to the Pollyanna stroll of topo map promise. My forty-six years, moderate Camel habit, and fifty-pound pack didn't make it any easier. No bloody mosquitoes, though; guess they couldn't take the lightning, thunder, wind, and hail that dogged us most of the way. With no trails leading in from any direction and no visible landmarks, I doubt I could have navigated here on my own with a dozen maps in a week of searching.

That experience under my belt, it's a lot easier to understand how a few acutely people-shy grizzlies—which Peacock and Sizemore believe the San Juan survivors have learned to become—could have survived anonymously up here all these years. Looking around, I rather envy them.

In the long view from where I sit—a mile or so to the south, across the whitewater-gashed gorge of the White—rises a chalky wall of naked sedimentary cliffs striped here and there with platinum ribbons of falling water. Above each fall, a brief, sparkling brook issues from a slow-melting patch of shaded snow. The beauty of this scene is heartbreaking. Behind me, Tolisano's camp—a dozen scattered tents and a communal fire circle at the edge of a big mountain park—is surrounded by a mixed old-growth forest of spruce, fir, ponderosa pine, and quaking aspen. Idyllic.

Amidst all this splendor, I've passed much of my time here so far in prowling the shadowy forests, alone mostly (the way I like it), searching for grizzly sign. And what a joy it is; with the thought that Griz could actually be up here with me, these familiar old safe San Juans have taken on a whole new excitement.

Nowhere nearly so exciting, I confess, as backcountry travel in Glacier or Yellowstone country or, especially, out on the Alaskan barren grounds where once a bold sow grizzly chased Bruce Woods and me off the fresh-butchered carcass of a caribou he'd shot and we'd planned to dine on for the next ten days. In our hasty retreat, we got away with only a couple of packfuls of meat, the bear claiming the rest. We didn't really mind: the experience was well worth the price of admission.

In such magical places as those, the certain knowledge of a constant lurking grizzly presence creates a surreal twilight zone of excitation that "elevates the mountains, deepens the canyons, chills the winds, brightens the stars, darkens the forests and quickens the pulse," as my Alaskan friend John Murray so perfectly bottles the essence in his anthology *The Great Bear.* Down here in the San Juans, the magic I'm feeling is far more subtle, reflecting only an anxious "maybe." But even that is enough to turn a routine hike into an adventure.

Further heightening the excitement, I've not been merely strolling along, but creeping cautiously through this ancient dark forest—striving to see without being seen, to hear without being heard, to scent without being scented, to discover without being discovered—thus becoming both the hunter and the hunted. It's the most profound way of going to nature I know, reflecting a long, slow evolution.

For almost as long as I can remember, each fall I've put aside most of the rest of my life in order to become for a while the best animal I can, a metaphorical cougar, using a simple longbow, handmade cedar arrows, and a level of concentration bordering on religious trance to experience an intensity of personal participation in wild nature to which I long believed there could be no equal. The challenge in primitive bowhunting is not just to collect meat or antlers, though both are welcome rewards for the considerable effort involved. Rather, the greatest satisfaction in this ritual—I detest and reject the concept of hunting as "sport"—comes from slipping breath-holding close, undetected, to deer or elk, the keenest self-defense mechanisms evolution has yet to hone . . . exactly as the puma must attempt to do every wild day of its life. Having been at it for better than three decades now, I've achieved a passable competence. Even so, far more often than not, I fail . . . exactly as must the puma.

Although I remain an avid bowhunter—it's a part of who and what I am—I have in recent years discovered an even more intense form of active participation in wild nature. By venturing unarmed into grizzly country, the old familiar hunter-prey roles are exactly reversed: In grizzly country I am no longer the puma, I am the deer. No other outdoor experience frightens me so thoroughly, humbles me so deeply, or makes me feel more alive and glad of it than hiking and camping in grizzly-quality wilderness.

Of course, there are those times when I—you, we— don't want the level of knee-knocking excitement that comes with sharing the woods with six-hundred-pound walking appetites. But for such timid times, we have the fields and forests and deserts and mountains of forty-three entirely grizzly-free contiguous states (as well as the bulk of the remaining five) in which to wander essentially unthreatened by nature red in tooth and claw. In such gutted, civilized, so-called wilderness, there's little more to fear than lightning, giardiasis, and the occasional human wacko. Colorado's silver San Juans are far too sublime to languish among that harness-broke majority.

That's why I'm up here, I guess, why I'm scribbling this meandering meditation on grizzer-bears and wilderness, why I agreed to attend Peacock's meeting in the first place—I wish to be part of an honest, earnest effort to renew in my own backyard the pulse-quickening aliveness I've found nowhere in the lower forty-eight beyond a few shrinking shreds of true wilderness . . . Grizzly Wilderness.

Call it enlightened self-interest, but measured against a Glacier or a Yellowstone or a Bob, the too-tame "backcountry experience" available in most of today's overgrazed, mine-polluted, logging-road-slashed, trail-tortured, ski-slope scarred, condo-littered, subdivided Colorado mountains is a big fat yawn. Try as I might to maintain objectivity, I can't get away from the fact that I *want* the grizzly here. Not just the bear, mind you, but the natural balance and ultimate wildness its presence signifies.

That's why I'm pulling for CGP. Win or lose in their efforts to bring about the San Juan salvation we all hope for, the project is doing important work. The educational aspect of the program alone, this trip has convinced me, justifies all.

Beginning this summer and continuing for as many summers as

necessary, small teams of highly motivated, tuition-paying student searchers will be up here, somewhere, everywhere, prowling the remotest niches of these sublime old rock piles with the Colorado Grizzly Project—hiking hard and high in snow, lightning storms, and blistering sunshine, sleeping on the firm sweet bosom of the rocky mountain earth, eating communal mush, slapping mosquitoes, drawing biotic maps, and bagging bear turds—the good life. After this fashion, the students achieve intense personal involvement with not only the project, but also the landscape, its wild inhabitants and—themselves.

Additionally, Round River students can earn six to sixteen college credits in the deal—provided they work hard, maintain constant good humor, religiously attend Jim Tolisano's graduate-level campfire lectures, successfully complete an individual research or writing project, and pass a comprehensive final exam. No freebies here.

Student tuition, in turn, helps to meet the project's growing operational overhead—food, transportation, insurance and such—plus laboratory expenses.

Success at the wildlife forensic lab is, in fact, CGP's primary goal at this stage. Toward that end, one of the basic activities of the searchers, me included, is collecting bear scats. This summer's pungent prizes—four of which I'm proud to have my name on—will be backpacked out and air dried, then picked through with tweezers and magnifying glasses by student volunteers in the biology lab at Fort Lewis College in nearby Durango.

What the Fort Lewis plop-pickers will be looking for are hairs lapped up and swallowed during self-grooming sessions or snatched from a hirsute hind-end by passing stools. Bear hair thus collected will then be sent for species identification to the Wyoming Game and Fish Laboratory, the acknowledged authority in such matters, then on for confirmation elsewhere.

So far, so good. Analysis of the 1991 take revealed that two of the samples likely had come from grizzlies.

The bad news last season was that the laboratory was critical of the way the samples had been documented and handled—the not-so-subtle implication being that, for all the laboratory knew, known grizzly hairs could have been collected in Yellowstone or Glacier and planted among the Colorado samples.

A lesson was learned, procedures refined.

A shimmering tangerine twilight fades to darkness. Time to get back to camp.

After dinner, while Professor Tolisano lectures and his students take notes by strobing firelight, I contemplate this summer's crew. There's carrot-topped Dan, at nineteen the youngest member of the expedition and the only one of us who can outpace that leaping gnome Tolisano at thirty-nine; Sara from Baltimore, who signed on, she tells me, in order to take advantage of this unique opportunity to immerse herself simultaneously in nature and intense academics; Steve, a gentle giant of a fellow from Indiana; Beth, a Cornell student and flowering artist; Chad, a quiet young hunter and trapper from Ohio, here in a conscious effort to better understand the workings of nature; and Martin, at twenty-nine the oldest and most worldly of the lot.

With the exception of Martin, none among these young men and women, easterners most of them, had ever laid eyes on the great blue rise of the Rockies before signing on with Round River and coming here. I sense that the light and space of this place, intensified by Tolisano's expert mentorship, are blowing their still-formative minds, transforming could-be yuppies and rednecks alike into committed wildlands stewards. This, I propose, is as good a way as any, better than a hell of a lot, to help ensure a future for American wilderness.

Tolisano kicks off this evening's lecture with a review of the tenets of conservation biology, then moves on to detail the technical distinctions between keystone, indicator, flagship, and restoration species, shifting finally into a Socratic exploration of ways to shake awake within the local citizenry (those all-important grass roots) a protective appreciation of the uniqueness of the San Juan ecosystem.

The project's ultimate goal, Jim reaffirms at the conclusion of his lecture, is to create a popularly supported vision for the San Juan Mountains wherein a long-term conservation strategy is built into all public-lands management plans. Proving the existence of the grizzly up here—"a big, sexy critter that gets people excited"—would go a long way, he feels, toward eliciting both local and agency support for that goal.

Hearing that, I fall to brooding. Unhappily, in light of long personal experience with both grass-roots and agency "support" for the natural world here in the rural West, I can only say . . . good luck, Jim.

Specifically, I fear that if those whom eco-philosopher Dave Foreman has dubbed the "bumpkin proletariat" (welfare ranchers and their Animal Damage Control sidekicks, loggers, miners, hunting outfitters, and other old-line public-lands profiteers) continue to get their way, which they're accustomed to getting and plenty willing to fight for, then Round River's kinder, gentler approach to wildlands stewardship is likely to be ridden out of town on rails of derision and intimidation. Bullying, after all, is the code of the rural West.

But then, local popular support for wilderness has been waxing hereabouts of late, strengthened by a rising flood of emigration from California and other places long since spoiled by "progress," people who have learned the difference between quantity and quality. (And people, ironically, whose very numbers are transplanting here many of the very problems they're running away from.)

Battle lines are forming.

At a public meeting held recently in my hometown of Durango—part of Round River's philosophy of informing and attempting to involve locals in the action—Montana writer Rick Bass told of the bitter war of wills, words, and worldviews being waged between preservationists and extractionists in his adopted northwestern logging community. Into the eye of the storm in Montana, Bass told the fifty-odd people in attendance, has been thrust the grizzly bear, a scapegoat for much larger problems there—exactly, he cautions, as it could become here. "Neither side wins with hard-line confrontation," Bass warned. "Keep your channels of communication open and don't let hate take over."

Well, we'll try. But division and derision are second nature to the rural western character, while objectivity and reason too often are shrouded under clouds of emotion and (perceived) financial necessity.

In this light, and sadly, when I think of grass-roots support for wilderness, I think of my old friend A. B. Guthrie, Jr.—the Pulitzer-winning author who gave Montana its Big Sky name and fame—and his long fight for wilderness and the grizzly. As reward for his efforts, Guthrie won local support in the form of hometown ostracism, including—most painful— the open scorn of his own rancher son.

Houses divided.

Nor, likely, will agency support for wildlands management reform come much easier. I'm thinking now of the intrinsic resistance of all government bureaucracies to change. And I'm thinking also, uneasily, of eco-warrior Dave Foreman's terrifying experience at the hands of a zealous Reagan-Bush FBI, that strident enforcer of the status quo, which decided to teach the eloquent rabble-rouser a lesson. And did. Ask Dave Foreman about "agency support" for the wilderness.

Even my own timid, faltering attempts to defend the natural world have generated hatred. There are people in my home county, individuals and agency employees alike, who wish me all bad things because of my outspoken support of the natural world and my public criticism of its enemies. Lacking the moral courage of a Dave Foreman or a Bud Guthrie, I sometimes grow weary and wonder—Why make myself a pariah in my own community? Why keep on fighting an increasingly bitter and apparently losing battle?

Why, indeed?

Were I able to ask that question of my late friend Ed Abbey—that eternal wellspring of moral courage—I believe I know just what he'd say: "And why the hell not?"

The Road to Eden
John S. Romain

1992—HANA, MAUI. SOME MAY RECALL IT AS THE YEAR OF THE mango. I'll always remember it as the year of the fishpond. The year was different, no doubt about it. Winter held back; the sunny, dry days produced a drought by summer. Everything seemed to double. The mynas nested twice, and the air was filled with constant bird babble. Vegetation of all forms grew, blossomed, and sprouted. But it was the mangoes that stole the show. Outperforming even the most bountiful of springs, mangoes dropped everywhere. Then, just when the air began to clear of the pungent smell of fermenting fallen mangoes, they dropped again. The seemingly endless harvest was picked, pickled, and preserved, ensuring, for a generation at least, edible mementoes of this auspicious year.

The fishpond is another story. It is a personal one that began more than seven years ago when good fortune and fateful circumstance brought me together with a piece of land wondrous beyond imagination—a genuine Eden in the rough, a piece of paradise with a history as mythical as its caves. Though just over a half acre in size, the land is a topographical gem, with lava tubes, shelter caves, and the crumbling rock-walled remains of an ancient Hawaiian fishpond. Back then, one could hardly call the overgrown, junglelike mess a pond, but the traces of past grandeur were undeniably there. It lay in quiet sleep, as if in a long hibernation, awaiting the rejuvenating breath of spring.

Owning such a remarkable piece of land transcended all sense of real estate as I knew it, and the price I paid proved to be more than the money that passed through escrow. Owning this property meant participating in a process that began in antiquity and would conclude long after my stewardship had passed. What I was to eventually give to the land would be returned to me in ways unimaginable. But with this privilege came the price of near total commitment. Fortunately, I didn't know all this then, otherwise the enormity of the task ahead would have been far too daunting. So, with the blissful ignorance of a drunken sailor willingly participating in his own shanghaiing, I signed on the dotted line. Seven years later, as the mangoes first began to appear with the resurgent spring, the pond did awaken from its slumber, but not without a long winter of preparation, perspiration, and prayer. For me, it was the completion of a long journey, so marked by challenge and revelation that it changed my life forever.

The fishpond project was the culmination of a series of events that began when I was vacationing in Hana in the spring of 1985. It was then that I fell under the disruptive influence of Sam Eason. Hana had been calling me back for years, and I had long envisioned it as my future home. I had always wanted to build my own house, and despite all of the obvious personal upheavals that would be involved, Hana seemed to be the place to do it. I had some money left from the sale of my Malibu home and was pondering this prospect when Sam arrived and interrupted my daydreams with a plan.

Sam Eason is an artist, in the broadest sense of the word, with the personality of P. T. Barnum. The brilliant renderings, sketches, and models scattered randomly throughout his cluttered studio testify to the wildness of his ways and the extent of his genius. We met there to explore the prospects of building my house in Hana. As I began to express my objectives, the wheels in his mind were already in motion. Before I could finish sharing my dream, we were in his car and heading for the land, which, it turned out, had long been the focus of his dream.

We arrived to find a piece of property so irregular and densely overgrown that many would dismiss it as unsuitable for a house site. But Sam's artistic vision cut through the vegetative shield like an x-ray, and he knew the beauty sleeping within. This was the perfect site to frame his architectural masterpiece! Sam's plan was to cluster a small guest cottage and office on the bluffs and a large two-unit residential building on the base adjacent to the pond. These were not to be just any structures; each was to be made of tropical hardwoods hand crafted by master carpenters and designed by Sam. Each dwelling was to be carefully positioned, appearing to have grown out of the land rather than being placed on it.

Sam's silver tongue conspired with the splendor of the surroundings to bait the hook. The line was cast when he led me into the main cave that stands as a sentry over the pond. It was there, while looking out across the pond's grassy camouflage at the surf pounding the shore of Hana Bay, that he reeled this mesmerized Pisces in. "Just imagine it, my boy. One day the fishpond will be restored, and you will have a cave with a view." Sam said this with such matter-of-fact certainty that my mind's eye opened to the brilliance of his vision. My heart was captured by the song of the land, and from that moment on there was no turning back.

THE MAGIC OF that moment in the cave sustained me for six years as Sam's vision gradually became reality. Overgrowth was trimmed and cleared to reveal hauntingly beautiful fern-covered rock formations. The buildings rose in graceful congruence with the natural contours of the landscape. Eventually, a small guest inn emerged, and the setting and architecture became a magnet for vacationing artists and nature lovers. The land was again being appreciated, and in return it offered its rich history and lovely serenity.

And as the land was restored, so was I restored. I learned to listen to a quiet voice within and to trust an invisible guiding hand. Living in Hana nurtured my soul, and I came to cherish the kindness of its people. Hawaiian history and culture became more than a passing fascination. I marveled at the people's eloquence; the more I learned, the richer my life became. Most important, I grew to appreciate the Hawaiian belief in the deep connectedness of all things. Much of this I learned from Parly Kanakaole. Parly comes from a family that has preserved the knowledge of ancient chants and prayers, and he has always been generous in sharing this knowledge. He opened my eyes to the Hawaiian world view and taught me the meaning of *Aloha*. The uniqueness of island living demands interdependence among land and people, and I learned this in Hana. Both

the land and I were now prepared, and the time for the fishpond had at
long last arrived.

I ALWAYS LOOK forward to the drive along the Hana Highway. To those
less familiar with its notorious twists, turns, and narrow bridges, it can be
an event as thrilling as Mr. Toad's wild ride. For me, it has become a time
for introspection and contemplation. Local residents refer to the journey
as "going over to the other side," and I have always found the reference
both amusing and appropriate. On a cool dry morning in February, I set
out on a trip to Wailuku to pick up the pond permit. I had long anticipated
this day, but its arrival brought with it the unexpected resurfacing of suppressed thoughts, feelings, and fears. Facing the completion of the task
that had launched this adventure also ironically meant facing the same
unresolved dilemmas that set me on the road to Hana in the first place.

As is probably the case with many who get involved in such inexplicable uprootings, mine is a story of being both pulled by dreams of the
future and pushed by events of the past. Living in Hawaii had been my
dream since as a child I arrived on a steamship in 1957. It took a conver-
gence of circumstances in the mid 1980s to provide the impetus that
brought me here. I was at a crossroads in my life when the opportunity
to purchase the Hana property arose. I had left a promising career in
advertising to try my hand at independent film production. The shine of
that yellow brick road soon tarnished, and I realized that the inner conflicts that caused me to leave advertising would not disappear with a
change of career. As I rounded the last series of bends before reaching the
straight stretch through Keanae, the frustrations and disillusionment of
that painful period all came rushing back. I was beginning to realize that
what I thought to be a new life direction was, in fact, only a temporary
detour around a personal conflict that would continue to reappear until I
thoroughly resolved it.

I pulled over at the turnout that overlooks the Keanae peninsula, got
out of my car, and took a deep breath. The ant-sized farmers below were
tending the taro fields in ways first taught to their ancestors by the gods.
I longed to have been born into a tradition so infused with the vitality of
life, feeling alienated from the way of life into which I was born. The culture I was educated and trained in is out of sync with the rhythms of my
heart song. In my life on the mainland, I had felt like a mercenary player
in a complex economic game that had no purpose beyond its own per-
petuation. Cleaning up my land and putting up the buildings were like the

educational deferments that kept many out of combat in the 1960s: they
bought time, and with it the chance to better prepare, but they did not
guarantee permanent exemption from service. There would be no more
deferments for me, I realized. I had to somehow reconcile the disillusions
of my past with my longing for future renewal. Would restoring the fishpond provide the link, the necessary means for reconciliation? I remembered my appointment with the planning department, returned to my
car, and, turning my thoughts to the road ahead, continued on to
Wailuku. Before water was to return to the pond, there would be many
more trips across the Hana Highway and many more bridges still to cross.

THE ISSUANCE OF the special use permit marked a milestone in my relationship with Doug and Mims Buck, the nearest neighbors and co-own-
ers of the pond. We had discussed the prospect of restoring the pond for
years, but the required time, resources, and collective will did not come
together until late fall of the preceding year. During our time of preparation, we had come to know each other as friends, and the trust and sense
of cooperation that grew out of this friendship greatly facilitated the
restoration. Together, we contacted the appropriate state and county
agencies, collected information, and formulated a plan. We brought
in Ron Hill, another of Hana's extraordinary characters, to head up the
project.

Ron's mark was evident on every phase of the work done on my land.
He did the big jobs: placing rocks, setting foundations, forming the walk-
ways, and building the driveway. His work is heavy, but his touch is light;
his embellishments are always respectful of the sanctity of the surroundings. Throughout it all, Ron kept his eye on the pond, carefully charting
a course for its recovery.

The scope of his plan was enormous. It required that we first fill in
large sections of the pond to provide access for the heavy equipment. The
rocks for the walls and gravel for the fill would be taken from the nearby
riverbed, its base first compacted to support the trucks that would work
the quarry. One heavy rain could mean a total washout. The material we
removed from the pond would have to be transported to a site about a
quarter of a mile past the same riverbed. Again, we were at risk of the
river flooding. With so many potential pitfalls and unproven methods
involved, there could be no guarantee of completion, even with Ron's
expertise guiding the way. Yet despite the odds, Doug and I knew that it
was now or never. Turning our backs on caution, we let the dice roll.

The grace of the unseasonable drought enabled us to complete the preliminary stages. It would take a near miracle to finish the job. Ron had anticipated that he could remove the grass and mud with a giant clamshell device attached to a boomcrane truck. The sixty-five-foot crane could be used to access the material from the banks and ramp that had been built into the pond. It didn't work out that way. The dirt banks and gravel-filled ramp were too soft to support the outriggers that kept the truck from tipping over when the boom was extended. I watched Ron's pained expression as he tried to nurse each scoop out of the pond. The consequences of the crane falling into the pond were unthinkable, and after a few near disasters, Ron literally threw in the clamshell.

We were seemingly at an impasse, but the dice were still rolling. Our only hope was to find an excavator with an operator daring enough to take it into the pond—and crazy enough to truck it along the narrow Hana Highway in the first place. But Ron had friends like that, and after more than a month of frustrating dead ends, he found the man with the excavator. It proved to be the answer, but its shorter reach dictated that much of the material dredged out of one place was used to fill in another. The procedure was not unlike a giant game of checkers, with some scoops of mud jumping many times across the pond before finally being taken out for good. The work was slow and tedious. The loud, muddy, messy process pushed the patience of many in our quiet community, and my own nervous system was on overload. Five weeks and nearly a thousand dump truck loads later, the job was finished.

AUGUST 20, 1992, THE day after the last scoop was taken from the pond, we were free at last of the noise and intrusion of heavy equipment. The water now needed time to settle, and I needed a break. I drove over to Lahaina and checked into the Pioneer Inn. The PI, as it is known to locals, is a living remnant of Lahaina's colorful past. The all-wooden structure was built in 1901 to house rowdy whalers on shore leave, and the tenants of today tend to honor and uphold the spirit of those times. Even before I made Maui my home, the Pioneer Inn had become my personal refuge, a change of venue where I could enjoy total anonymity and be alone with my thoughts. This was one of those occasions.

After checking into my room, I moved out onto the large veranda that overlooks the courtyard garden below. I pulled up a chair and watched the sun as it set slowly into the clouds that covered Lanai, the small sheltering island a few miles west of Lahaina. The sky turned purplish, though still bright enough to texture in the browns and greens of the silhouetted coconut palms that gently swayed to the subtle song of sunset. I sat and sighed.

Detailing and cleaning up aside, the pond was done! I was nearing release from the self-imposed servitude that had characterized the last seven years of my life. Realization of my accomplishment surfaced in a quiet and comfortable way; I felt good about the work I had done. I had discovered an inner well of strength and persistence, and though thoroughly exhausted, I had survived the undertaking and believed I was better off for the experience. Putting the experience in perspective, however, would be an equally exhausting process, as I was to discover throughout the next few hours.

The first star of the night appeared, and with it I made a wish for the wisdom and courage to face the challenge now before me. The restoration of the pond represented a healing process. I was now ready to confront the inner conflicts that had kept me isolated and had fragmented my wholeness. A moonless night fell on the torchlit courtyard, and the sky filled with the sparkling brilliance of stars. I sat back in my chair and let the process begin.

My mind raced, replaying my life up to this moment. Flooded with memories and images, I chose not to edit or direct them, but to feel them, to let them all in until I was full. There was no order to this chaotic collage of feelings, though occasionally the oddest connection occurred. Vows of "I'll never" in one moment collided with declaratives of "I did" in the next. Fears became desires, then reverted back to fears.

It was irony that eventually restored order. I stopped judging the fragments, and began to view them as parts of a larger whole. By accepting the contradictions, I found in my life greater clarity. For better or worse, my life was the sum of its parts. The restoration of the pond had depended on the cooperative efforts of a diversity of people and resources. Its future survival would rely on the various aspects of its ecosystem working together. My personal restoration hinged on seeing the fragmented pieces of my past as an interconnected body of wholeness. My future survival would rest with my ability to integrate the influences of two cultures into a balanced ecosystem of my own completeness.

Though in possession of this insight, I wasn't quite sure what to do with it. Awareness is a wonderful thing; translating that awareness into actual realization, still another. I was the product of one culture, but my heart beat in another. My own completeness was accountable to both.

What was missing in the life I had left in Malibu that I had worked so hard to find in Hana? My questions were suddenly interrupted as a fireball of sparkling blue-green light raced across the western night sky. My heart lept in passion, and a wave of awe jolted through me. I had never seen such a brilliant falling star before. Its colors streaked the sky like a star-dust rainbow, then vanished into a radiant flash of light. For an instant I felt a sense of oneness with a great mystery. And in this connection, I found an answer.

What drew me to Hana was that it still holds an underlying presence of a culture that lived in balance with the mysteries of life. The Hawaiian people, prior to Western contact, knew everything in closeness to one another. The separation between humankind, the gods, and nature was one of distinction, not distance. And though the ancient world view has been superseded with one of Western origin, Hana still carries the living essence of another way of life. *Mana* is the word Hawaiians use to describe this connection. *Mana* is a vital force that is acquired through inspired acts or spiritual attainments. Objects or places hold and reflect the *mana* of those who crafted or used them, just as the bones of a great chief or *alii* carry and preserve the *mana* of that person. Hana is rich with *mana*, and even visitors unaware of its meaning are moved by its pervasive presence.

The culture into which I was born is one of separation and distance from life's mysteries. It is a system based on rational knowledge and the preeminence of humans. I was born into a belief system that consolidates all that is outside scientific knowledge into a single God. But we are separated from our God by our disobedient act of free will at the time of our genesis. Tradition tells us that our God gave us dominion over all things of the earth and left his written laws to guide us; thus our world view is structured on dominance and hierarchical authority. It is a powerful system that has created a civilization of great magnitude, and our history is a testament to the scope and complexity of this culture's self-expression. But without the connection to that which is outside ourselves, our efforts are often devoid of meaning and in discord with the world around us. Perhaps because our belief system includes minimal reference to the female side of the mysteries, or perhaps because as a culture we lack the underpinnings of stewardship, our ignorance of this wisdom has put us in serious conflict with the natural world to which, whether we choose to accept it or not, we are irrevocably connected. The dogmatic attachment of Western culture to law and reason has blinded us to the Hawaiian understanding of our connection to the natural world. In short, the

Western intrusion has resulted in the subordination of one culture while compromising the integrity of another.

Yet I have to make this admission: although Hawaiian culture has been my spiritual beacon, by itself it seems incomplete in a technological world. As such, I believe that our collective future rests on our abilities to reconcile and heal the injustices of the past. If there is to be hope of future sustainability on our planet, it will be based on the acceptance of a new world view that combines the wisdom and essential spiritual truths known to indigenous cultures with the rational will of the Western way. For this to occur, the prevailing Western world view must accept the inherent sovereign rights of aboriginal cultures and recognize these cultures as equal, in every sense of the word, to ours. We must independently edit and strengthen the best of our respective systems and collectively grow in wholeness by building bridges of communication between cultures.

I have seen the best of both worlds and know that they are not mutually exclusive, but rather possess the potential to become productively interdependent. For me, it is not a matter of belonging to one or the other; rather, it is learning to combine the best of both. The restoration of the fishpond represents this belief. Its demise was the result of neglect brought by the weakened influence of Hawaiian stewardship; its recovery was made possible by the cooperative influences of both cultures.

THE HAWAIIAN WAY of learning is through observation, and for the next three months I observed and learned. The arrival of life to the pond was swift and sequential. Frogs, dragonflies, and small mosquito fish settled into territorial jurisdictions, and I watched in wonder as a primitive ecosystem grew. Each day the water turned a slightly different color as it stabilized into cycles of algae blooms and disappearances. But the most satisfying sight of all was seeing the pond rising and falling with the tide table, once again breathing and living. It seemed like a microcosmic rendering of earth before humankind, a window through which flowed the rhythms of nature.

The pond's surface is an ever-changing expression. Wind and rain texture it with complex patterns of waves and ripples, and passing clouds shade and heighten its many hues. On windless days, its silvery surface captures a world turned upside down. It is a mirror of truths and opposites, and like an Escher woodcut, it reflects both the viewed and the viewer. I find pleasure looking into this looking glass and seeing myself in relation to my surroundings. It is an interesting perspective, and seems to sum up my whole understanding of stewardship.

By early October, the pond was ready for stocking, and like everything else in that uncanny year, the fish arrived right on schedule. A newly formed Fishpond Foundation, in conjunction with the Oceanic Institute, was working with some other local pond owners as part of a statewide aquaculture program. One of the nearby ponds had a stock of juvenile mullet and ava in holding tanks, and the fish needed to be relocated. Our water was tested and found to be high in oxygen, with virtually no salinity. The water was suitable for raising the fish, but they would need saltwater to spawn. On October 14, precisely seven years to the day after taking title to the land, more than a thousand fish were released into the pond. Freedom was in the water, and their freedom was mine.

THANKSGIVING WEEKEND had long been targeted as the occasion to bless the pond. The Bucks and I first thought of holding a community-wide *luau*, but as the date grew closer, we took no action, as if we were waiting for something else to happen. My daughters Tiffany and Melanie were coming from the mainland for the holiday, and that alone was cause for celebration.

I received a phone call from Parly in early November. The Kanakaole family was planning a get-together over the holiday weekend, and Parly was looking for accommodations. I offered him one of the cottages and told him of our intention to have the pond blessed during that same weekend. Parly's only response was, "Ah, that is interesting." He accepted the offer of accommodations, and we didn't speak again until after our families arrived for the long holiday weekend.

Thanksgiving arrived, and we still didn't have a blessing scheduled. It was obvious that there would be no party, but with a house full of Kanakaoles, the blessing at least remained a possibility. There was a strange feeling about. The weather had been shifting and turning, and there was a general heaviness in the air. That night a terrific storm hit Hana. Within three hours, more than eleven inches of rain fell, three roads were washed out, four cars were swept away, and one life was lost.

The next day, as most of the community was out cleaning up and sharing stories, we began repairing the pond. The road on the other side of the Bucks' house had washed out, and a river of water had flooded the pond. The pond had overflowed its back bank, and the surface was thick with kamani nuts and leaves. By Saturday morning, the water had begun to subside, and the surface had been cleared of debris. I finally called Parly and asked him if a blessing could be arranged while our families were still in town. He said that he would check with his relatives and call back. My phone line went dead shortly after our conversation, so when Parly, his two sisters, and his brother-in-law appeared late Saturday afternoon to do the blessing, the Bucks, my daughters, and I hastily joined them in a come-as-you-are party.

I had never been part of something as sacred as the blessing. Positioned in front of the cave, and standing behind a protective *maile lei*, Doug, Mims, Tiffany, Melanie, and I watched in silence as chants and prayers were offered in words we didn't know but somehow understood. A light, steady rain fell on the pond like a crystal curtain, and gusts of wind suddenly swept the surface in perfect accompaniment to the prayers. After a closing prayer was offered to the cave as protector of the pond, Parly turned to us and announced that with the blessing, the pond had been named. He explained that before the ceremony, they had discussed myths and stories attributed to the area. They had also noted surrounding conditions, such as the direction of the winds, the cycle of the moon, and the feel of the air. Lastly, they had considered the efforts made to bring the pond back. The name, Loko Waihua, meaning heavy waters ready to bear fruit, was what they had decided on. Parly then looked straight at me and said with a slight laugh, "Just because the fruit is about to bear, do not think there is nothing left to do." And with a nod, he directed our attention to the water still in shock from the flood: "This is where the real work begins."

THESE THOUGHTS ARE written in the closing hours of the year of the mango. There is a misty haze on the pond and an anarchic chorus of exploding pyrotechnics in the air. Like most of the rest of the world, I have spent the past few days putting the year in perspective and looking ahead to the next. How can one explain a year like the one now passing? Though it marked the completion of a long personal journey, I sense that I was a player in a production much grander than my own personal drama. It seems clear to me that there are times when we must act in accord with an inner calling, even if it means a detour from our personal aspirations. Stewardship is a process based on change and circumstance rather than order and convenience. Restoring the pond next year would have been too late. The rain that held back in winter and spring returned in force and washed out the riverbed by fall. Learning to read nature's calendar starts by learning to read one's own self. Stewardship starts with reconciliation within, and in wholeness the connection to humankind and the natural world becomes self-apparent. These connections are truly our most sacred trusts, for in their preservation is our own.

A decade ago, I found a bumper sticker in a surf shop in Malibu, and I've carried it with me ever since. It is permanently affixed to the bulletin board above my desk and reads: "Primitive Future." In the past I have thought of these two words as a statement of vision, implying a future Eden where humans are at peace with themselves, and technology is in harmony with the natural world. I read it differently now. The future is now and my responsibility for the world is in the present.

On Stewardship
John Murray

As is the generation of leaves, so is that of humanity. The wind
scatters the leaves on the ground, but the live timber burgeons
with leaves again in the season of spring returning. So one generation of men will grow while another dies.

—Homer, *The Iliad*

I

STEWARDSHIP. THE FIRST TIME I HEARD THE WORD WAS ON EARTH DAY,
April 22, 1970. My father, a county engineer turned environmental manager with the Federal Water Quality Administration, was flying to Pittsburgh to speak for clean water at a Carnegie-Mellon student rally. As I
dropped him off at the Greater Cincinnati Airport—I was sixteen and had
just received my driver's license—he handed me a worn copy of Aldo

Leopold's essays. "Read this," my father said, "you'll like him as much as Thoreau. He writes about land stewardship." I remember thinking that no twentieth-century philosopher could possibly approach the manifold achievements of Thoreau, whose works had been my constant companions in study hall and after school for several years. Of course, I was a bit premature in that assessment. What a change that book wrought on my life and our times, as Leopold boldly took Thoreau's statement that "in wildness is the preservation of the world" and made it the basis for a unified philosophy of shared community. Here was the proposition: our role is not to be consumers of nature, as we had learned in Sunday school from the Book of Genesis, but rather to be caretakers of nature for the unborn, who should have the opportunity to see and enjoy the land as their fathers and mothers did. Every page radiated with Leopold's reverence and humility and love for the earth. Eventually, I worked my way through all of Dad's favorites, from Muir and Seton to Udall and Abbey, and came to treasure those volumes as much as my favorite hiking trails through the familiar oak and maple woodlands of home.

In June of 1971 the Murray clan packed up and moved west to Denver as Dad took a position with the newly formed Environmental Protection Agency. Here at last, in the Colorado Rockies, was an unspoiled landscape against which I could measure the extent to which culture had impacted nature, as well as study alternative strategies for living with nature. Nothing in the humanized countryside of southern Ohio could compare with the rugged grandeur of Wild Basin in Rocky Mountain National Park, where I spent that first summer hiking and camping and fishing. Each weekend my father, brothers, and I scrambled up a new trail into the high country, marveling at the clear timberline lakes and the permanent snowfields set among granitic peaks. Here were black bears and cougars, both long extinct in southwestern Ohio, and mule deer and elk, and rumors of fishers and lynx, and a whole new array of subalpine and alpine wildflowers to learn and hold dear.

After two class-cutting semesters at the University of Colorado I dropped out—much to the consternation of my parents—and for the next fifteen years, outside of a tour in the Marines, spent as much time as I could living and working in the mountains. In nature I found an order and harmony wholly lacking in those turbulent times. It seemed to me the mountains offered as much of an education as the classroom (an irony not lost on me now that I am a professor). Despite a passion for the Rockies, I became increasingly restless in the 1980s. Eventually the reason became clear: as soon as a part of the earth is designated a wilderness area, it ceases in some important ways to be a wilderness. Wilderness, after all, connotes an absence of civilization. During the 1980s, as visitor use burgeoned, wilderness areas unfortunately came to be associated with back-country hiking units, camping permits, campfire permits, trip itineraries, and daily trail quotas. More and more, through that decade, my eyes turned northward over the international boundary to the forty-ninth state.

Interior Alaska, my home now for the past five years, has been the natural culmination of a lifetime in search of both unadulterated nature and some solutions to the central problems of stewardship. Each summer since my arrival I have spent a month in Denali National Park, studying and photographing grizzly bears and subarctic wolves for my books *The Great Bear* and *Out Among the Wolves*. Denali is an extensive sanctuary with many virtues, but because the northern half is bisected by a heavily traveled road, the park has suffered a fate similar to that of Yellowstone and Yosemite. It was only this past autumn, when I flew north in a bush plane to the Arctic National Wildlife Refuge for a week-long caribou hunt, that I finally observed something like what George Caitlin and Washington Irving must have seen in the Frontier West of the 1830s. What was most incredible about this adventure was that although the land appeared to have never been touched by humans, it had actively supported a boreal culture of Amerindians since the Age of Mammoths. Here, some two hundred miles from the nearest road, caribou herds roamed as large as the buffalo herds of prerailroad Montana. Two or three grizzlies rambled around every mountain, and twelve to fifteen wolves ran along each major drainage. Braided rivers and birch-forest lakes brimmed with arctic grayling and migratory waterfowl. Moose were everywhere. Entire river drainages, from alpine headwaters to terminal confluences and beyond, were protected. Uncontrolled fires burned across the country from May through September, reshaping and reinvigorating the quaking aspen groves and white spruce stands.

Wherever I looked, from horizon to horizon, there was not one sign of the human race—not one sod-covered cabin, not one floating boat dock, not one smoke plume from one humble campfire. Here was the New World before the cross-bearing conquistadors, before the slave plantations, before Wounded Knee and the Dust Bowl and the Trinity Site. Here was a vision of a world long ago, and also of a distant future, and it gave me hope. Not a Panglossian hope, but a guarded optimism grounded in both wild nature and human nature. Somewhere, in the crowded centuries to follow our own, the human race would find a way to live in harmony with nature. We had only to look at places like the Arctic Refuge to see how.

II

THE ALASKAN WINTER nights are ideally suited, in their interminable length, for long indoor projects. Several years ago I spent an evening looking up the etymologies of words I frequently use in my nature essays, words like *park, nature, forest, refuge, conservation,* and *stewardship.* The last word, it turns out, is a lineal descendent of the Old Norse *sti-vardr,* which literally means, the "keeper of the house" (*vardr,* or ward, of the *sti,* or house). In Old English *sti-vardr* became *stig-weard,* again meaning the house-ward, or keeper of the house. *Stig-weard* subsequently evolved through *sti-weard* and *stu-ward* to become *ste-ward.* By 1465 a steward was an estate administrator or land manager, as in "the bayly [bailiff] of Hadley owyth hym ffor hys ffee off thy stewardsheppe off the same town." Shakespeare used the word occasionally in his plays, as when King Richard II turned to the Earl of Northumberland and said, "Shew us the hand of God, that dismissed us from our stewardship" (3.3.78–79). In the twentieth century, particularly after Leopold's book was published in 1947, the word *stewardship* began to take on a new meaning, if not a new spelling; it carried with it the sense of passing on the earth not as a jealously guarded plat of private property, but as a priceless shared gift to posterity. To a student of the history of ideas, this change represented a radical shift, the resanctification of the earth reversing a trend of secularization that began with the European Renaissance.

The tradition of regarding the earth as holy, of course, goes back long before the Renaissance quest to control nature turned the world upside down. We know, for example, that the pharaonic civilizations lived in equilibrium with the desert river for many thousands of years. Later, subsaharan African peoples set aside burial zones and restricted hunting areas that became de facto preserves, and they also practiced sustained yield agriculture. But let us linger for a moment on the Greeks, from whom so much of our culture directly originates. It was the Greek sacred groves, mountains, and forests—regions set aside to preserve nature— that first embodied the national park and protected species concepts in a governmentally sanctioned framework. Recall, for example, that Agamemnon's daughter Iphigenia was sacrificed to Diana, the goddess of the forest, on the eve of the Trojan War because her father's soldiers irreverently killed a sacred stag in the sacred grove. Today, the oracle of

Diana has been replaced by the federal judge, but the crime—killing a protected or sacred animal in a sanctuary—is still severely punished, whether a grizzly in Yellowstone or a panther in the Everglades. When a park ranger or federal land manager makes an arrest on these lands, he or she is carrying on a tradition that goes back to the priests of Diana in the forests of Greece thirty centuries ago. These preserves are vital to the notion of stewardship, then, because they serve both as benchmarks to measure change and also as reminders of the limitations of hubris.

III

YESTERDAY, DECEMBER 2, 1992, my father retired from the Environmental Protection Agency after twenty-six years of federal service, not including the four years he fought in Europe. Over the course of his career he worked in four regional offices, at the headquarters office in Washington, and finally at the National Enforcement Investigation Center. His professional life was dedicated to the proposition that clean water and clean air are inalienable rights, and he had a contempt for two sorts of people: those who recklessly pollute or degrade the earth in pursuit of financial gain, and those in and out of government who through incompetence or cleverness subvert the process of bringing environmental criminals to justice. At the time of his departure he was one of the last senior managers left who had been with the agency when it was formed by, of all people, President Nixon in December 1970. The Marine Corps band played at his farewell ceremony, which was part of an annual awards affair, and I wish I could have been there to thank him, because he taught me so much about respecting the earth and about our ethical duties to futurity.

   With our parents' generation retiring, this generation—I speak of the post–World War II generation—assumes a heightened set of responsibilities, both as citizens and as parents. One day soon, I will have to start teaching my four-year-old son Naoki some of the lessons of stewardship my father passed on to me. What will these be? First, I will share with him the importance of moderation, of avoiding extremes in the pursuit of life and the resolution of complex problems. Like most, I came by this creed two ways: through reading Aristotle, the Stoics, and the Founding Fathers, and through direct observations of nature, whether in studying which wolf pups survive to run with the pack or in unraveling the mechanics of forest succession. Second, because Naoki's mother is Japanese I must give him what I can of the Asian point of view on nature: the Buddhist haiku of Basho, the Mount Fuji prints of Hokusai, the notion of *torii* gates marking a passage to holy ground, the *kami* spirits inhabiting rocks and trees and animals and rivers, and the horrifying spectacle of atomic weapons.

Also this—I will teach Naoki what my father told me once when I was helping him plant a rosebush in the backyard. "Never put a dollar plant in a nickel hole," he said. "Always put a nickel plant in a dollar hole." Old grade school buddies report that the trees and bushes and flower beds Dad and I planted at 5572 Green Acres Court thirty years ago are still flourishing today. My father knew how to plant seedlings so that they would grow into healthy trees, and he knew how to nurture sons in their formative years so that they would mature into productive men. Stewardship is based on this principle of generational sharing, a verity Homer observed: "As is the generation of leaves, so is that of humanity."

IV

"OK. OK. I'VE HEARD your personal history. But how is stewardship relevant to *me?*" a skeptical student shouts from the back of the lecture hall. Good question. Any question that responsibly challenges the authority of received wisdom is worthwhile, and no idea should be accepted without examination. My answer is a question: Are we to live and perish like a petri dish of *E. coli* bacteria or green bread mold, destroying our world with unbridled population growth and accumulating waste, or are we rational beings capable of accommodating our numbers and our lifestyles to the narrow confines of this shrinking culture plate called Earth? The issue, it seems to me, is that simple, and nothing less than our future hangs in the balance. Extinction, as we know from even a cursory walk through the Natural History Museum, is an option nature is only too willing to exercise. It will not be an incoming asteroid that solves the riddle, it will be a sudden, brutal, total collapse, like the thriving penicillin colony that turns black overnight on the nutrient dish. Another interesting experiment gone awry, another pyrex dish to be sterilized in the autoclave, another species to be stirred by the rains back into the seething cauldron of life.

"All right then. Suppose I buy that," our critic asks, "What can *I* do?" A lot, actually. Above all, learn as much as you can. That means both in school and out of school. Learn to be the best writer and teacher you can. We desperately need more essays, articles, and books. And, always, more teachers. Study the masters. Spend time in the forest. Spread the word. Write a book. One good book—witness Thoreau and Leopold—can change the world more than any army ever assembled. An army grows old and undisciplined. Its bayonets rust and its gunpowder becomes unstable. The once-confident generals turn feeble, tentative, uncertain. A book lives forever. The words are always fresh and strong, winning converts, changing minds, influencing what Jefferson called the course of human events. Both Thoreau and Leopold proved, in their lives and writings, that you don't need to wear camouflage fatigues and a red beret to be a revolutionary. Through their essays and lectures these two brothers-in-arms forever improved the quality of human life.

V

I KEEP RETURNING to the Arctic Refuge experience of a few months ago. The images haunt me still: the broad timbered valleys where the beaver ponds backed the cold water up into tangled moose thickets, the stormy tundra hills where the ptarmigan huddled behind the wind-flagged spruce, the river otter that wandered unexpectedly into camp one day, as friendly as a pet dog I lost once long ago. This was their quiet legacy, the Indians of the north country, a land used and then returned, a stock of capital borrowed for investment and then faithfully repaid with generous interest. The generations to come would do well to make certain such places endure, places where the caribou roam freely and the blizzards last two weeks and the wolverines shuffle absentmindedly over the passes, places where the mountains and streams have no names, places that the human race leaves undisturbed as we leave undisturbed the hearts in our chests that beat and give us life.

Not Here
Bill McKibben

I LIVE IN THE SHADOW OF A MOUNTAIN. NOT A VERY LARGE MOUNTAIN; it's not among the hundred highest even in New York State, and out West it would be a valley. Still, for those who live around it, it is the mountain in our lives. At the turn of the century, a girl named Jeanne Robert Foster lived in a farm at its base. Her beautiful face helped her leave behind the poverty of the place (when the growing season is ninety days in a good year, a farm is a hard place to be). A man took her to the city; she became a Gibson girl, her face on the cover of *Vanity Fair*. She started to write— essays, reviews, then poems—and she became friends with Pound and Picasso, Eliot and Joyce. But she never for a day forgot the mountain where she had grown up. The mountain, and the Methodists, lumber- men, hunters who lived scattered around it, filled her poems. At the end of her very long life, she wrote a letter to a friend in the neighborhood. "If, when you go to the old Elliott Putnam place, you will walk toward the mountain directly from the point that would be about the exact location of the old Putnam house. You will cross the brook, of course, and keep on through the woods until you come to a stretch of the mountain where it rises *straight as a wall* from the terrain so that one may stand straight and lean against it. I found this stretch long, long ago and, in my young girlhood I would walk secretly and *lean* against the mountain, sometimes facing it and putting my hands out on either side. There seemed to be a strong force passing through me, so untamed, wild and beautiful that there are no words for it. But I know this force remained with me, helped me manage my difficult life, sent me to 'five seas' if not the 'seven,' flowed as courage in my blood . . . and never left me—not even today."

A year or so ago, our county decided it needed a new landfill. Actually, it hired some consultants, and the consultants decided it needed a new landfill, and having hired them, the county would have looked foolish disagreeing. Three hundred and seventy-five acres, the consultants said, to store the ash from the hundred-million-dollar incinerator, which was the last thing they'd sold the county on. Three hundred and seventy-five acres of landfill lined with two (2) giant rubber sheets, enormous landfill Trojans, to prevent unwanted leakage. Three hundred and seventy-five acres that would need to be kept free of trees, mowed twice a year for eternity, so no roots would ever rupture the rubbers. Three hundred and seventy-five acres—that's bigger than some golf courses. And of course the sodium vapor lights. Anyhow, the consultants were awarded a contract to figure out where in the county the landfill should go, and after a highly scientific search they announced their five final sites. And where were they? Not in the southern, urban part of the county, with 90 percent of the people and 90 percent of the waste. Four of the five were clustered forty miles from the city, at the very edge of the county, right around this particular mountain. The highly scientific consultants arranged for letters to go out to all the people who lived on the proposed sites, ninety families in all. Letters that arrived Christmas Eve and informed the residents that soon other highly scientific men would be arriving to drill holes in their land in order to make sure that if the condoms broke (but of course they couldn't, having been designed by men of science working in the public interest), the waste from the city wouldn't drop directly into a subterranean stream but would first have to travel a few hundred feet underground.

And we were not supposed to fight. Not supposed to fight because this is a poor backwoods place, and they were offering cash—a little tax relief, maybe some road funds. Not supposed to fight because we're not that kind of people. It's less apathy than a deep feeling of disempowerment, and what I mean by disempowerment is this. There was a meeting at the town hall, which is a sort of Quonset hut, where the impartial outside consultants were going to explain the mystery of why it was scientific to truck garbage forty miles in to the mountains. And it was winter, and still all the outside consultants were wearing suits and Italian loafer shoes without any laces. And if you are sitting there in your Sorels, you are allowed to get angry for a minute, but when the man in the loafers talks in his soothing way about the necessity of it all, you are supposed to sit down muttering and figure that it makes no difference, they'll do what they want, they always do.

But say you keep protesting a little longer. Say they suspect you too might have a pair of dress shoes home in the closet. They then say the magic word *NIMBY*, and you are supposed to be not disempowered but ashamed; you're just another of those people who say "not in *my* backyard." What if everyone was like that? It has to go somewhere, doesn't it. And so on. *NIMBY* is as powerful a mantra as *jobs*.

The NIMBY concept interests me. When I lived in New York City, I ran a small homeless shelter at my church, and before that I lived on the streets for a while in order to write about what people weren't even calling a crisis yet. (Nor are they calling it a crisis now. It was a crisis for a little while, but now it's a fact of life, and everyone would be amazed if there weren't people curled up in every subway station in America.) Anyway, the acronym was coined by people who didn't want homeless shelters in their neighborhoods because they might get mugged by people who lived in them, and even if they didn't get mugged, their property values would surely decrease, because who would buy a house where you might get mugged? And for a while everyone felt self-righteously angry about NIMBYs, especially all the people in the better parts of Manhattan where there weren't any homeless shelters. It was—it still is—a deep and difficult question. How can you justify damaging a working neighborhood? But how can you justify instead herding fifteen hundred homeless men a night into cots lined up in endless rows on a Harlem armory floor? (When you sleep there, you take off your shoes and you plant the legs of the cot in them so that they'll be there at five in the morning when the overhead lights flip on.) The answer, of course, arrived at not by deeply scientific consultants but by various contemporary saints, was that you designed small, decent residences where people could return to something like normal and which didn't blight the community in which they were placed. The same goes for homes for the mentally ill, the mentally retarded, and all the other kinds of places people fear and detest and then ten months later tell reporters aren't so bad after all.

But this NIMBY idea has taken on a life of its own, and now any time someone wants to put a shopping mall or a highway or a chemical factory or a radioactive waste storage facility someplace, they try to shut you up by calling you one. Happily, we are a few years behind up here. Most of my neighbors didn't understand that they were supposed to roll over paralyzed at this chunk of verbal kryptonite, and so they were undeterred in their organizing against the dump. We carried signs, we mailed letters (our upper school has two hundred and fifty kids, and two hundred sent letters; the little kids drew pictures), we assembled statistics, we met once a week to talk to each other.

The anger was about some of the usual concerns, like big trucks day and night, like noise, like odor. But an awful lot of it came from loving the land on which we live—not loving it in an abstract sense, but knowing it, gathering berries on it, cutting some logs on it, making syrup from maple trees on it, hunting on it, strolling through it. This mountain has had a hold on a lot of people. In the sixties, when Howard Zahniser, the great unknown hero of the American conservation movement, was writing the Federal Wilderness Statute, he was not gazing at the Tetons or the Brooks Range. He was looking out his cabin window at this 3,254-foot peak, which might soon command a view of the dump. Zahniser's son, Ed, wrote a book of poems about the mountain.

> There's only the rain to scatter stillness here
> like a baffle that no longer baffles me.
> Am I lonely? Not so: I take my shadow out for walks
> where the jeweled patch resounds
> with traffic sounds from Calvinistic hummingbirds.
> My nearest neighbors own the Putnam Place
> I own nothing, yet we hold in common
> a fool's love for these granite heights.[1]

But it was not just poets who knew the spell. This is a backward place—that is, it was only a generation ago that everyone knew how to fend for themselves off the land, and that connection has been slow to fade. We still *live* here, physically and emotionally, instead of residing in that grinning California-suburb nowhere that flows out through the cable. One cold night in February we reached the final scene of our battle, a meeting of the regional development agency that, after our hundreds of letters, was considering regulations that might block the landfill. One after another, my neighbors rose to say their piece. "Who's going to speak for the withered tree? Who's going to answer for the dead fish? Who will write newspaper articles about the nauseating effects of sulfur dioxide on the deer?" asked Ron Vanselow, who works seasonally as a forest ranger. Kelly Richards, an eighth-generation native of the area, said, "We get our water from spring-fed wells. We raise our eggs, meat, and vegetables, tap the sugar maples, harvest firewood, and rear our pets and children on the land. They told us we shouldn't worry because they weren't actually taking our homes. But my home doesn't just go to the walls and then stop. That land *is* my home." And then the Reverend Daisy Allen stood up. She is a Pentecostal Holiness minister, one of nine children (all named for local flowers) who grew up on one of the proposed dump sites, and though she is not feeling as well now as once she did, she has made a life's work of attending the dying, comforting the sick, providing for the hungry. She writes a weekly column for the local paper, the comings and goings on her road mixed with the new flowers in bloom or the birds that have arrived. "There's a beaver dam there," she said, "that's played a large part in giving beauty and a place for fish. Will the beaver lose their home? Will the fish die? . . . There's no florist in Baker's Mills, but will we lose or find endangered our trillium, our wild oats, our yellow, blue, and white violets? Will we lose our mayflowers and buttercups, and daisies and dandelions, cowslips, and adder's-tongue? Will the beauty of the apple blossom and pear trees be gone forever? Where will we pick our northern spies, our maidenblush, crabapples, yellow transparents, dutchesses? I just wonder how many people even know these apples." In this dark place, she said, "I can walk the country roads at midnight, able to see by moonlight. I study the Bible, and I'd like to give you an illustration from it. Naboth had a vineyard close to the palace of Ahab, king of Samaria. Ahab said to Naboth, 'Give me thy vineyard that I may have it for a garden of herbs. It's near my house. I'll give thee a better vineyard, or I'll give you money for it.' Naboth refused, because his father had had it. But Ahab pretended sickness, and his wife came in and said, 'Why don't you eat?' He said, 'I can't, because Naboth won't let me have the land I want.' And wicked Queen Jezebel said, 'Why are you so sad? Isn't it within your power and jurisdiction to take whatever you want, no matter whose it is?' And she wrote letters in Ahab's name—sealed with his name. And Naboth was stoned to his death. Jezebel heard of his death and said to Ahab, 'Go take possession; Naboth is dead.' And he went to take possession, but God spoke through his prophets and said, 'Where Naboth's blood has been licked by the dogs, so will yours be licked.'" And the $150-an-hour guys sitting in the back of the room in their loafers didn't say a word.

And we won. What do you know. It turned out that once the regional agency rejected the landfill, the county found out it needed a lot less space—ten or twenty acres, maybe. And the county next door was already building its own oversized monstrosity of a dump, and it turned out they were desperate to rent space in it for a fraction of what it would have cost to build our own, and the consultants went to work on that. And the mountain is more or less fine.

Not totally. Smaller things happen all the time. A new summer house here, a shabby logging job there, and things are always harder to fight when they aren't so clear-cut. But basically we won. There is *nothing* ignoble about protecting your backyard as long as it's the backyard you're protecting, as long as you're part and parcel of your backyard. Not once that whole long winter of debate did I hear anyone use the phrase "property values." (Not true. I used it, thinking it might summon us some allies. But of course I didn't grow up here.) The chance to protect your own ecosystem, your own watershed, your own navel of the world— that's ten times more awesome a thing even than the chance to protect the rain forest.

Here's a poem from Jeanne Robert Foster about this mountain:

> *How can I lift my mountain before your eyes,*
> *Tear it out of my heart, my hands, my sinews,*
> *Lift it before you—its trees, its rocks,*
> *Its thrust heavenward;*
> *The basic cliffs, the quartz of the outcrop,*
> *The wide water in the cup of the lower summit,*
> *The high peak lifting above the timberline*
> *Gathering the mist of fifty lakes at sunrise;*
> *The waterfall tumbling a thousand feet,*
> *White with foam, white with rock-flower in summer;*
> *The wreathing of dark spruce and hemlock,*
> *The blood splashes of mountain ash,*
> *The long spur to the north golden with poplars;*
> *A porcupine drinking, bending without fear*
> *To his image?*
>
> *When darkness shall be my home,*
> Eternal mountain, do not leave my heart;
> Remain with me in my sleep,
> In my dreams, in my resurrection.[2]

It did not feel to me like we were taking care of the mountain, protecting it. It felt like the mountain had nourished us when we needed it, and we were doing only what was natural—as if the boundaries between people and mountains were not so rigid; as if the real divide had us and the mountain and the trillium and the beaver on one side and the guys in the loafers on the other.

As we were leaving that meeting, one of those fellows snapped shut the locks on his briefcase, looked up at me, and said, "We think it would be more mature if you guys didn't deal with this on such a personal level. We try to keep things on a professional basis." Of course you do, I thought. But for once in my life I'm not going to be cowed by the abstract. Tonight I'm glad it's on a personal level. Tonight, in the neighborly shadow of the mountain, I'm reasonably proud of being a person.

1. *Way to Heron Mountain* (Rome, N.Y.: Night Tree Press, 1986).
2. *Crane Mountain* from *Adirondack Portraits,* edited by Noel Riedinger-Johnson (Syracuse: Syracuse University Press, 1986), 145.

About the Contributors

GEORGE ANDERSON has authored a variety of articles on fly-fishing for *Fly Fisherman, Trout,* and *Scientific Anglers Quarterly Magazine.* He is well known for his fly-fishing skills; he won the Jackson Hole One Fly competition in 1989 and 1990. He owns and operates the Yellowstone Angler fly-fishing shop in Livingston, Montana.

MARY CATHERINE BATESON is Clarence J. Robinson Professor in Anthropology and English at George Mason University in Fairfax, Virginia. Her books include *Our Own Metaphor: A Personal Account of a Conference on the Effects of Conscious Purpose on Human Adaptation, With a Daughter's Eye: A Memoir of Margaret Mead and Gregory Bateson,* and *Composing a Life,* as well as *Angels Fear: Towards an Epistemology of the Sacred* (with Gregory Bateson) and *Thinking AIDS* (with Richard Goldsby).

WENDELL BERRY and his wife, Tanya, live on a small farm in Kentucky. His most recent book is *Fidelity: Five Stories* (Pantheon). A new book, *Sex, Economy, and Community: Eight Essays,* will be published this fall by Pantheon.

STEPHEN BODIO has written the natural history books *A Rage for Falcons* and *Aloft* and the memoir *Querencia.* He has just completed his first novel.

ALSTON CHASE is the author of *Playing God in Yellowstone* and writes a nationally syndicated newspaper column on the environment. A contributing editor to *Outside* magazine and *Conde Nast's Traveler,* he has also written about conservation for the *Atlantic, Rolling Stone, New York Times, Wall Street Journal,* and many other publications.

YVON CHOUINARD is founder of Patagonia, Inc., outdoor clothing manufacturers. One of America's most influential mountain climbers, he has made numerous first ascents around the world. His essay on clean climbing helped form a new ethic among the climbing community. His book, *Climbing Ice,* has redefined the art of ice climbing.

GUY DE LA VALDÉNE, a photographer and filmmaker, is the author of *Making Game, An Essay on Woodcock.*

DAN GERBER is the author of three novels, *American Atlas, Out of Control,* and *A Voice from the River;* a collection of short stories, *Grass Fires;* a non-fiction narrative, *Indy, The World's Fastest Carnival Ride,* and five volumes of poems, the most recent of which is *A Last Bridge Home.* His poems, stories, and essays have appeared in numerous periodicals, including *The Nation, The New Yorker, The Partisan Review, Sports Illustrated, New Letters,* and *The Georgia Review,* and have been widely anthologized. He lives in northern Michigan.

JOHN GIERACH is the author of eight books, including *Trout Bum; Sex, Death & Fly-Fishing;* and *Even Brook Trout Get the Blues.* He writes regular columns for the *Longmont Daily Times-Call* in Longmont, Colorado, and *Fly Rod & Reel Magazine* and occasional columns for the *New York Times.* He is a recipient of the Arnold Gingrich Angling Heritage Award.

KRIS L. HARDIN teaches anthropology at the University of Pennsylvania and continues to do research in West Africa. She has published an ethnography on the Kono of Sierra Leone, *The Aesthetics of Action: Change and Continuity in a West African Town*, with Smithsonian Institution Press. She has also published numerous articles on her African fieldwork, as well as on topics related to contemporary American society. She lives on the outskirts of Philadelphia (where there are no mountains and few wild spaces) during the school year, and in Montana for the rest of the year.

JACK HEMINGWAY is the author of an autobiography, *The Misadventures of a Flyfisherman*. He is a past field editor of *Field & Stream* and is the only contributor to this book to have parachuted behind enemy lines in World War II with a fly rod. He is currently the host of the prize-winning television show "Incredible Idaho."

PATRICK HEMINGWAY worked for twenty-three years in Tanzania, the last ten of which he was an instructor at the College of African Wildlife Management, Mweka. He is now retired and lives with his wife, Carol, in Bozeman, Montana. He has three grandsons.

WILLIAM HJORTSBERG has published six works of fiction, including *Alp* and *Gray Matters*. His novel *Falling Angel* has been translated into eleven languages. Among his screen credits are *Legend* and *Angel Heart*. He has lived in Montana for over twenty years.

ROBERT F. JONES has written five novels, including *Blood Tide*, which was cited as a notable thriller by the *New York Times* in 1990, and three works of nonfiction, among them the prize-winning children's book *Jake*. His stories and essays have appeared in ten previous anthologies.

MICHAEL KATAKIS'S first book, *The Vietnam Veterans Memorial*, is a two-year study of the emotional impact of the memorial on its visitors. His photographs are included in *Seventy-five Years of Leica Photography* and will appear in an upcoming monograph on Kono culture, *The Aesthetics of Action*.

TED KOOSER is a poet and life insurance company executive living in Nebraska. His books of poems are published by University of Pittsburgh Press. A new collection, *Weather Central*, will be released in early 1994.

THOMAS J. LYON has taught at Utah State University since 1964. He was senior editor of *A Literary History of the American West* (1987), edited *This Incomperable Lande* (1989), and coedited *On Nature's Terms* (1992). He is at work on a study of the sense of place in western American writing.

BILL MCKIBBEN has written hundreds of pieces for *The New Yorker* and for other national publications, including *Outside, The New York Review of Books, Natural History,* and *Rolling Stone.* His first book, *The End of Nature,* is now available in seventeen languages. His most recent book is *The Age of Missing Information.*

JOHN MURRAY has published over a dozen books and a hundred articles, essays, and reviews. His works include *Wild Africa: Three Centuries of Nature Writing from Africa, Wildlife in Peril: The Endangered Mammals of Colorado,* and *Out Among the Wolves: Contemporary Writings on the Wolf.* He has taught in the writing program at the University of Alaska, Fairbanks, for the past six years.

GARY PAUL NABHAN is author of six natural history books and more than a hundred articles on ethnobotany and conservation. A MacArthur Fellow, he lives in Stinkin Hot Desert National Monument. Another version of "Hanging Out the Dirty Laundry" will appear in *Desert Follies and Borderline Fools,* a collaboration with photographer Mark Klett.

JOHN NICHOLS is a novelist best known for *The Sterile Cuckoo, American Blood,* and his New Mexico trilogy: *The Milagro Beanfield War, The Magic Journey,* and *The Nirvana Blues.* He has also published six nonfiction books, most recently *The Sky's the Limit* and *Keep It Simple;* both are environmental photo essays in defense of the earth.

DAN O'BRIEN is the author of two novels, *Spirit of the Hills* and *In the Center of the Nation;* a nonfiction book, *The Rites of Autumn;* and a collection of short stories, *Eminent Domain,* which won the Iowa Short Fiction Award in 1986. He has received two National Endowment for the Arts fellowships for fiction and lives with his wife, Kris, in the Black Hills of South Dakota.

DAVID PETERSEN has written several books of natural history, most recently *Among the Aspen* (Northland, 1991). He edited and introduced

Confessions of a Barbarian: Pages from the Journals of Edward Abbey, to be published by Little, Brown, and is currently writing a book about the Colorado grizzly bear to be published by Henry Holt.

C. L. RAWLINS combines outdoor work with writing. His wilderness studies won the National Primitive Skills Award from the Forest Service. His poetry has been recognized by Stanford's Stegner Fellowship and by the 1992 Blanchan Memorial Award. A recent book, *Sky's Witness: A Year in the Wind River Range,* blends art with natural history.

"The Road to Eden" is JOHN S. ROMAIN's first published work. Although most of his time is currently directed toward environmental media projects, he is also keeping a journalistic inventory of a planet and people in the midst of unprecedented change. If the Muse is willing, further writings will explore the challenge and wonder of it all.

FREDERICK TURNER is author of six books of nonfiction and editor of four others. His essays have appeared in such publications as *American Heritage,* the *International Herald Tribune, New York Times, Los Angeles Times,* and *The Nation.* He is the recipient of awards from the Guggenheim Foundation and the National Endowment for the Arts. He lives in Santa Fe, New Mexico.

JACK TURNER'S collection of essays, *The Abstract Wild,* will be published next year by University of Arizona Press. Turner has been climbing mountains for thirty-three years and has traveled extensively in Nepal, India, Pakistan, Peru, China, and Tibet. He lives in Grand Teton National Park, where he is chief guide of the Exum Guide Service and School of Mountaineering.

GERALD VIZENOR teaches Native American literature at the University of California, Berkeley. He is the author of numerous books. His novel *Griever: an American Monkey King in China* won the American Book Award. His most recent book is *Manifest Manners: Postindian Warriors of Survivance.*

A native Montanan, TODD WESTER received his B.A. in philosophy from Stanford University, only to return promptly home to guide fishermen on the splendid rivers and streams of southwest Montana. He ties flies for local fishing shops during the off-season, and has recently begun to write.

"The Only Last Best Place" is his first piece submitted for publication. He lives with his wife and their son in Livingston, Montana.

JOAN SALVATO WULFF is the author of two books: *Joan Wulff's Fly Casting Techniques* (1987), in which she pioneers a set of fly-casting mechanics as well as a casting vocabulary; and *Joan Wulff's Fly Fishing* (1991), which is written to and for women. The Wulff School of Fly Fishing, on the Beaverkill River in New York's Catskill Mountains, is where Joan can be found every spring, teaching the skills of her favorite sport.

"The Sirens," used as the epigraph, is from *The Collected Poems of Robinson Jeffers* by Robinson Jeffers. © 1941 by Robinson Jeffers. Reprinted by permission of Random House, Inc.

Wendell Berry's "Christianity and the Survival of Creation" is from his book of essays, *Sex, Freedom, and Community: Eight Essays,* published by Pantheon Books, New York and San Francisco, © 1993, printed by permission of the author.

Stephen Bodio's "Passion, Gifts, Rages" appeared in the *Los Angeles Times Magazine.*

Jack Turner's selection of poetry by Onitsura and translated by R.H. Blyth originally appeared in *Haiku,* vol. 4 (Tokyo: The Hokuseido Press, 1982). Reprinted by permission of The Hokuseido Press.

Robert Jones' excerpt of "Big Yellow Taxi" by Joni Mitchell used by permission. © 1970, 1974 Siquomb Publishing Corp. All Rights Reserved.

C.L. Rawlins's "Grandpa's Horse" appeared in the *North American Review.*

Gary Paul Nabhan's excerpt of *Landfill Meditation: Crossblood Stories* by Gerald Vizenor appears courtesy of Wesleyan University Press. © 1991 Gerald Vizenor. All Rights Reserved.

Gary Paul Nabhan's "Hanging Out the Dirty Laundry" appeared in the *Tucson Weekly.*

Bill McKibben's use of Jeanne Robert Foster's poem *Crane Mountain,* from *Adirondack Portraits: A Piece of Time,* edited by Noel Riedinger-Johnson, is reprinted by permission of the publisher. © 1986 Syracuse University Press.

Cover oil painting and interior crayon illustrations: Russell Chatham
Cover design: Sharon Smith
Interior design and typesetting: Philip Bronson
Text & Display type: Monotype Dante medium & Adobe Centaur
Production coordination: David Peattie
Printing and binding: Data Reproductions, Michigan